Good People

BOOKS BY DANNY SIEGEL

Mitzvahs and Jewish Values 1980 ANGELS*
1982 GYM SHOES AND IRISES: Personalized Tzedakah*
1987 GYM SHOES AND IRISES – Book Two*
1988 MUNBAZ II AND OTHER MITZVAH HEROES
1989 FAMILY REUNION: Making Peace in the Jewish Community
1990 MITZVAHS
1993 AFTER THE RAIN: The Book of Mitzvah Power for Adults and Teens
1995 GOOD PEOPLE

For Children 1993 TELL ME A MITZVAH *(Published by Kar-Ben Copies)*
1993 THE HUMONGOUS PUSHKA IN THE SKY

Humor 1982 THE UNORTHODOX BOOK OF JEWISH RECORDS AND LISTS *(With Allan Gould)*

Poetry 1969 SOULSTONED*
1976 AND GOD BRAIDED EVE'S HAIR*
1978 BETWEEN DUST AND DANCE*
1980 NINE ENTERED PARADISE ALIVE*
1982 UNLOCKED DOORS (An Anthology)
1985 THE GARDEN: Where Wolves and Lions Do No Harm to the Sheep and the Deer
1985 THE LORD IS A WHISPER AT MIDNIGHT: Psalms and Prayers
1986 BEFORE OUR VERY EYES: Readings for a Journey Through Israel
1991 THE MEADOW BEYOND THE MEADOW
1992 A HEARING HEART

Midrash and Halachah 1983 WHERE HEAVEN AND EARTH TOUCH – Book One*
1984 WHERE HEAVEN AND EARTH TOUCH – Book Two*
1985 WHERE HEAVEN AND EARTH TOUCH – Book Three*
1985 WHERE HEAVEN AND EARTH TOUCH SOURCE BOOK (Selected Hebrew and Aramaic Sources)*
1988 WHERE HEAVEN AND EARTH TOUCH – Combined Volume: Books One, Two and Three*
1989 WHERE HEAVEN AND EARTH TOUCH – Combined Volume *(Jason Aronson Hardcover Edition)*

*Out of Print

Good People

by

Danny Siegel

&

THE TOWN HOUSE PRESS
Pittsboro, North Carolina

ON THE COVER: Ms.Erin Broadbent descending a cliff.on a leisurely
outing with Wilderness Inquiry in Australia. (See page 16: *The Poster*).

Credits for photographs and illustrations:

Cover: Greg Lais of Wilderness Inquiry, Minneapolis
Page 12: Robert Gamer, United Synagogue Youth Central Staff, New York City
Page 71: Jerry Davis–photographer, Seattle
Page 83: Av Rivel, White Plains, New York

Library of Congress Catalog Card Number: 95-60904
International Standard Book Number: 0-940653-40-0

For ordering:
CMS Distributors / Eisenberger
384 Wyoming Avenue
Millburn NJ 07041

For
Reb Shmuel Munk,
My Torah Teacher

לכבוד מורי ורבי
שמואל
בן הרב אברהם הכהן
בן הרב רבי עזריאל הכהן מונק

A good, sweet Jew
א גוטער ייד, א זיסער

And

For My Uncle and Aunt,
Herb and Phyllis Kamm,
Who Have Believed in My Talents
As a Writer
For Many Years
And Who Gave Me
The Encouragement to Continue

Kind permission has been given by the following:

Acknowledgments

Many people have helped make this book possible. I thank them all for making this a successful venture. Their insight and suggestions have contributed greatly toward making this a complete book. My gratitude to: Michael Bohnen, Rabbi Debra Robbins, Dr. Zoltan Gondos, Gordon and Myra Gondos and their children, Gary and Brian, Naomi Eisenberger, Steve Vinocor, Professor Ron Wolfson, Vikki Bravo, Debbie Friedmann, Abraham and Shulamit Gittelson, Toby Pollack, Dr. Lou Marmon, Rabbi Danny Grossman, Dr. Jay Masserman, Sandy Andron, Aviva Kieffer, Jeff Liberman, Laura Rubin, Louise Cohen, Dr. Diane Jacobstein, Dani and Aaron Shneyer, Ms. Trude Holzmann, Allan and Merle Gould, Irene, Stewart, and Scott Bolton, Robert Gamer, Professor Daniel Sperber, Ms. Regina Carmel and her Shabbat morning classes, Arnie Draiman, Linda Hines, Maureen Fredrickson, Rabbi Gordon Tucker, Karin Levine, Neal Gold, Jenny Sherling, Ari Newman, Dr. Judith T. Fine Dach, Dr. Elizabeth and hannah Feldman, Jonathan T. Howe of Howe and Hutton Ltd., Chicago, Marilyn Moses, Leonard, Adele, David, and Michael Morris, Greg Lais, Sarah Toffler, Erin Broadbent, Ms. Betsy Pietriyk, April Rozboril, Av Rivel, Mark Stadler, Janet Rickles, Dr. David Schwartz, David and Darryl Kuperstock, Rabbi David Golinkin, Victoria Ginsberg and her students at the Ramaz Lower School, Ms. Beverly Cheuvront, Melissa Klein and Linda Kaplan, Sarah Gutin, Sara Simon, Rick Meyer and the people from the Milwaukee Jewish Federation leadership who reviewed the *Jewish* Jewish Leadership article, and Rabbi Keith Stern, whose special coffee, The Rabbi's Blend, was the only brand in the freezer that could get my creativity going full speed early in the morning.

And of course, my special thanks to my mother, Edythe Siegel, who has been my inspiration for many of these ideas as well as my faithful editor, Lo, these many years I have been a writer.

There is joy for people who make plans to do good
—PROVERBS 12:20

...וּלְיֹעֲצֵי שָׁלוֹם שִׂמְחָה

Rabbi Levi said,
Whoever thinks to himself or herself
before going to sleep at night,
"When I wake up tomorrow,
I will do good things for So-and-So."
That person will ultimately share great joy
with The Good People
in the Future, in the Next World,
as the verse states,
"....There is joy for people
who make plans to do good."
(Midrash Mishlay [Proverbs] 12:1)

א״ר לוי....
כל מי שהוא ישן על מיטתו בלילה ומתחשב בלבו ואומ׳
למחר אני משכים ועושה טובה עם פלוני
עתיד לשמח עם הצדיקים בגן עדן לעתיד לבא
שנאמר וליעצי שלום שמחה

Table of Contents

Introduction

This book is about Good People.

It is about the many ways they use their human talents to make good things happen in this world. That explains why lofty words such as *astonishing, glorious, magnificent,* and *majestic* appear so frequently. Through Mitzvahs, Good People are capable of doing astonishing and glorious acts, kind deeds that are at once just and beautiful.

Many of the Good People are intellectually brilliant. They could hold their own in discussion or debate with the brightest professors in their field. Indeed, in their "other lives," some of them are part of the university world; a few are world renowned for their academic achievements. But *who they are* is defined by *what they do*: provide for those who have no food or clothing or shelter or friends or hope. They are forever unlocking the chains that — for whatever reason — immobilize the bodies, minds, and souls of others.

Some of the Good People are fabulously successful in business. For example, Dave Thomas, the man who made Wendy's fast food restaurants an American institution, has built a corporation worth more than $3,000,000,000. Even though I live in Washington where a common topic of conversation is billions of dollars are, the number still staggers me. I cannot imagine how much $3,000,000,000 is worth to any individual. Yet, what really defines Dave Thomas is his work on behalf of children in need of adoption. He, himself, was an adopted child, and now he moves Heaven and earth to find loving homes for children who would otherwise be lost in an often neglectful, apathetic world. At my lectures, I tell the audience that, if Dave Thomas were told he could never go back to his corporate office, never move hundreds of millions of dollars by a phone call or stroke of a pen, he would still be a very happy man. He would have that much more time to make children happy. I am certain he enjoys his work as the Ultimate Boss of Wendy's, but he knows that balance sheets, profitability, and cash flow *ultimately* mean nothing unless they are linked to some higher values. *Ultimately*, what more could Dave Thomas want in Life than to make children happy?

Good people are our Teachers. They answer the questions, "What is our purpose in Life?" and "How may we most meaningfully use our talents?"

I have written this book to encourage all of us to get more involved, to *do* more and more of these acts of Tzedakah.

I believe the *meaning* of Tzedakah becomes clearer the more we engage in substantive good deeds. Others have written most eloquently about the meaning. I prefer action, watching human beings at their finest, when they relate to each other decently, pleasantly, and fairly. I watch them as they do their Mitzvah work, but not as an objective observer. I am, rather, their student, seeking instruction about the Good Life Well Lived.

Everything else by way of introduction is purely editorial:

1. Because of my 20 years as a student of the Good People, I often get overly enthusiastic in my retelling of the stories. When you read this book, if

you come across a phrase as strong as "we must," for example, feel free to insert something like, "It would appear to me that..." or "It would seem that...." I most certainly make no claim to absolute insight.

2. I use the term "Mitzvah" very loosely, usually to express the idea of "doing something good." Literally, it is defined as a commandment from God, binding on Jewish people, but I often employ the broader meaning which derives from the Yiddish connotation: "Do a Mitzvah," i.e., "Do something good." I have coined the phrase "Mitzvah heroes" with the broader definition in mind: Good People who perform extraordinarily fine acts of human kindness, and I apply the term to all human beings, though, again, technically, "Mitzvah" in its sense of "obligation" would apply only to the Jewish people. Good People see something wrong in this world, some unjust situation, and apply their powers and skills to set things right. "Tzedakah-צדקה" means "Justice," "The Right Thing." "Tzaddik-צדיק" carries a broad range of meaning. The most frequent translation, "Righteous Person" is beyond the grasp of many people, so I now tend to translate it as "Good Person," "A human being who personifies the quality of Tzedakah."

3. Some of the Good People and some of their projects, as well as some of the relevant Jewish texts, are mentioned in more than one place in this book. The reason is twofold: (1) several of the articles were written for different occasions, and (2) the Good People and their work, and Jewish texts, teach us different insights in different contexts.

4. There are two kinds of articles in this book: essays about Good People and their work, and several text studies that attempt to bring to light the distinctly Jewish element in Mitzvah work.

5. The invention of the computer and its many peripherals such as the CD-ROM drive and the growing library of Jewish texts on disk have allowed me much greater range and flexibility than in any previous attempt I have made to write on this subject.

6. On the issue of appropriate terminology relating to people with disabilities: Things are still in flux and will no doubt remain that way into the near future. "Individuals with disabilities," "physically/mentally challenged people," "retarded people/exceptional people," "people with special needs" are all "in" and "out" at different times and in different places (particularly in different English-speaking countries). When I wrote this book, I tried to consult with others concerning which terms are current and acceptable and which are not. It is still difficult to make final determinations in all cases. A woman I met, Ms. Pat Broderick, a skier, a "physically challenged" or "disabled" person, made a most emphatic point about this issue of vocabulary. She said, "If you're still into naming it, you haven't dealt with it." The precise choice of words is certainly essential. I, as a poet, with more than 25 years of experience choosing words, can attest to that. But the critical issue is the people, the human beings the terms represent. Let us stay current with the struggle to find the best words, but, in the meantime, please forgive any slips that may have occurred.

נזכה למצוות-May this book lead to more Tikkun Olam.

The Helen Keller of Israel

I. Helen Keller

We all know the story. We have either read it in books or seen it as the play or movie, "The Miracle Worker":

In 1880, in a town called Tuscumbia, Alabama, a healthy child was born. When she was 19 months old, she suffered an attack of some kind of fever in the brain that left her blind and deaf.

Somehow, some way, her parents eventually found a teacher — Anne Sullivan — for this very unruly child.

We all know the rest of the story:

Through Ms. Sullivan's ever-patient teaching, this child grew up to be the famous Helen Keller, graduate With Honors from Radcliffe College, Class of 1904, author, lecturer, inspiration to millions of people.

And we all know the famous breakthrough scene:

One day when Helen was a young child, Ms. Sullivan finger-spelled the word "water" into Helen's hand, and, out by the well alongside the house, Helen realized that the word "water" spelled from Ms. Sullivan's fingers into her hand (and by a marvelous neurological pathway further up to her brain) was that same wet liquid pouring all over her hands.

The rest is history.

II. Yossi and Shoshana

A. Yossi's Birth and Early Childhood

Sometime in the 1970's, a tainted batch of DPT[1] vaccine made its way into the Israeli medical inventory. By the time the Israelis had realized what had happened, many infants had already received the shots. Each one reacted according to his or her own immune system. Many of them died; some suffered severe physical and mental damage.

One such child, Yossi Samuels, lived, but it soon became clear to his parents, Kalman and Malky, that their son had been seriously injured. Besides his seizures, it was evident that he was blind.

The family moved to New York. Kalman and Malky felt that the famous Lighthouse for the Blind would be the best place for Yossi to receive his education.

One day, a teacher called Malky and said that she thought Yossi was also deaf.

It would be difficult to imagine how Yossi's parents must have felt at that moment. And it would be nearly impossible for anyone to imagine what was going on in Yossi's mind since the toxic vaccine entered his system and battered it so badly.

As loving and caring and insightful as Yossi's parents were, they were in despair. They simply didn't know what to do to break into their son's mind.

For all they knew — for all their efforts, their incredible love, and their day-to-day struggles to make something happen — they felt they were at a dead end.

And...all the time they were in America, they realized how much they missed Israel. Kalman said, "If we are going to move back, we should move back now. But if we return to Israel, we will stay for good." So they came back.

In Jerusalem, their efforts continued. Being such devoted parents, Kalman and Malky gave Yossi every possible chance to live a full, rich, and fulfilling life. But, as often happens with so many children (and adults) who have sustained setbacks to their health, progress was measured slowly, despite special schools and all kinds of programs for exceptional children. Every new thing Yossi accomplished was greeted with moments of parental happiness and some small feeling of hope. But still, there was no breakthrough. I would imagine by a certain time in Yossi's childhood, Kalman and Malky resigned themselves to the fact that there never would be anything radically or awesomely different about this child. He would always remain blind, deaf, and — for all they could tell — very slow (or as people used to say, "retarded").

All this time, other children were growing up "normally," learning to read and write, playing with their toys at a predictable pace, perhaps beginning their first attempts at jacks or soccer. Their parents anticipated the time when they would become teen-agers, complaining about exams, learning to drive a car, maybe playing some heavy metal Israeli or American music on their tape decks or boom boxes, going to the beach for a pleasant day with their friends, just hanging out. They could look to the future when their children would worry about their complexions and whether Sara or Rivka or Yaakov or Shimon would find them attractive enough to ask them out on a date.

And throughout all those early years, Kalman and Malky never said, "וויי איז אונז-Woe is us," or, in secular terms, they never cursed their fate or bad luck. Being religious people, they accepted their situation, despite all the challenges and frustrations, and lived their lives raising Yossi and the rest of their growing family as best as they knew how.

B. Enter Shoshana, The Anne Sullivan of Israel

When Yossi was eight years old, Kalman and Malky found Yossi a teacher, Shoshana Weinstock.[2] They had heard about her from the network that exists among parents with exceptional children. And still they had to wait. For a number of months Shoshana refused to take on Yossi as a student, Though they didn't know why. It was because her own husband was not well, and she wasn't free to spend the enormous number of hours with this child.

Then she was free.

Then she began to work with Yossi.

And you would probably guess that, just as one day Annie Sullivan finger-spelled the word "water" into Helen Keller's hand and she knew that what was spelled in her hand was what was out there in the world all wet and drippy and wonderful and cool to the touch and tasty to those who are thirsty —

"water" — so, too, one day, in Jerusalem, when Yossi Samuels was eight, Shoshana Weinstock spelled

"שׁ (Sh)→וּ (u)→לֹ (l)→ח (ch)→ן (n), שׁוּלֹחָן-Shulchan"[3]

into his hand.[4] She spelled "שׁוּלֹחָן," and Yossi knew that the four-legged thing with a top on it where you can eat or play or pile things in heaps like laundry or books or dishes — that that very "שׁוּלֹחָן" was the same one he knew had been spelled-by-touch on his body by Shoshana.

And now you know who the Helen Keller of Israel is: Yossi Samuels.

And now you know who the Annie Sullivan of Israel is: Shoshana Weinstock.

And now you know the infinitely obvious connection in this world between water and tables. And I couldn't even tell you if it was a living room table or a card table propped up alongside a wall where the Samuels' throw their coats instead of hanging them up in the closet or on a hook, or if it was a high table or one of those kiddie tables where children eat their meals until they are tall enough to sit in a real chair without their feet dangling too high off the floor.

It's enough that we can put them all together: Yossi and Shoshana and the Hebrew word שׁוּלֹחָן and some kind of table in their apartment in Jerusalem.

And, as it happens, Yossi is a very bright young man, somewhere now in his upper teens. He has a wonderful mind and great talents...which no one could get to — not Kalman, not Malky, not the brothers and sisters nor the best teachers around — until that one unique Shoshana Weinstock came along and found the way.

The story of Yossi and Shoshana is a story about faith and human goodness and decency and persistence and potential and hope inspiration, and we are fortunate to have learned the story.[5]

III. What We Can Learn From Yossi and Shoshana And, Most of All, What We Can Do

Alef — and obviously — not all stories of despair are destined for despairing endings.

Bet — and just as obviously — I am not naïve in these matters....Not all stories that begin in despair end in exhilaration.

Gimel —

With whom do we identify in this story?

With Kalman and Malky: the distraught parents, helpless, groping for some shred of positive possibilities, some infinitely gentle touch?

With Yossi: Bound within terrible limits, screaming to get out, to achieve, to be himself,...if only we had the key, the right word, the magic, magnificent touch?

With Shoshana: To be The Miracle Worker? This is the one I like the most, ever since, as a little child, I would make a cape out of a towel and think of Superman doing all those good things.

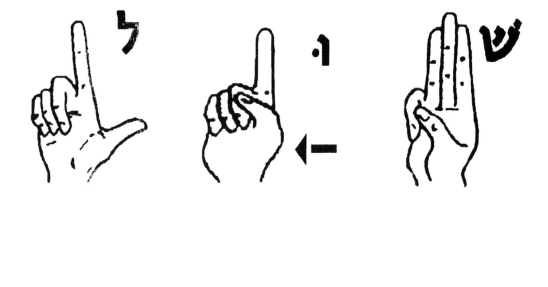

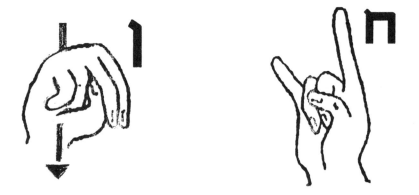

Finger spelling Yossi's magic word "שולחן – *shulchan (table)*".

With all of them?

So — Dalet would be that we, as Jews, I believe, are put on this earth to be, as it were, God's Sorter-Outers, sorting out what is changeable and what is beyond our powers, or anyone else's powers to change. And once we have differentiated between the changeable and the not-changeable, we should set about changing what can be changed, making note that many things need not be changed completely, nor all at once, but we could do part of it, or part of it now, and the rest later. In many, many situations, *part* is much closer to completely than to zero.

As this applies to human beings, this means that we are to look at whomever it is we are with —*including ourselves* — to look that person square in the face, and then see just how much of the Shoshana Weinstock/Annie Sullivan is in each of us. And as Jews, we are, I believe, required by God to take whatever Weinstock-Sullivan powers we have and try to bring out the brightness, the wisdom, and the uttermost potential of those around us.

In fact, it is really a well-known fundamental principle of special education that we need to extend into the Big Wide World: special education starts with looking at the individual and asking — above all else — what are this particular person's special needs?

We all have special needs.

We all have our strong points and weak points.

We all have our *mishigossen*, our quirks and idiosyncrasies.

We all have our own cravings and desires, sweetnesses and bad moments due to any one of an infinite number of life-circumstances, from losing a job all the way down to eating an overload of candy or missing a night's sleep.

And we all wish to be treated as someone special. God wants us to be treated as someone special, and God wants us to treat others that way...special.

And for all of those people out there who need us, to be opened up — as Yossi was opened up by Shoshana —

1. *They* are waiting for us.

2. *We* become who we are, we as Jews, when we use our God-given powers to make these things happen.

We can sort out the unchangeable from the changeable in people. A person with a hole in his or her chest a mile wide from an accident who comes into the emergency room with no vital signs whatsoever....There really isn't much that can be done. Almost anything other than that, is waiting for us to be fixed, which is the meaning of תיקון עולם-Tikkun Olam, Fixing the World, piece by broken-but-fixable piece.

IV. *Projects, Insights from Torah*

A. Relating to individuals with disabilities:

1. The Book of Proverbs (31:8) says פְּתַח־פִּיךָ לְאִלֵּם — Open your mouth on behalf of those who cannot speak."

a. On one level, we could consider becoming a speech pathologist, speech therapist, or ear, nose, and throat doctor or a physical or occupational therapist.

b. On another level, this is a verse that means we should speak out on behalf of all individuals with disabilities whose right to full integration into society might be denied. The Americans with Disabilities Act was passed to insure all citizens of the United States the possibility of access. We should become more familiar with this law and work toward implementing it in our society.

2. One of the most well-known verses in the Book of Leviticus is: וְלִפְנֵי עִוֵּר לֹא תִתֵּן מִכְשֹׁל, "Do not put a stumbling block before blind people." (19:14)

a. The greatest stumbling block placed before individuals with disabilities is making a prejudicial assumption that they are incapable of doing certain things. While there are certainly limits to what some disabled individuals can do, *all* people have limits...but we shouldn't begin by assuming limits until they have been tested.[6]

b. In our prayerbook, one of the blessings at the very beginning of the service is, "Blessed are You,...O God, Who opens the eyes of blind people (בָּרוּךְ...פּוֹקֵחַ עִוְרִים) If we are supposed to be God's messengers or partners in the work of תִּיקוּן עוֹלָם-Tikkun Olam, Fixing the World, we should be literally and metaphorically doing the same: bringing out into the open all the abilities of individuals with disabilities[7]

c. My friend, Mark Mannis, is an ophthalmologist in the Sacramento area. His specialty is doing cornea transplants. In many years of practice, he has literally given (or given back to) people the ability to see. We are not trained ophthalmologists, but we have other ways we can use our talents to remove the stumbling blocks before those people who have visual impairments. The easiest project to do is to insure that our synagogues have large print and Braille prayerbooks and a large-print and Braille section in the library. And by extension — we should make certain that our synagogues and other Jewish communal buildings have special sound systems for hearing impaired people, and that synagogue and community events have a sign language interpreter for people who will only understand the content of the event by watching hands speak the language.

3. Four classic examples of the Weinstock/Sullivan Principle of finding the right key to unlocking human potential:

a. The Full Circle Program of the Clearwater, FL, Marine Science Center[8] brings together children with disabilities and disabled sea animals such as dolphins (Sunset Sam being the most famous) and giant turtles. (One of the dolphins had been attacked by sharks.) The interaction produces many incredible results, not the least of which is the children's new way of thinking, "If *they* have disabilities and can survive and do well, so can I."

b. At the Chase Memorial Nursing Home in New Berlin, NY, Dr. William Thomas, discovered that some of the residents with Alzheimer's disease no longer needed special medication to counteract a tendency to wander. It is a truly *classic* example of how a diagnosis may mislead people to assume that more is wrong with someone than is really wrong with them....All you need to do is keep trying other methods — like Shoshana with Yossi — to discover what the other person really *can* do. To find out how Dr. Thomas' program transforms the lives of the elderly residents at Chase and other homes, call him at 607-674-5232. We hope that his methods will be used in many more old age homes.

   c. Sometime in 1994, Anita Shkedi, founder of the Therapeutic Riding Club of Israel was conducting a lesson with a child who was diagnosed with a condition of almost total agenesis of the corpus calossum. This means that there was very little connective tissue between the two hemispheres of the child's brain. For some people with this condition, the symptoms may be relatively mild. Perhaps the right hand won't know what the left hand is doing. Other people experience severe problems, including an inability to speak, behavioral problems, and a series of other disabilities. This particular child's situation was of a more extreme nature. Among other things, the child, age five or six, had never spoken. And so, this one day, as they were riding along, Anita pointed to a building that was a school, and said, "ספר זה בית- Zeh Bet Sefer-This is a school." The child replied, "אני בגן-Ani BaGan-I am in kindergarten." The miracles of therapeutic horseback riding are relatively common, and while this was an extraordinary moment, it was not totally unexpected. They continued the lesson, carrying on a conversation, as if it were the most natural thing in the world to do.

   d. A group based in Minneapolis called Wilderness Inquiry explains its mission as "to empower people to reach beyond perceived limitations to achieve things that they never thought possible. We provide opportunities that integrate people with and without disabilities in experiences which inspire personal growth, instill confidence, develop peer relationships, and enhance awareness of the natural environment. These experiences inspire all people to maximize their vocational, educational and leisure potentials." It all sounds very idealistic, and you might be at least a little skeptical about their accomplishments. After a few rounds of communication with the Wilderness Inquiry staff, and after careful examination of their catalogue of trips out into the wilds of America, I have become increasingly impressed with their work. When they sent me a poster of a woman named Erin Broadbent tied by cable or rope to other climbers or safety equipment going up the sheer side of a cliff — in a wheelchair! — I became convinced that they are really on to something. Call 612-379-3858 (voice or TTY) to find out more.

   B. Relating to people-in-general:

   1. The Weinstock/Sullivan Principle can be stated another way, based on a passage in Jewish literature:

לא ישתמש אדם בפניו ידיו ורגליו
אלא לכבוד קונהו שנא'
כָּל פָּעַל יְהוָה לַמַּעֲנֵהוּ

One should use one's face, hands, and feet only to honor one's Creator,
as it is written, "God made everything for a purpose."
(Tosefta Brachot 4:1, Proverbs 16:4)

      2. Teen-agers have shared with me a wonderful project, sometimes called "Senior Prom":

      a. There is so much ageism in America, i.e., prejudicial thinking about and prejudiced actions against older people, particularly by younger people. The Mitzvah וְהָדַרְתָּ פְּנֵי זָקֵן, "You shall make certain that the faces of the Elders are radiant" (Leviticus 19:32) would entail two things on *our* part: (1) recognizing that Elders[9], by definition, have an aura of glory about them, and that, if, sadly, some misfortunes have ravaged their physical presence, we are not to dwell on them, but always to go beyond, and (2) *doing* things with them that will bring out the radiance that may be hidden or hiding, due to past circumstances. Ageism is the opposite of this Mitzvah.

      b. A few years back, someone had the brilliant idea to hold an event they called "Senior Prom". For this function, the high school students invited the elders from a local old age home to a prom at their school, complete with fancy dresses and suits, boutonnières and corsages...the whole story. And surprise of surprises! Many of the people they would have otherwise thought were semi-comatose or foggy or lost forever in their own shattered worlds — when they were asked to dance, they not only danced, but they dazzled the Young and the Restless and Vibrant and Cool and Smart, who just couldn't believe it. But now they know. They know that some people just lose their will to live because no one has asked them to dance! And if you ask these same high school students if they were ever at a family bar or bat mitzvah or wedding and the band started to play and Aunt Sophie or Uncle Harry (age 85 and above) started *really* moving out on the dance floor — Many would no doubt respond, "Why, yes. Now that you mention it, that's exactly what happened." All that was needed was for someone to make the connection with the prom! *Now* it seems so obvious.

      c. Senior Prom reinforces what has been stressed all along by the Weinstock/Sullivan Principle: if we start by considering *what is best for the other person*, without imposing our own personal agendas about what might be best for them, the potential for progress and development on their part can — maybe — go far beyond anything we might have ever considered possible. (There is always that *maybe*.) We just have no way of knowing how far the Weinstock/Sullivan Principle extends until we try it in our own lives, becoming Shoshana/Annie at certain moments, doing whatever we can with our own talents to actualize in others we meet what Shoshana and Annie achieved when they applied their own talents to bring out the best in Yossi and Helen Keller.

V. A Brief Summary

      If we are to be God's sorter-outers, we should remember to view everyone as needing nothing more than a good look at them-as-themselves. What is most important is what is good for them...and then we should ask them to dance, if that's what they need; or for (God forbid) a suicidal teen-ager — to go for a walk and a leisurely lunch away from it all, to be listened to, heart and soul; or, for lonely people — a ride to synagogue for a class or to the art museum, or a horseback ride, whatever it is that equals "water" and "שילוח".

On Rosh HaShana and Yom Kippur we want God to look at and evaluate us as individuals, not as a cluster or mass of creatures.

We want God to consider each one of us a real, live breathing human being with specific needs and wants and glorious triumphs and disastrous failures and disappointments and talents and readiness to do God's work. In that context, just as we want God to look at us as individuals — our promise to God, in turn, should be to look at ourselves and at the people right next to us and all around us and set ourselves the task of making sure that Yossi becomes Yossi, as Helen Keller became Helen Keller, and Randy Nussbaum or Alissa Reinhardt or Max Schlossberg will become whoever they are supposed to be, in some way, at least, because of us.

The Story of Helen Keller and Anne Sullivan and Yossi and Shoshana is really the story of the Human Touch, and how we are defined by that touch that makes us human.

VI. *A Chassidic Story*

The story goes that, when the great, sweet Rabbi Zusia of Hanipol was on his deathbed, his students gathered all around him.

This is what he said to them:

When I get to the Next World, I am not afraid if God will ask me, "Zusia, why weren't you Moses, to lead the people out of this land where Jews are so oppressed and beaten by the people?"

I can answer, "I did not have the leadership abilities of a Moses."

And if God asks,

"Zusia, why weren't you Isaiah, reprimanding the people for their sins and urging them to change their ways, to repent?"

I could answer, "I did not have the eloquence of Isaiah, the Great Master of powerful and dazzling speech."

And if God should ask,

"Zusia, why weren't you Maimonides, to explain the deeper meaning of Judaism to the philosophers of the world, so they would understand the Jews better and perhaps treat them better?"

I can answer, "I did not have the vast intellectual skills of Maimonides."

No, my students, I am not afraid of those questions.

What I fear is this:

What if God asks me,

"Zusia, why weren't you Zusia?"

Then what will I say?

VII. Conclusion

There is something very appealing about the story of Zusia of Hanipol. Zusia is right: he was created to be Zusia and not Moses or Isaiah or Maimonides. Whatever his gifts and talents were, *those* were the ones God wanted him to use for his specific Life's work.

In some ways, we are *not* Yossi, but we are *like* him: in the dark about many things, unable to hear or see some of the glorious things in life. If we want to truly be ourselves, we should be aware of the Yossi Samuels that is a part of us, and hope to find some Shoshana Weinstock who will play a part in our lives.

And while we are *not* Shoshana, we are *like* Shoshana in that we should take that Shoshana-part of ourselves and bring it into our daily lives: we are teachers, we are sorter-outers and sifters, taking all Life's experiences and all our connections with others and saying, "This is beyond my powers to change (at least at the moment); *that* however, I can manage — even though others say it is impossible."

We are our most true selves when we are as much the Shoshana-within-us as we can be.

So we are both Yossi and Shoshana...and more. All that remains is to live our lives every day as if that שולחן-moment, that moment at the Samuels' table, were going to happen at any moment, and that we, somehow, made it happen.

VIII. What To Do Now

1. Learn how to finger spell the word "שולחן".

2. Learn the story of Yossi and Shoshana well enough to re-tell it to one of your friends.

3. Finger spell שולחן into the hand of this friend while you tell the story.

4. Have the friend spell שולחן back into your hand while re-telling the story to you.

Mitzvahs have a way of being remembered better if we feel them with our fingers.

It is our human touch that makes us human.

Life

Tzedakah is Life.
Life is Tzedakah.
Tzedakah is even more than Life. It is immortality.

בְּאֹרַח־צְדָקָה חַיִּים וְדֶרֶךְ נְתִיבָה אַל־מָוֶת:

In Tzedakah's way is Life;
on its path is immortality. (Proverbs 12:28)

Life is a road.
Tzedakah is a road.
The road of Life and the road of Tzedakah are the same.
The road of Life may be dark at times and troublesome to negotiate; at other times it may be slippery, frightening, or treacherous.
Tzedakah clears the way and allows the walker and the wanderer to continue on from any starting point to the final destination with confidence, peace of mind, and hope.
Two possibilities: (1) the road of Tzedakah takes us to the right destination; (2) the destination is of secondary importance...the very fact that human beings are on this particular road means that they are on the right road.
Three more possibilities: (1) even though it may be a well-worn path, our going that way makes the way smoother for others who come after us; (2) even if the road is paved and our footsteps make no noticeable impression, still, we know we are on the right road, (3) sometimes we are called upon to be trailblazers, opening up new trails for others.

אֹרַח חַיִּים לְמַעְלָה לְמַשְׂכִּיל

For the person who uses all human powers [for Mitzvahs],
the road of Life leads upward. (Proverbs 15:24)

וְאֶל־הָעָם הַזֶּה תֹּאמַר כֹּה אָמַר יְהֹוָה
הִנְנִי נֹתֵן לִפְנֵיכֶם אֶת־דֶּרֶךְ הַחַיִּים וְאֶת־דֶּרֶךְ הַמָּוֶת

Say to this people:
Thus says God,
"I offer you the way of Life
and the way of death." (Jeremiah 21:8)

The way of Life is Tzedakah.

הִנֵּה תָּאַבְתִּי לְפִקֻּדֶיךָ בְּצִדְקָתְךָ חַיֵּנִי

I love your Mitzvahs.
Give me Life through Your Tzedakah. (Psalm 119:40)

One must be passionate about Tzedakah and Mitzvahs, no less passionate than about the things we crave as human beings that are no more than that: things.

One must love Tzedakah and Mitzvahs, no less than we, as human beings, love other people: spouses, soul-mates, friends.

No less than we love Life itself.

תּוֹדִיעֵנִי אֹרַח חַיִּים
שֹׂבַע שְׂמָחוֹת אֶת־פָּנֶיךָ נְעִמוֹת בִּימִינְךָ נֶצַח

Teach me the path of Life.
In Your Presence is overwhelming joy;
eternal pleasantness is in Your right hand. (Psalm 16:11)

Torah guides us like a map: which way to turn, how steep the hills, how difficult or dangerous the way on a night of raging storm, how our unique stature somewhere between Heaven and earth allows us to use the tools of Tzedakah to find our way, planting gardens and orchards along the roadside, removing the stones from the path so others may walk with greater ease and enjoy the exquisite view.

Torah shows which Mitzvah tools work best, and when, and teaches the feel of each tool, no less than the expert carpenter knows one saw's blade from another, a particular kind of wood's resistance to the plane, the awl, and the massive and mechanized hole punch that works its wonders through the toughest steel plate, no less than the surgeon must know which blade, scissors, or laser will ease the tumor from the kidney's wall.

Tzedakah is Life.
Life is Tzedakah.

גמילות חסדים נקרא חיים שנא'
כִּי־טוֹב חַסְדְּךָ מֵחַיִּים

The act of caring, loving kindness is called "Life,"
as the verse states,
"Truly, Your caring, loving kindness — ever reliable —
is better than Life." (Avot DeRabbi Natan 34, Psalm 63:4)

Tzedakah is what gives Life its meaning.

The meaning of Life, if we would use such a phrase, is using our Divinely given gifts to serve as God's agents...to save the lives of those who should not die for the wrong reasons, to renew a sense of The Good Life in those who have lost hope, to give dignity to those who may have forgotten who they are, magnificent people, so important in God's eyes they are barely lower than angels, glorious, the work of God's own hands.

וַתְּחַסְּרֵהוּ מְּעַט מֵאֱלֹהִים וְכָבוֹד וְהָדָר תְּעַטְּרֵהוּ

You have made them — at times nearly imperceptibly so —
barely lower than the Divine, gracing them with glory and majesty. (Psalm 8:6)

Your care, Your need to know that this thing called "Life" is truly good, and that these human beings You created will work things out; that we people can be partners with You in making a human-and-divinely decent world — *this* is what gives Life meaning.

A Life of Tzedakah is Life.

The Poster

I. The Poster

She is going down a nearly perpendicular wall. There is a rope — standard procedure in wall climbing — secured around her waist, and she is clearly intent on making this experience work.

At first I am uncomfortable with the poster. I am afraid of heights, both in real life and particularly in dreams. I was once on vacation in Honolulu and they put me on the 30-somethingth floor, complete — standard procedure in Hawaii — with a balcony. One of the things I like most about my vacations is the opportunity to sit on a balcony, facing the water, drinking a cup of coffee and thinking about nothing in particular. I couldn't do it this trip. It was much too high up for me.

(She's in a wheelchair.)

I particularly remember when I took my Mom to Cancún for vacation. We hired a driver to take us to the magnificent Mayan ruins at Chichen Itza. When we got there, I saw that the "in" thing to do was to climb the steps to the top of the temple you see in all the travel books and tourist brochures. There are many steps up, and then a platform. Up there, you get a wonderful view of the entire surrounding area. A vanished civilization stretches out in all directions. It is something not to be missed, a sight to tell your friends about when you get home.

But the steps were narrower than I had expected. Still, I kept my eyes firmly on the next step up and managed to make it up to the platform. I took in the view and was pleased at how well I was doing considering how high up I was. I suppose having so many tourists around me made it easier. *Then* the problem really began: getting back down. I was terrified. I did it, but I did it facing the steps, crawling, and stopping every five or six steps...*never looking down.* Had I known how terrifying it was going to be coming down, I would never have gone up the steps. Instead, I would have bought a picture book back at the hotel.

She's in a wheelchair.

I really don't know why people want to climb rock walls. I imagine there is a thrill to it, but it doesn't thrill me. Still, if they want to, I say, "Let them do it." And if they want to do rock walls that are nearly smooth and as close to absolutely vertical as is geologically possible, I say again, "Let them do it if they want to." While I admit being jealous of figure skaters at the ice rink in Rockefeller Center (just the intermediate skaters; the Olympic-class athletes are too far above and beyond to make comparisons) and some baseball players in sandlot leagues who can hit (apparently effortlessly) home runs deep into the stands, my jealousy doesn't extend to rock climbers. I suppose I admire their achievement; it's probably the same admiration I have for water skiers at 50 miles per hour. But it's too dangerous for me, so I'll admire them, but I won't be jealous.

She's in a wheelchair. This woman, Erin Broadbent, right there on the poster going down the rock wall, that almost perpendicular rock wall, is in a wheelchair.

And her hands are on the wheels doing the work.

And the story goes that, when Ms. Broadbent was asked if she was sure she wanted to do this, she said, "It's OK. I already broke my neck once."

II. Some Questions About the Poster

1. When did Ms. Broadbent decide she wanted to take on The Cliff? At what point in her life did it have such significance that she was willing to put herself at additional great personal risk?

2. Why did Ms. Broadbent decide to do it at all? Just because it was there? Because she is a compulsive person? Because she wanted "to show them" (whoever "them" is)? Is it because she is a maniac and has a long history of risking her life for the right and wrong reasons?

3. Does it matter at all when or why she wanted to do it, or is it enough to know that at some time she made up her mind to do it?

4. When you look at the picture, do you know if Ms. Broadbent is going up or down the cliff? (She is going down. I asked her.)

5. Would she have done it if there weren't any groups that take people with or without disabilities out into the wilds?

III. Some, But Not All Answers; What We Can Learn From Erin Broadbent on the Face of the Cliff

Above all else, before we consider this poster *a symbol* of anything — of courage, or drive, or the will to succeed — we must keep in mind that this is a *real* event in someone's *real* life, in the life of one Erin Broadbent. After we consider that fact thoroughly, we are entitled to move it up, up into the upper spheres of symbolism. But when Ms. Broadbent decided to take on The Cliff, I am certain she did not have symbolism in mind. She just wanted to get up and down that wall as best as she could — for whatever reason she, or anyone else, would want to do such a thing.

Now we can continue with other lessons from the Poster.

1. If people are crazy enough to want to go up and down rock walls — even traveling all the way to Australia as Ms. Broadbent did — there is no ethical or moral reason in the world why they shouldn't be allowed to do it, as long as all the appropriate safety precautions are in place.

2. Since there are great differences in the body, mind, personality, and talents of every individual, then, no matter how each person's body, mind, personality, or talents are different — if these (in my mind) crazy people want to climb rock walls, they should do it for whatever reason within reason, as long as all the appropriate safety precautions are in place.

3. If there are no facilities available that will allow people who use wheelchairs (for example) to climb nearly 90° rock walls, it is *our* job to start a program that will make it happen. Which is one of the reasons why Wilderness Inquiry[1] of Minneapolis, whose poster this is, exists. Wilderness Inquiry has done quite a job of it: in a fax from February, 1994, Greg Lais, the director, mentions the following statistics — "Since 1978, Wilderness Inquiry has served over 30,000 people, approximately half of whom have some sort of disability. Last year we served about 3,500 people. Again, about half of these folks have disabilities."

4. What *can* be accomplished is more often than not more than we had originally thought possible. On occasion it is astoundingly more than we would have considered possible. Accomplishing less than some world-famous feat, on the other hand, is *not* a failure. Any accomplishment in the world of Tzedakah moves things, changes things, brings benefit. We need not push ourselves to such astounding levels as Ms. Broadbent did. It is enough that we have done what we can, if we have done *all* that we can. *All* Mitzvahs make a difference. The balance is this: on the one hand, we might not want to take on gigantic projects, because we may be setting ourselves up for failure; on the other hand, taking on big projects should not deter us just because they are on the grand scale. We'll never know what we can do until we try it. It comes down to this: either we believe changing one thing big or small, one moment or event in Life momentous or a little less cosmic than momentous, or one opportunity for a human being makes a difference...or we don't. *I* most certainly believe it does.

5. Once upon a time, Nikolai Ivanovich Lobachevsky decided to question one of the basic principles of Greek geometry. He said that two parallel lines *can* meet somewhere. That's all I know. I don't really understand the implications of non-Euclidian geometry. It doesn't make any sense to me, and I don't know why Nikolai Ivanovich Lobachevsky came up with this crazy idea, but it changed many different aspects of reality. We are supposed to be thinking like Lobachevsky, coming up with ideas like his...in the world of Tzedakah and Mitzvahs. If we could make breakthroughs as great as Lobachevsky's — so I am told by the mathematicians — we would have a much more decent, fixed-up world.

So, the next time we set out to do some Mitzvahs, let's keep the picture of Ms. Broadbent on that cliff in our minds. I think it is a fine place to start.

Eyal Sherman's
Bar Mitzvah Speech

Eyal Sherman is the son of my good friends, Rabbi Charles and Leah Sherman of Syracuse. When Eyal was four years old, he was diagnosed with a brain tumor and the prognosis was very bleak. It was Purim Day.

Last Spring was the first time I saw Eyal since the time he was using a high chair and stroller. His Bar Mitzvah was in a couple of months, and he was hard at work finishing his preparations. It was going to be a large affair, so large in fact, the Shermans had to limit the number of invitations. They knew long ahead of time that the 750 seats in the sanctuary would be full.

Eyal uses a wheelchair and needs a respirator. He has tutors and attendants. Beyond that, there is no need for details other than to say that I am grateful he sent me a copy of his speech — and gave me permission to reprint it — and to say that knowing him makes my own life a געבענשטע לעבן, a blessed experience.

This is what Eyal said on the day he assumed full command of his Life of Mitzvahs:

Shabbat Shalom! Some people never thought I would have a Bat Mitzvah because I'm in a wheelchair and on a respirator. But this day proves them wrong! You might think this day is like a miracle, when something happens that you don't expect. Here I am today on the bimah (pulpit), an honor and a pleasure to be where my father stands every week. I prepared for my Bar Mitzvah at home for a long time starting when I was very young. I've learned to say the kiddush, blessing over the wine, and Birkat Hamazon, grace after meals. My family builds a Succah and we put on our ski jackets and eat in it. I learned the prayers by coming to services every Shabbat with my family. It was harder for me to prepare than other kids. The Cantor had to learn to read my lips.

Having my Bar Mitzvah means I am a man and now my father can call me on the phone to help make up the minyan when they are short. The happiest part of this day is having my relatives and friends from all over America and Israel here with me.

Even though my Bar Mitzvah is different, or awesome or radical, being high tech, I never really thought about that. I just always knew I'd be up here on the bimah and have a Bar Mitzvah just like any other kid.

Eyal's speech stands on its own, a brilliant statement, inspiring words. I didn't want any of my thoughts to interfere with Eyal and his words, so I saved my comments for the end —

A stylistic note: Young people tend to overuse exclamation marks when they write. (Teen-age love letters are filled with them.) I am particularly moved by the ! Eyal used after "But this day proves them wrong!" So much is expressed by that single punctuation mark.

Rabbi Sherman is the Rabbi of Temple Adath Yeshurun in Syracuse, NY. He is mentioned in another part of this book in the chapter called "How to Solve All the World's Problems (Well, Almost All of Them) By Making Just One Phone Call." His phone number is 315-445-0002, and I included it under the heading "Building a Ramp to the Bema (Even for High Bemas)". The Adath Yeshurun sanctuary is a very large one. The Bema is high. Someone who enters the sanctuary for the first time would assume it is a nearly-impossible task to build an access ramp for people who use wheelchairs or who have difficulty walking or climbing steps. It would appear to be an architectural and aesthetic nightmare, but the ramp is, indeed, there. Since this book has a very practical purpose — to change things — I would hope that, after reading Eyal's astonishing speech, a few dozen more people will call Rabbi Sherman to find out how they can build appropriate access ramps in their own synagogues. I would hope they are more determined than ever to do so. What good, after all, is being deeply moved by words if we don't *do* something?

I had originally thought to append Eyal's speech to a section of miscellaneous items I had collected and which I use during my speeches, i.e., the chapter called "From Newspapers, Magazines, Letters from Friends, Or Just Heard or Seen Around". For the grand irony of it all, I was going to place it right after the crazy story of a Bar Mitzvah party at a Miami dog track, complete with a mock gambling casino, whirling roulette wheels, clanking slot machines and green felt crap tables. I just couldn't do it. Eyal's words, so eloquent, simply had to be given a place of their own.

The Three-Wheelchair
Lending Service Mitzvah Project
For Synagogues
And Other Jewish Communal Institutions

I. The Project

1. Put three wheelchairs in every synagogue, Jewish Federation office, Jewish Community Center, Jewish Day School, and other Jewish Communal Buildings.

2. Whenever people need to take home a wheelchair, they call, sign their names, pick up the wheelchair, and take it home with them. When they are finished, they return it.

3. No charge for the service.

II. The Miscellany

1. It has been going on for years in Israel, through the Yad Sarah organization. My friend, Ari Newman, thinks it is eminently adaptable on a smaller scale to American Jewish institutions.

2. It works in Israel; it can work here.

3. Most places don't have to buy wheelchairs. Many congregants and community members still have wheelchairs somewhere in the house from previous use. Many would be delighted to donate them to this project.

4. Some synagogues in North America are already doing it.

5. If a community agency decides to expand into (a) a bigger supply of wheelchairs, or (b) other kinds of equipment (Yad Sarah has hundreds of different kinds of supplies), they are welcome to do so. If they can't go beyond the three wheelchairs, we are still way ahead of the game: in any given year, thousands of people will have access to wheelchairs with no hassle. One phone call, one pick-up.

6. And if they are unable to pick up the wheelchair, the Jewish agency can have a staff member or layperson deliver it.

7. Inevitably, people will appreciate this Mitzvah project so much, when they return the wheelchairs, many people will make a donation so the project can be expanded.

It's just another Mitzvah project waiting to happen on a larger scale.

Call Rabbi Gerry Walter at Temple Sholom in Cincinnati. 513-791-1330. He'll tell you how they did it and how you can do it.

All we have to do is do it.

How to Solve All the World's Problems
(Well, Almost All of Them)
By Making Just One Phone Call

I. *What to Do*

1. Pick a problem in the world, almost any problem — brightly colored T-shirts for kids living drab lives, lonely people, people who cannot afford to get cataract operations, getting medical supplies to Jews in Cuba, finding used cars for recently-arrived immigrants.

2. Start asking anyone and everyone you know who's doing the best job getting it done. Use the Yellow Pages, too, if you are stumped. (For example, for Mitzvah Clowning — I am surprised how many cities have a listing for "Clowns".)

3. Start making phone calls (sending faxes, working the Internet).

4. Meet as many of the people who are doing The Great Things as you can within your own personal schedule.

5. Make a phone number sheet of your own, print it up and start passing it around so that others can be part of your network.

II. *To Remember*

Remember — if it's being done in one place, most likely it can be done somewhere else (allowing for necessary adaptations and adjustments).

Remember — the critics can't say, "Impossible!" as long as you have the Magic Phone Number for them to call to see and hear that it is possible. A perfect example is donating leftover food from a hospital cafeteria to soup kitchens. "Impossible!" Not so — Rose Medical Center in Denver does it. The phone number is: 303-371-9250.[1]

III. *Keeping Track of Things*

1. I only know how to solve things easily.

2. There are experts on how to solve the difficult problems in Life, people who understand power structures and power plays and horse trading, the high and low art of lobbying, War and Peace and conflict resolution. If that is your forté, start making your calls and doing your research.

3. The trap: I remember all our guests at Thanksgiving dinner praising Mom's pumpkin pie. She told them it was easy. Sure it's easy, if you're a great baker, as good as my Mom. (All my Challah-baking friends say the same thing.) It's just like the glitches with your VCR or toaster oven. One of your mechanical friends comes over and does this and that with a screwdriver or a knife or tweezers, and the VCR goes its merry way recording all your favorite

programs, and the toaster turns out bagel after bagel exactly to your taste. They, too, tell you it's easy. But that's the trap: for *them* it's easy. *They* have the touch.

4. Trust me: Some of these Mitzvah endeavors are *very* easy. Distributing 50 pairs of shoes to people who need them isn't as difficult as it sounds. In most cases, taking the leftover food from a Bar or Bat Mitzvah reception to a shelter isn't so hard. Try one project. If it doesn't work, try another. Something will work, and all through the first few rounds, make notes, reminding yourself how easy it was. From there, it's a piece of cake (or as my Mom would put it, "A piece of pie.")

IV. My List of Phone Numbers

1. Phone numbers change.
2. Mitzvah projects end.
3. People doing Mitzvah projects move on to other-things-to-do-in-their-lives, though they rarely retire from Mitzvahs.
4. Some of these names, places, and phone numbers will no longer be of use after the text is frozen when this book goes to press. Try one or two of them, anyway, in case the numbers are still good. But at the same time continue building your own Mitzvah phone number list.

Danny Siegel's List of Mitzvah Phone Numbers

*How to Make Your Old Age Home a More Menschlich Place
(While Reducing the Cost of Medications by 50%,
Cutting the Infection Rate Dramatically,
and Offering the Residents The Opportunity to Live
Longer, More Fulfilling Lives)*

The Eden Alternative: Dr. William Thomas, 607-674-5232.

Saving Lives

Bone Marrow Testing: Arlene Feinberg, 1-800-9-MARROW
What It's Like to Be a Donor: Joyce Juda, 617-964-8210
Infant Car Seat Drive: Merrill Alpert, 818-788-6000

Off-Beat Mitzvah Projects

Mitzvah Crib: Merrill Alpert, 818-788-6000
Mitzvah Clowning: Sweet Pea and Buttercup (Mike and Sue Turk),
　　201-376-2885
Mitzvah Manicures: Ethel Shull, 813-960-1321
Gathering Millions of Pennies for Tzedakah: Teddy Gross
　　(Common Cents), 212-PENNIES, 212-877-3738 (h)

Mitzvah Mall (Channukah Mitzvah Gifts): Sharon Halper,
    914-723-7727
Mitzvah Co-op (Bringing Down Catering Prices):
    Marilyn Moses, 617-598-4331
Planting a Mitzvah Garden: Rabbi Roy Walter, 713-771-6221

The Big Time

Incredible Poster (take my word for it): Wilderness Inquiry,
    Greg Lais, 1-800-728-0719; 612-279-5972 (fax)
Starting a Jewish Community Food Bank:
    Bobbie Carr, 303-691-6136
Starting a Jewish AIDS Project: 213-653-8313 (Project "Nechama")
Starting a Jewish *Pro Bono* Legal Service: Joy Rothenberg,
    617-277-6090, Ralph Gottlieb, 213-939-0506
Starting a Jewish Battered Women's Shelter:
    Sherry Berliner Dimarsky, 312-583-HOPE
Starting a Group for Jewish Substance Abusers:
    212-397-4197 (JACS)
Starting a Jewish Free-Loan Society: Mark Meltzer, 213-655-6922
Starting a Mitzvah Heroes Column in Jewish Newspaper:
    Arthur Horwitz, Detroit Jewish News 313-354-6060
Becoming a Volunteer Dentist in Israel: Trudi Birger
    011-972-2-436-628, fax: 433-623
Becoming a Volunteer Ophthalmologist in Israel: Project Vision,
    Dr. Stephen Kutner, 404-577-8670, fax: 586-0843

Projects That Would Benefit Poor People

**Getting New Shoes to Donate Shipped to You
    (You Only Pay Shipping Costs):**
    Ranya Kelly, 303-431-0904
Donating Leftovers from Community Events:
    Ari Newman: 401-861-3474
Leftovers — Jewish Day Schools: Victoria Ginsberg,
    212-427-1000 (Ramaz Yeshiva)
Leftovers — Public Schools: David Levitt, 813-398-1766
Leftovers — University Cafeterias: Ari Newman, 401-861-3474
Leftovers — Restaurants: Operation Food Share, Don Cook or
    Bruce Feldman, 513-224-7283
Leftovers — Professional Sports Stadiums:
    Steve Chaikin, 410-528-1637, 301-983-0816
Community-wide Pick-up Service for Food Donations:
    Rachel's Table, 508-799-7600
Hotel Shampoo and Soap Drive: Elana Erdstein, 313-541-6997
Truckloads of Potatoes: Ray Buchanan or Ken Horne, 1-800-333-4597

The Mitzvah Menagerie

Getting Pets into Hospitals: Holly Pfau, 818-397-3495
(Huntington Memorial Hospital, Pasadena, CA)
or Donna Miedema, 303-861-6286 (Denver Children's Hospital)

**Delta Society (Projects Involving Animals that Benefit
Human Beings):** Linda Hines, 1-800-869-6898 (V/TTY)

Mitzvah Dog Program/Demonstration: Becky Duncan or Nancy Foust,
Canine Companions for Independence, 707-579-1985

Getting Birds into Old Age Homes or Synagogues: Carol Hutton
(The Bird Woman of Indianapolis), 317-630-3063 (day), 845-8829

**Mitzvah Horses (to locate your nearest therapeutic riding
group):** NARHA[2,] 1-800-369-7433

Giraffes (meet, bring in Mitzvah heroes): 360-221-7989

Mitzvah heroes, also: The Caring Institute, Marian Brown, 202-547-4273

Dolphins and Kids with Disabilities: Marianne Klingel, 813-441-1790

Kids bring Pets to Synagogue for Program:
Mark Hyman, 310-546-3962

The Great Stuffed Animal Mitzvah: No phone number needed. Just
gather 100 teddy bears and other stuffed animals from friends, then
distribute them to kids whose families cannot afford to buy them toys.
(Idea from Aviva Kieffer.)

Projects That Would Benefit People With Disabilities

Large Print Siddurim: Rabbi Matthew Simon, 301-881-6550

**Sound System in Jewish Communal Buildings for Hearing
Impaired People:** Dr. Mark Ross, 203-429-6688

Organizing a Drive to Gather Used Hearing Aids:
Dr. Mark Ross, 203-429-6688

**Getting a Telecommunications Device for the Deaf (TTY)
into Jewish Communal Buildings:**
Dr. Mark Ross, 203-429-6688

**Almost Anything You Need to Know About Jewish Hearing
Impaired People:** Rabbi Dan Grossman, 609-896-4977 (o)

Building a Ramp to the Bema (Even for High Bemas):
Rabbi Charles Sherman, 315-445-0002

Learning How to Braille Books: Betty Lukinsky, 212-928-3510

Designing Useful Items for People with Disabilities:
Julie Grubaugh, 216-368-8765

Organizing a Jewish Community Disabilities Fair:
Elaine Albert, 213-476-0512

Adopting Children with Down Syndrome:
Janet Marchese, 914-428-1236

Synagogue Projects

Starting a Synagogue Mitzvah Committee: Mindy Agler, 407-395-2721
Synagogue Mitzvah Projects Newsletter: Mindy Agler, 407-395-2721
Starting a Telephone Reassurance Program in the Synagogue:
    Naomi Eisenberger, 201-763-9396
Starting a Wheelchair-Lending Service Through Your Synagogue:
    Rabbi Gerry Walter, 513-791-1330
Sell a Torah, Use Proceeds for Tzedakah:
    Naomi Eisenberger, 201-763-9396
Welcoming Guests and Strangers into the Synagogue
    ("Blue Cups/White Cups"): Temple Emanuel, 617-332-5770
Non-Shabbas Bat/Bar Mitzvah with Tzedakah Fair:
    Sarra Alpert, 818-996-1360
**Bat Mitzvah Person Doing Mitzvathon to Raise Tons of Money
    for *Dreams Come True*:** Ilana Gildenblatt, 513-984-4415

Miscellaneous Projects

Mitzvah Projects on College Campuses: Rabbi Albert Axelrad
    or Ora Gladstone, Brandeis University Hillel, 617-736-3570
Starting a Recycling Program in your Community:
    Laura-Beth Moore, 713-862-5487.

The Mighty Mitzvah Horses of Israel

Horses?

I am 50 years old and I am in the horse business.

Being 50 isn't all that bad, although so many people who turn 50 in America worry that their lives are going too fast and they are running out of time. They get depressed. Some people — usually people in their 30's — give them those dumb T-shirts that say, "It took me 50 years to get this good looking!" And there are always people, usually in their 30's or early 40's who secretly buy them their first year's membership in the American Association for Retired Persons, and, if they are particularly brave — some of us might say foolish — one or two start calling you, "Grandpa" or "Gramps."

But I don't mind. I'm in the horse business, and I feel terrific.

My first horse was a very big one, a white one, named "Quickie," but the Israelis changed its name to "Nur," which is one of many Hebrew words for "Light". Israelis will do that. Once you get settled in Israel, there is an urge to take on a more Jewish name, and, anyway, this wasn't going to be a racehorse, so they didn't need a horse with a name like Quickie.

Now I am up to four horses. I added three more this year: Little John, Katie, and Comet. And the reason I feel so good at 50 is that I have a goal: By the time I am 55, I want to have a whole herd of them, and I hope they'll have all kinds of exotic and weird and run-of-the-mill names like, "Moshe" and "Ora" and "Yaffa" and whatever the Hebrew equivalent might be for "Wind-in-Your-Mane".

In fact, if I were a millionaire, I wouldn't even wait until I was 55. I'd buy the rest of the herd right now. But I am a little short of ready cash, so I'll have to do it more slowly.

But I know I can do it.

I just know it.

After all, another Jewish kid has a big herd of them, though they are different kinds of horses, and he uses them for different things than I do. William Shatner is his name, or, in his other life, Captain Kirk of the Starship Enterprise. From all I have heard, he has one of the biggest horse farms in Lexington, Kentucky, and he seems to me to be a reasonably happy man. So why shouldn't I be happy with my horses?

It really doesn't make much sense that I should be dealing in horses.

I was raised a nice Jewish kid from Arlington, Virginia, doing my homework, playing ball with my brother and friends in the afternoons and evenings and all day, sometimes, during the Summers, prizing my new glove or a fine bat I got for my birthday. I would go to synagogue, first with my family, then with friends and family, and I got involved in youth groups. We were fairly pleasant kids, and I see some of them now and again, most of them

Nur, a Mighty Mitzvah Horse.

with AARP cards in their wallets. One, Gordon Gondos, is My Oldest Friend in the Whole World, and you'll hear more about him later.

If you were to go back with me then to around 1960 or 1961 and asked what was I going to be when I grew up, I probably would have said something like "professor" or "Hebrew school teacher" or maybe even "Rabbi". I remember I once had an assignment to interview someone who had a job like you wanted to have "when you grew up," and I picked a friend's father who was a nuclear physicist — a rather famous one, I believe —, but by a year or two later I knew I had picked that occupation only because it sounded long and neat to say. (I became a poet, besides a horse businessperson, so I always liked the sound of words more than their meaning.)

Thirty-three years ago, if Jack or Wayne or Marilyn or one of The Twins, Randy or Brett, had said to me, "I'll bet when you're over the hill and 50, you'll be in the horse business..." — I'll bet we would have had a good laugh and probably worked off the joke with a round of miniature golf or a movie and a Coke afterwards. Why, I had never been near horses except once or twice — though I had watched a lot of Westerns on TV, all the way back to the black and white days, and many, many movies, all the way back to the days when the bad guys wore black and the good guys wore white and had holsters shiny with studs and more studs on the horse's stirrups and saddle and reins. But the only time I had been near real horses was as a typical suburban kid forced up on a pony's back at the local carnival by Mom (me dressed in Roy Rogers gear, of course) so she could take pictures for the photo album, so in our old age we could look back on that day and enjoy another one of Life's Good Laughs.

I think I cried when they put me up on the horse, and I'm *sure* I made them walk me around the ring *very* slowly. For me, it wasn't easy making the transition from TV and movies to the real thing. I'm sure I even had a wooden hobby horse as a three-year-old, but that didn't help much, either.

At that age of riding a pony, I was definitely no more than a cat and dog person.

How I Got Into the Horse Business

Someone sent me an article about Mitzvah horses in Israel.
That's all it took.
I was hooked.
Actually, that's not the whole story. I began with Mitzvah dogs, and, I suppose, worked my way up.

Somewhere along the way, about 20 years ago, I began to read about how money can make miracles happen. People started giving me money to give away, so miracles could happen. It's now almost $2,000,000 worth of miracle money, and as I worked my way through articles and videos and meetings and visits to miracle workers, I began to see how many ways there were to do it, and how little money it took to make it happen.

I became a Matchmaker, taking the money, and matching it with people who knew how to touch the lives of many people and make them feel better, or to get them to walk if they couldn't walk or to get them to smile, even if they were so sick that no pills or injections or intravenous drips could make the pain go away.

I soon found out there were Mitzvah heroes everywhere, and they did their great Mitzvah heroics in so many ways I lost count. They used every kind of tool: time, hands, computers and CD-ROMS with full-color movies, singing, card tricks, six-day treks out into the wilds and wilderness of America in canoes and wheelchairs with and without backpacks...just about anything.

I mean, listen to this: I just got in the mail this huge poster of a woman in a wheelchair, safety rope tied securely around her body, going down the al-most-absolutely-vertical, nearly-ninety-degrees side of a cliff!

Talk about miracles!

And that's how I became fascinated by Mitzvah dogs, which eventually got me to the horses.

A few years ago I was giving a talk at a synagogue in Northern California, in that part of the state known as The Wine Country. The next morning I had a few hours free before I had to present my next lecture one or two counties South, and my hosts said, "Do you want to go to the wineries?"

I said, "I don't think so." Wine never did anything for me, except for Kiddush. I wouldn't know a fruity taste from a tawny color, and I still would-n't know if I were in a fancy restaurant, if my friends would need to order white wine to go with fish or red for pasta, and whether 1983 was a good year or a bad year for Bordeaux.

So they said, "Do you want to see the dogs?"

And I said — remembering Bruce, our German shepherd when I was very young, and Pokey and Flopsie when I was older — I said, "Sure."

So they took me to see the Mitzvah dogs at a place called Canine Companions for Independence. These are the dogs that pull wheelchairs, that pick up things for people who use wheelchairs because their bodies don't work as well as mine...things like paintbrushes if they are painting, or a five dollar bill if they are in a store and drop it by accident. And they turn light switches off and on and press elevator buttons, and at least 85 other things. They even have dogs for people who can barely hear or can't hear at all, gentle, gorgeous dogs that can tell their owners if someone is ringing the doorbell with a package from UPS or if there is a fire engine blasting away with its siren outside the window so the human partner can go down the steps to safety along with ev-eryone else.

I was hooked.

People who had been in car accidents and people who had been born with the wrong genes and couldn't move like other people, and people who had had diseases that took away their hearing were all getting a second, better chance at living The Good Life, because of a bunch of dogs, every one of them rigorously trained. So tough is the course, in fact, some of them flunk, and have to live the rest of their lives as house pets instead of as Mitzvah dogs. I know, from personal experience. Canine Companions for Independence honored us by naming one of its puppies "Ziv," after Ziv Tzedakah Fund, my nonprofit foundation. I recently received a letter from Corey Hudson, the Executive Director, with an update. "Ziv was released from the program because of an uncontrollable urge to chase cats. He is living with a family that worships him. He has his own swimming pool to play in, goes running often and even gets along with the cat he lives with."[1] I suppose if I were a dog in the middle of training, and I were just lounging around during a break with my friend Max the Golden Retriever, I might say something like, "I'll bet this is as hard as trying to get a Ph.D. in Chemistry from Harvard." As I said, the training is *very* rigorous.

But the ones that make it — what a marvelous life they have, making Life so much better for their owners. And all for the mere price of $10,000 per dog, though the owners only pay something like $125 for the backpack and bowl and little things like registration fees. Why, for a few bucks — $9,875.00 to be almost exact — miracles could happen.

I was really hooked.

What a cheap price to pay for miracles!

I mean, just think about it. Besides the very high-sounding fact that people can now be more independent, some of them may no longer have to feel like outcasts or freaks. I especially remember one of the graduates say that, after he had broken his neck, and after he had been in the hospital and rehabilitation for months, he decided to get his life together and go back to college, but, one day, when he was in a class of 200 people — he said — no one saw *him*. All they saw was *the wheelchair*. Now, with this gorgeous dog at the side of his wheelchair, can you imagine everyone ignoring him? Can you imagine people averting their eyes from the sight of a human being in a wheelchair whose legs, or arms and legs, may not be working so well or at all? Can you imagine not wanting to ask, "What's the dog's name?" Or not wanting to ask, "May I pet him/her?" Just think of the pleasure of explaining why this dog is so special. He'll never have to feel lonely again. And for only $9,875.00, that's a cheap price to pay.

I mean, how hard can it be to raise that kind of money so someone can get around by himself or herself and never be lonely?

A piece of cake.

So, from the dogs to the horses was an easy step, with a few side trips along the way, like:

Reading about and seeing all the birds, cats, dogs, and fish in old age homes, and how their presence gives people a sense of why it is so wonderful to be alive.

And like: Reading about and seeing dogs in hospitals, some as visitors to be petted and do tricks and lie in bed to be warm next to a scared kid who has just had an operation on her eye; and others as resident pets of the hospital, playing in the hallways and helping out in physical therapy or fetching a ball out on the grass when someone who used to be feeling fairly lousy throws it, and then the person doesn't feel lousy anymore because there is something alive that isn't sticking her with needles or taking his temperature or asking about her medical history at 2:00 in the morning. It's just something natural: play and fun, a dog and a human being, innocent, lively, and alive.

And like:

Reading about and seeing videos about those marvelous Mitzvah sea animals down in Clearwater, FL[2] — the dolphins and sea turtles and other wet wonders who do so much for kids with disabilities. Miracles. They're real-live miracles! Not the least of which is the fact that the dolphins and huge turtles have their own physical problems — one dolphin is blind in one eye, one turtle has a damaged flipper, and one of the most recent additions to the teaching staff — another dolphin — survived a shark attack. And listen to what the staff has been hearing lately from the children, something like: "Look at them! If they can survive and do so well, So can I!"

All those Mitzvah animals doing their thing, just like people!

And that's not even counting The Great Stuffed Animal Drive. That's the project with kids in schools everywhere, the little little kids especially, bringing in their teddy bears and tigers and penguins and raccoons and giving them away to kids who don't have a single stuffed animal in the whole world! (Just to give one example: the kindergarten class of the Solomon Schechter Day School in Skokie, IL, collected more than 120 stuffed animals. All those happy kids, just because other kids decided to *do* something to make a difference!)

So you can see how — when that article about Mitzvah horses arrived in the mail — you can see how ready I was to go into the horse business.

Mitzvah Horses

What the article said:

There is a place in Israel, near the city of Netanya, where they are doing therapeutic horseback riding.

Why it rang a bell with me:

Remembering that My Oldest Friend in the Whole World is Gordon Gondos, I pictured his son, Gary, who had been taking therapeutic riding lessons since he was six years old, and I just knew that there was something special about these horses and the way he rode.

Gary is a fine young man now. He's in his early 20's and in college. But when he was an infant, his parents — my friends Gordon and his wife Myra — were told there was something wrong with his heart, and surgery would be the best thing.

The surgery went well, tricky as it was, but Gary had a stroke. For the next number of years, there would be visits to physiotherapists and all kinds of other specialists to make sure Gary would do well in Life, including Myra's discovery of the Mitzvah horses in Northern Virginia.

For years he rode, and one day I went out to see what it was all about, little suspecting that I would have to do some of the work actually leading the horse. I think it was the closest I had been to a horse since I was a kid myself playing Roy Rogers on the little pony, except maybe once or twice when I ventured out on vacation for an hour's ride. But that doesn't really count. We barely slogged along, never cantering or galloping or doing anything tricky, since I was too scared. But there I was, myself in front of this big, powerful, gentle horse, Myra to one side, the special therapist on the other stretching Gary's leg, and The Kid way up high, following the teacher's instructions and having The Time of His Life.

And the fact of the matter is, when it was all over, Gary could walk better and stand straighter, and do many other things more easily, because of whatever it is about this special horseback riding that made his nerves and muscles and balance system kick into high gear and get themselves back into more fine-tuned working order.

Ah, it was miraculous! Not like the Parting of the Red Sea, and not exactly like forty years of Manna coming down from Heaven to feed the Children of Israel all those many miles through the Wilderness until they reached the Promised Land. Not Biblical, but still a miracle to behold.

That's why, when my friend sent me the article from *The Jerusalem Post*, it rang a bell with me. I couldn't wait until I got back to Israel that Summer to see the horses in action.

The Mitzvah Horses of Israel

I made it.

My friend drove me to the place where it was happening, The Therapeutic Riding Club of Israel. You could smell it was there, even before we turned off the road. It was a very horsey smell, so I knew we were in the right place.

There were about a dozen horses around, a tin shed for an office, a flimsy kind of corral or something that resembled a corral, another shed for storage, and a big riding ring, where some people were having their lessons. It was nothing like I had imagined it: no deluxe accommodations for the horses like I was used to seeing when the TV reporters would interview the jockeys and trainers at the Kentucky Derby. There was nobody in a thousand-dollar riding outfit. The other difference was of little real-Life consequence: most of the students moved their bodies in a different way than I did.

We met Anita Shkedi, the founder of the Therapeutic Riding Club of Israel, and her husband, Giora. We sat and talked and watched the riders, and as we talked, she'd explain this and that about the essence of the program: how a horse walks the way people walk, how they have special saddles for different kinds of riders, Western saddles and English saddles, and even one with two seats so a therapist can ride right behind the rider, and one that's particularly comfortable when they lay some of the students stomach-down on it so they can flop along and loosen up every bone and muscle, ligament and tendon in their tight bodies, how there's a difference between hippotherapy ("hippo" is Greek for "horse") and therapeutic horseback riding (though I can't keep them straight), how sometimes you need three or four therapists walking alongside one rider, how the nerves that sometimes can't be brought back to life by aquatic therapy or work with the Big Ball in the physiotherapy room at rehabilitation hospitals are brought back to life by the horse's movement — how they come alive, even though some people thought they were dead forever — how it feels to interact with a warm body, such a huge, muscular, awesomely powerful body, how it must seem to a kid who can't learn in school the right way because of irregular connections in his brain, how her friends used to make fun of her, but now she is sitting on top of the world and no one can make fun, how the idea got started in Europe a couple of hundred years ago, but how it didn't really have a worldwide impact until Lis Hartel came along....

The 1952 Olympics

As if I weren't already convinced.

Here's where I *really* got hooked.

Helsinki, Finland, the Summer of 1952. A young woman named Lis Hartel of Denmark wins the silver medal in dressage, one of the horse events, the one where the rider puts the horse through all kinds of paces and the judging goes by how closely the rider and horse work together and how good their time is while they are making all those turns and doing all those particular moves.

The moment of triumph has arrived.[3] Something incredible happens when it is time for the winners to mount the platform to receive their medals.

Lis Hartel can't do it by herself. Until Henri Saint Cyr of Sweden, the gold medal winner, helps her up to her place on the victory platform, she just can't climb those two steps.

Because her legs won't work right.

Because she had polio a few years before, and, even now, at the Olympics, she had to be helped on and off her horse.

Because after she had polio, she was determined to get back on horseback, as she had done when everything worked just right with her body,

before she had to start crawling around the house, then learning to walk with crutches and re-learning how to lift her arms,

despite the pain and exhaustion.

It was one of those Magic Moments in History with the news cameras and reporters all around, wondering just why this vibrant young woman, this Olympian, couldn't climb those two steps.

Now the word was out, and millions of people would know about the spectacular possibilities of that unique interaction between a horse and a rider who has something not-quite-right with his or her body or mind or both.

And she took the silver medal again in 1956 in Stockholm, once again on Jubilee, her Mighty Mitzvah Steed.

And I would imagine that Mr. Saint Cyr, who won the gold medal for a second time, knew exactly what to do when it came time for Ms. Hartel to get her medal.

What a glorious moment it must have been!

The Mitzvah Horses of Israel, Part II

I was so fascinated by the story of Lis Hartel that I have had Anita tell it to me many times over the past few years. I have read books on the Olympics, looking for more of the story. I have written to Ms. Hartel and received an answer from her and her husband. I even carry her address in Fredensborg, Denmark, in my wallet, just in case. In case I ever decide to just get on a plane to Copenhagen and drive the hour or so to Fredensborg to meet this most extraordinary woman.

Anita really hit home with that one.

Then she went on to explain the many kinds of people that come to ride: people who have had car accidents and other kinds of accidents, blind people — including one child who wouldn't hold her head up, didn't have any reason to hold it up because there was nothing to see, but now she holds her head up and her neck and spine are just fine, thank you — and nearly-blind people, kids and adults who are severely hearing impaired, people born paralyzed in one way or another, learning-disabled people (like myself, but only mildly so), mentally slow individuals including some people with Down Syndrome, people from an old age home in their seventies and eighties who had never been on horseback before, people with bad spines and crooked spines, people with spina bifida and cerebral palsy, Israeli soldiers — so many soldiers — with every kind of injury, Israeli citizens injured in terrorist attacks piecing their lives back together, and people with one leg, just like the woman I once saw who unscrewed her artificial leg at the bottom of the chair lift pick-up, went up, skied down, and put her leg back on then went her merry way, and people who had to be lifted by a special lift from their wheelchair onto the horse's back, and people who walked — not the way I might want perhaps — slowly up the ramp, mounted the horse, took a lesson, got off, walked back down the ramp and went home...a man who couldn't walk at all eight months before. Or so Anita explained to me.

And many, many of them didn't feel very good about themselves...until they started to ride the Mitzvah horses.

Miracles. The last one — feeling good, and feeling good about themselves — not the least of them.

How it all works, using all the long words of science like "neurologically" and "vestibular" and other textbook words — that's important, too, and it's all there in the journals, including articles by Anita. But it's only secondary. It doesn't count as much as the man in the video who has to use a wheelchair because of an accident or war wound who said, "I used to be six feet tall. When I would walk into a room and come up to talk to you, I could look you straight in the eye. Now I look at your stomach. But here [he's talking to the reporter while sitting high on the horse], here, I am on top again. I am somebody."

I could see miracles happening right in front of my eyes, and I knew that if I came back the next day or next week or next year, I'd see more of them, and hear about more of them, like how in some places in England, three weeks after some people have had a stroke, they put them right into therapeutic horse-back riding: special horses, special teachers, special equipment, and a great deal of love and caring and gentleness. And there would be more miracles in England with people who had lost their power to speak or to move one arm or one leg, even though those horse therapists, and Anita and Giora and I know that where no miracles could happen, they wouldn't happen. There would just be some plain old impossible situations where nothing would work. Nothing.

But that thought didn't ruin the time I spent there that first time, nor the second, nor the third time. Too many wonderful things were happening. I was even there once when Abir was only about six or eight weeks old, and I stood there and watched him munch away on his feed, and petted him, and thought, "This horse is going to grow up to be a Mighty Mitzvah Horse." And when I saw him the next year, he was already one, huge, gorgeous horse, ready to do his thing. "Abir" — the "Knight," the "Valiant One," "Courageous One."

I even wondered if parents sometimes might not take a look at their young children that particular way, picturing them all grown up, doing their Mitzvah work, full strength, in all their glory.

There was no question that I was hooked.

And you would be hooked, too, if you went to see them in action, the horses and the people working together. You could just stand there or sit there and watch, and be deeply moved.

Getting Into the Horse Business

That first time, Anita went on to explain how many people came to ride each week. Such-and-such lessons a day, so many available riding hours (except for mid-day in the Summer heat, except Shabbat and holidays), and how many more riders could come to ride if they only had more horses.

But I was slow to pick up on her hint.

I started using my friends' Tzedakah money for different things: one year we bought them a special lift, for example, so Giora wouldn't have to pick people up out of their wheelchairs and put them on the horse's back, painful to Giora, painful to the horse, painful to the rider. Or another time, we purchased a tractor for them, to make the riding arena better suited for the lessons, and yet another time we paid for some particular items the Riding Club needed so blind riders could have an easier time going around the track. And, of course, we donated scholarship money to pay for people who couldn't afford the riding lessons, even though Anita and Giora charge less than they should to make a go of it financially.

But I never thought I'd actually get into the horse business, and the way it happened, well, it was like so many other things that happen in Life. It's what they say in Yiddish, "אריינגעפאלן אין קאפ-Areingefallen in Kup" — one day it just fell into my head to do it. It was probably sitting there in some room or box in my brain since the time Anita told me they needed more horses, but it just wouldn't come up to the "Boker Tov-Good Morning! Wake Up!" part of my mind.

Until that day, whenever it was a couple of years ago when I handed over $8,000.00 and said, kind of with a flair and a bit of Mitzvah swashbuckling, "Go buy yourself another horse. My friends would like that. And they don't even want their names on a plaque on its mane or tail or flank or withers."

That $8,000.00 became Quickie, the big white one who likes to roll in the dirt to have fun or scratch its back, the one they re-named Nur because it made more sense to call it "Light" than making up some name that suggested its Life's Purpose was to win a $1,000,000.00 purse at the Belmont Stakes.

It took them a year and a half to find exactly the right horse, the one with precisely the right personality: gentle and patient, in good health, the right size, the right age, with a strong back and a sense of nobility, and full of a horse's Joy of Life and love of human beings.

They bought it some time during the Winter or Spring months, and I couldn't wait to get back during the Summer to see my first Mitzvah horse.

When I did, I knew I was *really* hooked.

I knew that this was how I wanted to spend more of my time, getting more of the Tzedakah money — frequently in $1.00 and $2.00 and $5.00 shots at my lectures. I wanted hundreds of people to play a part in the Mitzvah work of this living, breathing, stunning Mitzvah animal.

A Dream I Must Have Had, Or How I Wound Up Buying Little John, Katie, and Comet And How They Got to Israel

After Nur settled into the new life as a Mitzvah Horse, I must have had a dream. I never used to dream about horses, but, one night I must have dreamed about a white one, probably Nur. This is what the Talmud has to say about white horse dreams:

הרואה סוס לבן בחלום
בין בנחת בין ברדוף יפה לו

If one dreamed about a white horse —
whether it is resting or running —
it is a good sign. (Berachot 56b)

And as if that weren't enough to push me full tilt into the horse business, I subsequently found out from my friends, the Gondoses, that there is a Hungarian phrase that goes like this, "Fehér lovat látni, szerencsét találni," which means, "If you see a white horse, you will find good luck." So whether Nur appeared in my night dreams, or whether I saw this magnificent white steed in a daydream, I knew I was on the right track. And clearly, after the first one, the next equine beauties were going to be easy. A piece of cake, or, more appropriately, a feedbag of oats.

It happened this way: Anita was in New Zealand giving some talks at an international conference on therapeutic horseback riding, and she decided to stop back in the States before returning to Israel. She spent some time with my

Two of the Mitzvah horses preparing to board an El Al cargo plane for Israel, with Giora Shkedi of the Therapeutic Riding Club of Israel.

Little John, Katie and Comet —Mighty Mitzvah Horses.

friend, Naomi Eisenberger, who is deeply involved in my Mitzvah work. Just out of curiosity, Naomi had started asking around New Jersey about horses that might be for sale, and might just be the right kind of horse for Anita's program.

Sure enough! After looking over a few of them, there was Comet, a *big* Appaloosa, the right age, the right size, with the perfect personality.

Anita went home, and now the fun began: Naomi had to figure out how to get our Mitzvah horse to Israel. And, in the meantime, she had found out it wasn't so much more expensive to send three than it was to send one....So we bought two more horses, Little John and Katie.

You couldn't fax them.

You couldn't send them in the mail. There would be too many problems trying to do it that way: (1) at 50¢ for the first half ounce, 45¢ for the second half-ounce and 39¢ for each additional half-ounce up to the first 925 pounds, it would simply cost too much money, and, even if we did it that way, (2) what happens if the largest stamp they have in the post office that day is only $2.00? Think of all the stamps! And worse (3) what happens if the post-person's sponge isn't working right and Naomi would have to stand out in the hallway licking away $2.00 at a time? She wouldn't be able to speak for weeks. That's for sure. And even if she finally got all the stamps on them, imagine (4) how difficult it would be to get even the small ones, Little John and Katie through that tiny slot in the wall. She probably couldn't get more than one hoof through at most.

It just wouldn't work.

And we couldn't send them by boat, because they'd go stir crazy by the time they got to Israel, and it would probably take months of a different kind of horse therapy to get them into working shape, and we would probably get a bill for the broken couches from the horse psychiatrist because they weigh so much the furniture would just crumble when they would lie down on them for the therapy sessions.

And we couldn't send them by the regular plane — even though I have a picture of them standing at the bottom of what appears to be an El Al ramp exactly like the ones we climb to get on board for the flight over. First of all, they are too big to fit in coach class. And Comet was definitely too big even for Business Class, and we didn't want to put him up in First all by himself, and we couldn't get him up into the big bubble in a 747 anyway, because the windy staircase up to First Class is just too curved for a horse. And besides, we had already discussed their dietary requirements with the previous owners, and El Al wasn't prepared to negotiate with us beyond providing Kosher, vegetarian, low salt, bland, or fruit plate for our three horses. And then there was the issue of blinders big enough for them, in case they wanted to sleep through the movie so they'd be rested when they got off the plane at Ben Gurion airport.

No, a regular plane just wouldn't work.

So we finally settled on EL Al Cargo. Giora flew over to accompany them, and Naomi went out to the airport to see them safely off, saying Shalom as they went up the ramp into the plane. It was a six-tissue moment.

Later we got a fax that they had landed safely, and that, after a while, they had passed through the quarantine, and were ready to start work as Mitzvah horses.

All for a mere $21,000.00, purchase price, preparation charges, and transportation.

I say "a mere $21,000.00" because if you use a $6.00 calculator, you work it all out this way:

Let's say each horse works 275 days a year. (No Shabbat, no holidays.)

Let's say they do two lessons a day = 550 lessons. It could be more, it could be less, but let's say two a day.

And there are four horses in all....(We paid $8,000.00 for Nur, so our total bill was $29,000.00.) Four horses X 550 lessons = 2,200 lessons a year.

Let's say they can work about 13.2 years before they retire to green pastures and frolic and play in the grass: 13.2 X 22,000 = 290,040 lessons, or, rounded out, 290,000 lessons.

290,000 lessons ÷ $29,000.00 = $.10/lesson we invested.

Now, when you get down to it, that's not really that much money, is it?

Without Really Knowing a Lot About Horses,
You Can Still Be an Owner of a Mitzvah Horse

As anyone who knows horses can tell, I don't know much about horses, even though I have a couple of books about them.

I am told that Katie is a mare and Little John and Comet are geldings, and that they were all eight years old when we bought them, and that Comet is an Appaloosa and the other two are Quarter Horses. (I can't remember what kind of horse Nur is.) And even though I just checked *The Complete Book of Horses* so I could know the difference between one kind and another, I am sure I will forget, just as I can't remember if a filly means not only a female but also a mother horse. I know they aren't old nags, but I still couldn't tell the difference between a Thoroughbred and a Quarter Horse, though I *do* know that some people who know everything about Mitzvah horses think the Icelandic breed is the best.[4] (Well, maybe, I would know a Clydesdale, those big, big ones with the furry hooves you always see pulling the big Budweiser wagon through the snow during time outs in a football game.) That's about all I know about breeds. And "mare" and "foal" and "hoof" and "mane" and "saddle" and "bridle" are as far as it goes with my horse vocabulary.

I couldn't tell you if they should be eating more hay than oats, or if high fiber oats are better for their digestion or if some particular horses like it crunchy and others prefer it soggy in water. I don't even know if they only eat breakfast and supper or if they like to snack all day long.

I don't know the name of a single horse disease, and, if I did, which ones are serious and life-threatening, and which ones are only little things like a human's cold. I just don't know.

I've heard that they never sleep, and I've heard that they sleep only 60 winks; that they sleep standing up and that they sleep lying down on their haunches (do horses have haunches?) And I just know that if I were on a quiz show and the $25,000 Prize was mine if I could only answer the question, "Do horses give birth standing up or lying down?" — I'd be out of luck. I just don't know.

What I do know is this: there is something magical about them, about them and their riders working together. It's not magic like Pegasus the ancient Greek mythological horse with wings, and it's not like comic book horses that can leap over incredible chasms a hundred feet wide to rescue their owners who have been captured by The Bad Guys in Black Hats. Those are fantasies. And it's not like a magician's magic when he or she makes something like a Lincoln Town Car disappear in front of an audience of thousands by saying some magic words and waving a big cape in the air. These horses certainly don't jump through flaming hoops or juggle rings or cups and saucers or bowling pins, and they won't turn into a prince or princess if you kiss them on the forehead at midnight under a full moon. They don't play guitar and sing rock and roll songs from the Sixties. Why, they can't even talk.

And still, they are magic, and what they do is magical.

Here are the endorsements of just two physicians, quoted from a publicity package sent out by NARHA, the North American Riding for the Handicapped Association[5]:

(1) "A horse's walking action mimics your body action. So, when you put somebody on a horse, in order to keep their balance, they have to move their trunk, arms, shoulders, head and the rest of their body. Only a live creature can make happen what is so beneficial. Nautilus™ and other exercise machines work only one group of muscles at a time. They don't require you to respond to them with natural body movements. A horse makes your whole body respond in a smoothly rhythmic, progressive way." (Dr. Louis Wagner, chest and vascular surgeon, Franklin, PA.)

(2) "Therapeutic riding is extremely effective with:
— adult stroke victims
— adults or children with brain injuries
— children with cerebral palsy.
"In addition to the physical benefits, therapeutic riding offers psychological benefits because riders feel a sense of achievement and control.
"Therapeutic riding requires balance and muscular control that often enhances or expedites recovery. The slow, continuous, rhythmic motion of the gait of the horse is therapeutic and helps develop the muscles around the spine." (Dr. Walter Bobechko, Director of Humana Advanced Surgical Institute, Orthopedic Center of Dallas.)

Mitzvah horses give dignity to so many people who feel they are worthless human beings.

And Mitzvah horses give hope where there is little hope or no hope at all, and they give Life where Life was going out like a candle with barely enough wax or wick left to burn.

And that's why, if I were a millionaire, I would buy a whole herd of them right now.

And that's why, even though I am not a millionaire, I promised myself I'll find the money, somehow, to buy a whole herd of them.

It's really not that much money, is it?

Not when you are buying Dignity and Hope and Life.

Postscript: Horse #5

The herd of mighty Mitzvah horses grows.

I had already finished writing and revising this article, and I was confident that I had covered everything.

Then I got a call from a friend who told me that Jeffrey, Dori, and Michael Schwartz, children of my long-time friends, Joe and Gloria, had just bought a horse for the Therapeutic Riding Club. I had met all three of the kids off and on since the time they were teen-agers, and then, last Summer, the entire family was in Jerusalem. We shared some good times together, including a long, lovely, leisurely walk one afternoon.

Recently, Great Aunt Lillian Karpa Chabner passed away, and Jeffrey, Dori, and Michael (and Michael's fiancée, Kimberly Miller) decided to do some act of Tzedakah in her memory. Now, even as I am writing this, their horse is giving Dignity and Hope and Life to many people.

As the Talmud tells us (Bava Batra 10a) — and as Jeffrey, Dori, Michael and Kim remind us by their very great Mitzvah — "Tzedakah is mightier than Death."

The Therapeutic Riding Club of Israel, c/o Anita and Giora Shkedi, POB 3168, Bet Yehoshua, Israel, 09-697-776 or 698-289, fax: 09-696-103.

From Newspapers, Magazines, Letters from Friends, Or Just Heard or Seen Around

Wolfman, The Awesome Mitzvah Cat[1]

Wolfman is "an 18-pound, plant-chomping, spaghetti-slurping feline who has his own cozy corner at St. Anthony Hospital Central" in Denver. The article explains that, "Research has shown that animals can provide walking, squawking therapy to people in nursing homes and people with mental illnesses." The article's author, Bill Briggs, describes the situation, "And he's been able to pounce on a few tough cases, like the psychotic patient who wouldn't make eye contact or talk to any nurses." Now here's the part I like — he quotes Debra Matzinger, the cat's owner who brought Wolfman in to live there and do his good Feline Mitzvah Work. "He was just real guarded. Then he saw the cat and *you could see life come into his eyes.* [Italics mine.] He started talking about how he used to have a cat like that."

A New Posse for the Chicago Cops[2]

The Chicago Police Department — famous over the years for other not-so-Mitzvah-oriented deeds — formed an 11-member special force: individuals with disabilities whose job it is to ticket people parked in spaces that have those cute little signs with wheelchairs on them. Down in the Loop in 1993, the take was 29,000 tickets @ $100 each, plus 17,000 tickets (@ $30 each) for people who parked across sidewalks that have special bevels for wheelchair access. That was with the "regular" police at work. The new force, established May 3, 1994, had issued 600 tickets by the time the article was written in early June. Not a bad start.

One Person's Idea[3]

Every American must remember that day, the day all our mailpersons asked us to leave a can or package of food by the mailbox, so they could take them to the local foodbanks.

A brilliant idea. One mail carrier somewhere must have thought of it. We don't think it was the CEO of the postal service. Probably just someone with sore feet or calluses on his or her hands from driving the delivery truck to all those stops along the route. If you think about it, who visits more American homes on any given day than the mail carriers?

In Golden, CO, near Denver, some of the carriers had so many donations, it was difficult to deliver the mail. In that area alone, approximately 33 tons of food was collected for the Food Bank of the Rockies the first year of their drive.

Gobs of Arsenic and Goo[4]

USA Weekend Magazine sponsors Make a Difference Day. Hundreds of communities, thousands of people are out there doing their thing for Tikkun Olam. On their fourth annual volunteer day in 1994, 527,000 Americans did some form of volunteer work in their communities. Some of the stories are featured in brief articles, and I find the variety of Mitzvahs fascinating. The students at Goddard High School in Roswell, NM, caught my eye this year. Dressed in uniforms that protected them from the toxic substances, they went out to collect tons of hazardous waste. "Gobs of Arsenic and Goo" is the caption of the students' picture. Used oil: 200 gallons, waste paint: 220 gallons, latex paint: 200 gallons (recycled for paint-overs of local graffiti), and *a ton of pesticides*. What a gutsy thing to do!

Radiation Experiments-The Wrong Approach to Tikkun Olam[5]

More and more documents are being uncovered about radiation testing since the 1940's. 11,000 new documents were made public, some telling the sad tale of tests as recent as the 1980's. The Department of Energy, Office of Human Radiation Experiments, spokesperson, Ellyn Weiss, explained that these documents were selected because the experiments they describe had "no potential therapeutic benefit to the subjects themselves." The most grizzly one in the article — pregnant women injected with radioactive iodine-131. The purpose was to see if there would be any effect on the fetus. All of the women in the experiment were scheduled for therapeutic abortion. After the abortion, tests were performed to determine the effects of the radiation on the fetus.

Clown Doctors Come to Israel[6]

Two clowns, Laine Barton and Michael Christensen, came to Israel to conduct a week-long workshop for Tel Aviv University theater students. The graduates of the course would use their talents at the Children's Medical Center to fight pain, fear, and despair with goofy tricks and stethoscopes that blow bubbles, and yes, even rubber chickens. There are 25 clown doctors like them in the Big Apple Circus Clown Care Unit.

The 102-Year-Old Man Who Had To Find a New Place to Live Because He Had a Cat[7]

Mr. Konrad Dornberger, 102 years old, had to vacate his apartment in Alexandria, VA, along with Mizzen, his 7-year-old (diabetic) cat. No pets are allowed in his building. "...the management recently gave him an ultimatum: Get rid of Mizzen, or we'll get rid of you." Mr. Scott Sterling, Vice President of the rental company, said, "...the rental office receives numerous tips about pets in the complex and tells all violators to get rid of the animals or move."

The article continues by stating that, while this was not the case with Mr. Dornberger's apartment, "Apartment complexes that receive federal funds — such as those in which rents are subsidized for elderly or disabled tenants — cannot bar pets."

Serra's Miracle[8]

A letter written by a bird breeder to her veterinarian. It was accompanied by a picture of a man with a cockatiel sitting on his shoulder:

Hello,

This is a picture of JS...,We had talked about his recovery with "Serra," one of my hand fed teils.

Serra's name comes from (Serandipity) meaning prize found when looking for other things.

J. goes by the nickname Bob — he had a stroke 1-3-86 retired military, his speach was lost, he'd mainly hollor & was hostile (no words) very frustrated. His heart attack was in '89, still no words Mother's Day weekend he has a new bird - in fact this is a bird I accendently broke the wing and you fixed it. That same week he was talking to Serra saying "Pretty Bird" & "Bob"!

Now he strives to say things clear to his bird so it may learn to speak...

An Interesting Insight into Maimonides' Explanation of Loving Others as One Loves Oneself, Namely, "Whatever I want for myself, I want the same for other people."[9]

Dade County, FL, is putting in closer parking and a ramp over the sand, so that people who use wheelchairs can get to the nude section of Haulover beach.

Pizza Hut Donates Leftovers[10]

All 32 Pizza Hut outlets in Palm Beach County are donating the leftovers to a group of agencies that feed the 28,000 people in the county who come to shelters, soup kitchens, and similar places. Try your own Pizza Hut. Tell them how proud you are of their corporation. If they balk, have on hand the phone number from one of the Pizza Huts in the Palm Beach area. Give them the number. (Try one of them in West Palm Beach: 407-684-2552. Ask for the store manager.) Offer to pay for the call. After your local Pizza Hut does it, take on some other corporation.

The Elders in Cyberspace - Part I[11]

It's really nothing new in the field. It's also perfectly logical. But only a few places are doing it...getting residents of old age homes hooked on computers. At the Maimonides Hospital Geriatric Centre in the Côte St. Luc suburb of Montreal they are doing it. One cleverly-stated sentence in the article says it all, "Staff in occupational therapy are using the technology to reboot memories in the elderly who are confused and to give others software that challenges their imagination." Call 514-483-2121 and ask them all about their program. Then start your own.

The Elders in Cyberspace - Part II[12]

Online and over 55? Try SeniorNet, with 13,500 members, though there is some suspicion that a few under-55's are at the keyboard. Another interesting statistic: the three major online services have a membership that is approximately 85% male. On SeniorNet, it is roughly 50-50. My friend, Charles Savenor, thinks it would be a wonderful idea to set up e-mail pen pals between high school students and residents in nursing homes. The ever-increasing numbers of Elders using computers and electronic mail indicates that this program would show great promise, benefiting (and educating) both people at the keyboard. In a different article (November 23, 1994), Ms. Mia Moody of the Cox News Service reported that Clara Fentress, age 92, a poet, began writing verse after she took a computer course at a community college at the age of 89.

Melissa Klein of Farmington Hills, Michigan,
Eloquently Describes The Meaning of Her Bat Mitzvah,
April 8, 1995, Temple Israel, West Bloomfield

In December of 1993 as a member of the Temple Israel Junior Choir, I was privileged to participate in a Chanukah musical program at the Hechtman Senior Apartments. As I witnessed the joy that our singing provided to the residents, I immediately knew that I wanted to do more to enrich the lives of others. After meeting with the social workers and college interns at Hechtman, I developed an ongoing project entitled "Someone Special" in which I interview, photograph and spotlight a different resident each week.

In beginning my Bat Mitzvah process, I began to realize that this activity which I cherish and enjoy so much is called a Mitzvah. As I thought about my own Bat Mitzvah, I knew that I wanted to dedicate the occasion to continuing the act of Mitzvah, extending these acts of kindness to the giving of charity also known as Tzedakah.

The Bar Mitzvah Celebrant Who Loved to Gamble[13]

A story about reaching the age of Mitzvah responsibility, possibly the bash to end all Bar/Bat Mitzvah bashes: Mother and grandmother own a dog track in Miami. After the ceremony at the synagogue, the 450 friends, relatives, and guests, played the greyhounds. The track doesn't open until July 1st, but, if you own the track, you can open it whenever you want. They also set up inside the building an enormous 20,000 square foot casino. Using play money, the winners could then claim prizes. Mom's line says it all, "For this kid, this was the perfect party. He doesn't like girls and he doesn't like to dance, but he loves to gamble. He loves math, he loves the business. It's in his blood."

Picture Pals[14]

A letter from Sandy Gruenberg, Director of the Learning Center at the Solomon Schechter Day School of Westchester, NY, reminding the parents about a new Mitzvah project:

Dear Kindergarten Parents,

אַל־תַּשְׁלִיכֵנִי לְעֵת זִקְנָה כִּכְלוֹת כֹּחִי אַל־תַּעַזְבֵנִי׃
"Do not throw me away in the time of old age,
When my strength fails me..."

Here at Schechter, we use this verse as a guiding principle to introduce even our youngest students to the obligations of Mitzvot that we as Jews are required to fulfill. Towards this end, our kindergarten children are each assigned a "picture pal," a senior citizen who resides in an area nursing home. The children will be drawing and sending a picture to their pal each month from school, and hopefully they will receive some communication back from the senior. The program will be introduced to your children through literature accompanied by an explanation of the how, whys and wherefors that will make the program work.

Below you will find the name and sometimes the birthday of your child's picture pal as well as the address of the nursing home. We encourage you to discuss the program with your child and to send a birthday card to her/his pal, or other special holiday card at the appropriate time. Thank you in advance for your enthusiasm and encouragement with all of our "special" curricular activities.

Those Cute Little Soaps and Shampoos from Hotels[15]

You can collect them from your friends or have a major drive like Elana Erdstein did in Michigan. (She gathered 25,000 of them and donated them to shelters.) *Or* you can be someone like the ad executive who says he's worth $20,000,000 and has thousands of them in his collection, adding, "And I don't even have hair." He even said, "There's something sick about this whole thing." (It's hard to disagree with him on that one.) But he says, "I'm helpless." (A new defense in court for possession of cleaning substances?")

Zack the Super Mitzvah Dog[16]

Peter Steen has a Mitzvah dog, Zack. He is a Labrador/golden retriever that was trained by Canine Companions for Independence to work with people who use wheelchairs. I have seen them in action, know the story as told to me by Dr. Bonnie Bergin, the founder, herself. They graduate knowing 89 commands (more than most children follow, by far), and learn more as they spend more time with their human partner.

Zack wins the Super Mitzvah Dog Award for this one: Mr. Steen is prone to bedsores. He has to be rotated in bed periodically to prevent these terrible (medical term:) decubiti ulcers from forming. Pre-Zack, the 3:00 o'clock in the morning choices included: not getting turned and suffering from the sores, having a family member turn him, or hire someone to do it. None of those appealed to Mr. Steen. A little ingenuity, a little tinkering, a pulley, and one Mitzvah dog later — Zack turns him whenever he needs it.

Cat Food[17]

"Applicant is 80 year old white female living in high risk neighborhood on fixed income with little or no discretionary income..." This is a familiar description to people involved in front-line Mitzvah work. The report continues with a list of 6 diseases and disorders, and describes the specific needs that this Tzedakah organization might meet.

The P.S. is the most important part. "The $45.00 per month for animals is for food and care of 2 dogs and 2 cats. These animals are this lady's 'life.' She can not, would not live without them. (The dogs provide protection in high risk neighborhood and are her true friends and companions.)"

The Mitzvah of Crocheting

My friend, Charles Savenor, a rabbinical student at the Jewish Theological Seminary of America, wrote me the following story:

There is an African-American woman who panhandles around JTS. She used to make bookmarks out of used clothes, which she sold for a $1. When this idea grew old and the winter came on strong, she started just begging for money. Day and night she stood outside and asked for donations. Recently a rabbinical student, Matt Eisenfeld, spoke to this woman and discovered that she knows how to crochet. Matt informed her that with this skill she could make money by making kippot. She now makes a few kippot a week [$10 each], and she has enlisted other needy ladies to help. The kippot are quite nice.

Poor Elders[18]

In 1992, nearly 20% of New York's elders lived below the poverty line.

The Lover of Life

Part of a letter I received describing how a contribution from Ziv Tzedakah Fund was used in one old age home:

Dear Mr. Siegel,

Thank you so much for helping I.S.L.C. realize a dream. Your gift allowed us to purchase 150 frames — one for each resident. I know A.R. explained their intended use to you.

I want to thank you from a staff perspective. You see, we only know the residents often after their bodies have betrayed them. I'll give you an example — A bedridden 80 year old with dementia who is often difficult to care for is how we have seen Mrs. C. for two years. Today, I hung her picture taken at her college graduation as she toasted the photographer with a glass of wine. I now care for a LOVER OF LIFE as I know Mrs. C. was and would probably want to be....

Life Is The Good People

עשרה נקראו חיים...
צדיק נקרא חיים שנא'
פְּרִי־צַדִּיק עֵץ חַיִּים

Ten are called "Life"...
A Good Person is called "Life,"
as the verse states,
"The fruit of a Good Person is a tree of Life." (Proverbs 11:30)
(Avot DeRabbi Natan 34)

Good People are what makes life Life.

Life is being with The Good People, because they personify Tzedakah in everything they do. They affirm the goodness of Life, the incredible, at-times-miraculous power of human beings to bring sweetness and pleasantness and kindness and justice and decency into the lives of others.

In the verse from Proverbs, it doesn't state, "A Good Person is a tree of life," but rather, "The *fruit of a Good Person....*" Human goodness, righteousness, is defined by a person's acts, not by his or her thoughts. It is what they *do* and not what they *think* that makes them who they are.[1]

They live well, they feel their lives are very rich, because of their relationship to others, tied to the rest of Life by acts of justice and decency...and humbly so. They are simply doing what is expected of them.

One such Good Person was the late father of one of my Ultimate Torah Teachers, Shmuel Munk. This man, learned in Torah, held a very important position for many years at a bank in Israel. His job was to get people who were slow to repay their loans...to repay them. This immediately conjures up seedy or sleazy images of investigators and heavy-handed tactics, repo people taking back cars purchased with the bank's money.

Not so. Shmuel's father was a person of such stature, so pleasant and sweet a human being, he established a record so impressive that when he retired, the bank could find no replacement. Borrowers repaid their debts because it was the right thing to do, the only thing to do.

הצדיקים שאפי' במיתתן קרויין חיים

The Good People, even though they have passed away,
are referred to as "alive".
(Ecclesiastes Rabbah 9:4)

This is immortality.

Shmuel's father is no longer alive, yet he lives, through this story, the many other tales of his righteousness, and through his descendants who live by his ideals and the standards he offered them of what is humanly possible...and through the descendants of all those who benefited from his life of good deeds.

This is immortality.

The descendants of the descendants of those who benefited will continue on, living a different, better life, because of Shmuel's father, and because of how he chose to live his life.

This is immortality — the cycle continues until the end of time, because of his kindness, caring, and decency...like the rings of water that move outward and outward and all the way to the outer reaches of a pool or pond, because of one pebble dropped in the water, even a leaf fallen from a tree.

From such prosaic work — loans and repayment of loans — the fruits of the labors produce grand and everlasting results. It is exactly like the life-giving fruit we eat to give us strength. And if, sometimes, we bring the fruit to one who is starving, who is near death, and this is what restores the body to good health, that person and all who are touched by him or her and all those who come afterwards who are touched by them, will have benefited.

As the scientists think of it: when the butterfly in Asia moves its wings, the weather in North America changes.

Nothing in Life is static. Whatever we do changes the course of people's lives and of Life itself and history itself. Grand thinking this is, intimations of eternity and immortality...and very Jewish thinking.

As to what makes Good People who they are, I have discovered (up to this point) what appears to be only two of their so-called "secrets," which are not really secrets at all. Both of these insights come from Shmuel Munk, as he explained to me the essence of living the Life of the Good Jew:

וְצַדִּיק בֶּאֱמוּנָתוֹ יִחְיֶה

A Good Person lives by unwavering trust in God.
(Habakkuk 2:4:)

Shmuel has an extraordinary sense that God has the best interests of human beings always in the forefront of the Divine Plan. While the Hebrew word אמונה-Emunah has come to mean "faith" in modern times, in its ancient philological context it really carries the weight of "absolute trust". This does not preclude the need to raise questions, and to raise them with great passion. Shmuel's kind of אמונה-Emunah is not naïveté or simplemindedness. It does not imply surrendering one's critical powers to become a slave, a cultist, or a lemming-like person. To the contrary, it allows full play for the Good Person's personality to be harnessed to brilliant Mitzvah activities, and it is a wonder to behold. As best as I can tell, some seem to achieve it with a degree of ease; others, after an inordinate struggle, and still others never do reach this ability to trust, though they never surrender the worthiness of the goal: acquiring deep in the soul the quality of אמונה-Emunah. People like Shmuel Munk who have done it — inspired people — are often inspiring to others.

The other "secret" comes from a verse Shmuel explained to me:

הַשְׁלֵךְ עַל-יְהֹוָה | יְהָבְךָ וְהוּא יְכַלְכְּלֶךָ
לֹא-יִתֵּן לְעוֹלָם מוֹט לַצַּדִּיק

Cast your substance on God, Who will sustain you,
God will never let the Good Person stumble. (Psalm 55:23)

This verse's interpretation depends on the meaning of the word יהבך.
The best I can make of Shmuel's explanation is that he understands the verse to
mean, "Put everything in Life in the Hands of God." Once a human being has
done that, recognizing everything is from God, then all human reactions to
Life's events, good and bad, uplifting or discouraging, will come as reactions
of a person who believes God has the person's best interests in mind.

Once again, it is a difficult human quality to acquire. The same statistical spread holds true with this verse as with the one from Habakkuk: some
seem to achieve it with a degree of ease; others, after an inordinate struggle, and
still others never do reach this ability to hand everything over to God, though
they will not surrender the goal as being a most worthy one. Shmuel brought it
down to very simple imagery for me:

It is like a child and a parent at a street corner. They are about to step
off the curb to move to the other side. There is a great deal of fast-moving
traffic, a din, perhaps wild, frightening sounds coming from the cars and
buses. There may even be a reckless or lunatic driver, or a drunk behind the
wheel, approaching the intersection. Yet, the child puts his or her hand in the
mother or father's hand, and crosses the street, confident that it is safe to do
so...the parent will watch out for the wellbeing of the child.

This makes more sense to me. I like the feeling of return-to-childhood.

And the image can be taken much further, and each individual should
review this image from as many aspects as will produce more results. Surely
the child is not a fool for trusting the parent. Surely the very shoes the child
walks in were bought with the parents' money. Certainly things go wrong
crossing the street — the light changes suddenly, someone runs a red light,
pedestrians in a hurry push and shove from all directions, rain, snow, sleet, and
ice make the street slippery (for parent as well as child).

Surely it is fine Torah Shmuel teaches, and like all good Torah-insights,
we come back to it again and again, discovering new things each time.

Now we can understand two texts from the 2nd Century. One day hundreds of years ago, in one of the many great places of Torah study in ancient
Israel, in one particular discussion, Rabbi Akiva brought great words of wisdom to the attention of the assembled Rabbis. Overwhelmed with emotion,
Rabbi Tarfon responded:

עקיבא כל הפורש ממך כפורש מן החיים

"Akiva, being too far away from you
is like being too distant from Life itself. (Kiddushin 66b)

So intense was the moment, Rabbi Tarfon realized that simply knowing
this man, just being in his presence, brought home to him a grasp of the feel
and touch of Life itself. Note that Rabbi Tarfon does not say, "...from *the*
meaning of life itself." His reaction is more fundamental than "meaning".

In a parallel passage in another part of the Talmud, our printed texts record Rabbi Tarfon's comment slightly differently:

עקיבא כל הפורש ממך כפורש מחייו

"Akiva, being too far away from you
is like being too distant from one's own life. (Zevachim 13a)

This phrase is as immediate as the other one, but it is personalized even more. Rabbi Tarfon feels that being close to Rabbi Akiva touches *his own Life* very deeply. He sees that his own Life is defined by his relationship to this genius of Life, Akiva ben Yosef, who was, after all, no more than a simple illiterate shepherd until middle age, who, only at age forty, and through the most unexpected circumstances, assumed his Self and destiny through Torah study.

This is not magic. Nor is it mysticism, nor some form of hokey parapsychology. It is intimacy and connectedness in the highest form.

Rabbi Akiva himself very passionately expressed the intensity of this רב-Teacher/תלמיד-student relationship and חיים-Life. It was at a high, joyous moment in his personal life:

מעשה בר' עקיבא שעשה משתה לבנו
על כל חבית וחבית שפתח אמר
לחיי רבננא ולחיי תלמידיהון

Once, when Rabbi Akiva made a feast for his son,
every time he opened a new barrel of wine
he would offer the toast,
"Here's to the lives of Torah teachers,
and here's to the lives of Torah students." (Tosefta Shabbat [Lieberman] 7:8)

We are accustomed to saying "לחיים-To Life!" as a toast. For Rabbi Akiva, Life is the relationship and interactions of teacher and student and student and teacher.

Returning now to the end of a verse mentioned at the beginning of this article, we read —

וְלֹקֵחַ נְפָשׁוֹת חָכָם

Wise people attach themselves to these Good Souls. (Proverbs 11:30)

— it would follow that being with the Good People would lead us to Life at its most profound, most intimate and most intense.

And they are everywhere to be found. Commenting on the verse —

וּמַצְדִּיקֵי הָרַבִּים כַּכּוֹכָבִים לְעוֹלָם וָעֶד

"And those who bring the people to do the right thing
shall be as the stars, eternal" (Daniel 12:3)

— one Jewish text offers the following insights:

ומה כוכבים רואים אורם מסוף העולם ועד סופו.
כך צדיקים רואים אורם מסוף העולם ועד סופו.
מה כוכבים פעמים נגלים פעמים נכסים. כך הצדיקים
ומה כוכבים כתות כתות שאין להם מנין
כך צדיקים כתות כתות שאין להם מנין

Just as one sees the light of the stars
from one end of the world to the other,
so, too, one sees the light of Good People
from one end of the world to the other.
Just as the stars are sometimes visible
and at other times hidden,
so, too, with Good People.
And just as the clusters of stars
are so numerous they cannot be counted,
so, too, the groups of Good People are innumerable.
(Sifre Devarim, Ekev 11, 47)

It is probably very bad form to quote myself, but I believe this poem from one of my earlier books[2] summarizes the place of צדיקים-Good People, in the Grand Scheme of Things:

The Good People everywhere
will teach anyone who wants to know
how to fix all things breaking and broken in this world —
including hearts and dreams —
and along the way we will learn such things as
why we are here
and what we are supposed to be doing
with our hands and minds and souls and our time.
That way, we can hope to find out why
we were given a human heart,
and that way, we can hope to know
the hearts of other human beings
and the heart of the world.

This is the heart of the matter.

How to Make Your Old Age Home
A More Menschlich Place
(While Therapeutically Slashing the Quantity of Medications,
Reducing the Rate of Infection Dramatically,
And Offering the People Who Live There The Opportunity
To Live Longer, More Fulfilling Lives)
Dr. William Thomas' Eden Alternative Project:
The Revolution Has Begun

My Favorite Statistic

In the first full year of his Eden Alternative at Chase Memorial Nursing Home, a residence for 80 elders in New Berlin, NY, Dr. Thomas reduced the cost of medications from $220,000 to $135,091, a savings of $84,105.

Version #1 of the Story

No one dies at Chase.

Well, that isn't exactly true.

What *is* true is that no one dies at Chase Memorial Nursing Home for the wrong reasons.

It would appear to me, son of a physician who served Northern Virginia's people for more than half a century — it would appear to me that the only right reason for an old person to die is because his or her body (as we would say in my native Virginia) "just plain wore out," without help from even the most well-intentioned institutions that function essentially on a medical model.

The *wrong* reasons, on the other hand, make up a long, long list, a scary list, a list sad with too few people to say, "This has got to stop." On that list are:

loneliness;

powerlessness;

uselessness;

chronic unhappiness;

fatigue of the spirit and weariness of the soul;

will-to-live gone all to hell;

a sense of abandonment;

wariness of those who mean well but perform hypocritically, downright poorly, or maliciously (openly or otherwise) for reasons only the most skilled and insightful therapists can imagine — all their energies being exhausted fighting off the good intentions of those who harm them in the name of their personal health and welfare;

despair, a fate worse than loss of eyesight or gangrene in a limb;

and being-unlistened-to...a worrisome, sorry state.

The Talmud[1] (Sotah 46b) tells the story of a town named Luz where people never died. When people who lived in Luz dug deep down into their souls and considered that their time had come, they would go on their own outside the city walls, where they would die, at the hands of the Angel of Death, who is, after all, an Angel.

The Eden Alternative is Luz in our own day. It is where people come *to live* until it is time to die for the right reasons, because no one dies there for the wrong reasons.

Now it is time for the statistics:

At Chase, there are more than 100 birds at the home, most of them living in the rooms of the Elders.

2 dogs, including Target, a retired racing greyhound destined for Death Row until rescued, and a plain old mutt with a warm and friendly personality named Ginger.

4 cats (I am a cat person), including Chase and Sanborn.

Many, many kids. Including Summer Camp on the grounds of Chase. Infants and little and middle-size kids everywhere..

Plants, gardens, light. Plants and more plants.

Oxygen.

Still more plants and more oxygen.

Pure air.

No stink.

Just fresh and natural smells.

The pleasant smell of real-live vegetation.

Flowers.

(Did I mention many, many kids?)

Did I mention that I am writing this as I approach my 50th birthday, and wouldn't for a moment think of being depressed because I have seen, as it were, The Light, which is to say, the way the Eden Gang uses light, physical light, and uplifting human, warm light.

Now it is time for the hard-and-fast statistics — comparing to a similar home of 80 elders not too far away (erroneously referred to by some as "an 80-bed facility" — God help us):

People at Eden have a 15% lower mortality rate than residents of the other place.

Nurse aide turnover — a grizzly problem for people working in a depressing job — slower by 26%.

Medications. Ah, medications: Eden reduced the medications by a half in 2 1/2 years.

Infections: 50% less than the other place.

Now, isn't it time to call 607-674-5232 and ask for Dr. William Thomas[2] (Harvard Medical School graduate), and find out just exactly what is the scientific and statistical relationship of having birds in your own room to a lower rate of infection? Wouldn't it be good to find out why some people with Alzheimer's disease who tend the birds seem to have lost some of their ostensible Alzheimer's symptoms while in-the-act of feeding the parakeets and cockatiels and finches and cleaning their cages? Wouldn't we want to know why the staff smiles, smiles naturally, is cheerful, naturally cheerful, is not looking to "move on" so quickly to another job? Wouldn't it be important to find out exactly how people live less infected and less frequently infected and less drugged because of a bunch of animals, kids, ficus and geraniums, and how, along the way, they just lost the habit of dying and picked up a bunch of other habits, like talking to the birds or telling stories to the kids, or just plain sitting in the sun, their wrinkles all aglow with pink, their radiance, well, so real you can touch it?[3]

It's all about the difference between "care" and "treatment," and if you want to know more, you will have to call visit an Eden Alternative or read the book or call Dr. Thomas, or, best of all, do all three.

Version #2 of the Story

Some Foreign Language Lessons and Their Relation to
The Wellbeing of Elders Everywhere:

"Quod erat demonstratum." I always liked that phrase when I heard it. It had a certain finality to it that the initials Q.E.D. never quite carried. "As has been demonstrated..." with a nice deep tone meaning, "Don't you dare mess with us. We proved it."

As a kid, I could go for days teasing my brother and friends and anyone else I might run into — "Ha, Ha, *Quod erat demonstratum* to you, Buddy."

It had more zip than *terminus ad quem, corpus delecti,* and it's more titillating cousin, *in flagrante delicto.*

The Eden Alternative works, and, if anyone else comes along and says it doesn't, it is clear that their wards, their patients, their interns, their clients and their welfare are not their primary concern.

Sunday Morning

If it were Sunday morning, and a Christian friend of mine was on his or her way to church, and if it were a wonderfully Bible-thumping church service complete with no air conditioning and all those people decked out in their finery like in the movies, and fanning themselves with fans just like in the movies, and the sheet listing all the service's Psalms and readings and the topic of the sermon right there like in the movies, and if the topic were indeed the Eden Alternative, I would fully expect many Amens and Glory Glories, for the sermon, "The Dignity of the Elders" would be so very true it would be revelatory. No less. And yet so obvious.

If I Were the Host of a Famous TV Game Show

If I were a game show host with its big spinning wheel and band and cymbals in the background punctuating the high moments, with the flashing lights and the network employee with the big card with the word "Cheer!" and "Clap!" on it ready to be flashed when the winner wins big, I'd certainly make it easy on Mr. Anderson and his opponents Ms. Renfrow, the nautical engineer from New Orleans and Charles Biederman, the collector of small rocks of many colors from all over Arizona. I'd let them choose one of two for the big award, "Would you, Mr. A and Ms. R and Mr. B like to play all or nothing? Spin the wheel, one of you. Eighteen slots for dying, and one for living. Give it a whirl."

Oh, wouldn't the audience go wild! Wouldn't they be tense on a 19-to-1 odds that the needle will come to rest on Life.

Oh, I would want to make it easy for them, I would, let the spinner know that if you flick your wrist just about 23 degrees and don't push as hard as possible, it'll most certainly land on Life.

I wouldn't want anyone to die for the wrong reasons.

How I Buy my Cars, Which Is to Say, Where:

Why, from the Kaplan Boys, of course, way down in Salem, VA, a good five hours from where I live in Rockville.

And I do it because they haven't got a dishonest bone in their bodies, neither Bob, the short, one, nor Andy, the one who's got to be 6'4" tall, and I've known them both since, well, since they were just boys, and I know that if they sell me a car it'll be a good one and if something goes wrong they'll stand by it and make sure it runs well and if they did something wrong, I won't have to go shlepping through Chrysler Motors' equity line of command nor the courts, and that even if they charge me $500 more for the car than I might have paid down the road, well, it's worth it, it's worth $500 not to have to wake up in the middle of the night every Monday and Thursday to worry about whether or not my car is going to work the next morning when I have to go out and make a living.

And if I keep the car until it is on its last legs, I will know for sure that it wasn't dying because of faulty or sleazy parts or because the maintenance manual lied to me or I got grade-C service at the service center. It'll be because it just plain wore out and was ready to die, having served me well and brought me great joy in Sunset and Sunrise and on the long-hauls down the highway at 2:00 a.m. to see a friend who was just as lonesome as could be. They'll just tell me "It's time, Danny" and I'll know, because of who they are, I'll know it's time. But only if *they* tell me.

You can be so sure of it, you can bet your pension funds on it and never lose a moment's sleep that you'll have nothing to retire on.

Get the analogy?

Which Is the Point:

Namely, that if there's no need for subtleties, and, indeed, this is all so obvious that — if you have to have a home for the Elders at all — it should be a natural place to live, a pleasant place, a respectful ambiance being the rule of the day. If that makes as much sense as it sounds like it does, wouldn't it make sense to get in the car or on a train or plane or to return to the '60's when everyone was searching for truth and hitchhike up there to New Berlin, NY, (which the natives accent "Bérlin," accent on the first syllable) to see it with your own eyes, and to touch it with your own hands, remembering not to forget to scratch the kitties behind the ears, if you can tear them away from the Elders, and to hear The Great Truths (often in the form of birdsong) with your own ears. And if you can't get to Chase, call Dr. Thomas at the Eden office and he'll give you a list of other places that have "Edenized". Then just get in the car and see it with your own eyes.

If I Hear One More Person In the Audience Say,
 "Who's Going to Feed the [Damn] Birds and Clean the Cages!"
 I'm Going to Scream.

Let's answer that one with one of a hundred answers, namely, — if your Eden is as Paradisical as any of the Eden Alternatives, then you will have eliminated so much of the drugs (as they did) that you can release at least two of the medications nurses from their duties (get them re-assigned somewhere where they are shorthanded), and can hire the finest bird cage-cleaner and food and water changer in the county. (Maybe we should consider that Great Day at The End of Time when all our sorrows will be no more, and bird cage cleaners for elders will be paid as much as medications nurses.)

And now that I think of it, consider all those nurses who will be forced into early retirement, leaving them only a few options, including, (a) getting re-trained for some other occupation like a car dealer or antique salesperson or pilot for NW or CO or UA or AA, or (b) they could retire early to some home for retired people, and after they have unpacked their bags, they should sit on the bed, close their eyes, breathe deeply, and pray to whichever God is their own God in whatever language is dearest to them: Hebrew, Greek, Latin, or English, they might want to pray that the place they have settled their bones into is one that is Edenesque.

And, of course, part of the Eden package is assistance in finding retraining programs or new jobs for the nurses who have been phased out of their positions.

It is the ethical, Menschlich thing to do.

And, Finally,
    If I Were a Hard-Nosed, Brazen-Foreheaded Animal Hater

and I saw those shimmering statistics about how much money is being saved on drugs and all the adjunct costly items that seem to cling to drug/med culture like a plague of some Miasmic Crud;

if I felt that America is sinking deeper and deeper into debt and we're just not going to have enough money to make the Founding Fathers' and Mothers' dream stay alive much longer;

if I felt that, and saw that with a simple calculator two birds + 1 dog + chow and seed = 1 nurse and 243 Prozac and 92 anti-inflammatories, multiplied by 35,897 old age residences in any given 14,000 square mile radius in the Northeast (as a statistical sample, all things adjusted for midwestern temperament and California moods), if I just multiplied it all out and saw that we'd save another $2,000,000,000 a year (make it $1,800,000,000, allowing $200,000,000 for retraining of staff who have become irrelevant) —

I think I'd most certainly get on a train or Greyhound bus, or in my car or a friend's car, or fly to Binghamton or Syracuse or any place there's an Eden Alternative nearby, so I could go see this place.

I most certainly would.

Even if I were resistant to change.

Even if I didn't have a green thumb and could never appreciate the enthusiasm of all my gardening and house plant-loving friends.

Even if I were allergic to fur.

Even if I thought all household pets were nuisances.

Even if,

Even if...

Since this isn't about *me*, but rather about the wellbeing of the people in residences for the Elders, I most certainly would go to see the Eden Alternative.

Dr. William Thomas, c/o The Eden Alternative, RRI, Box 31B4, Sherburne, NY 13460, 607-674-5232, Fax: 607-674-6723.
Dr. Thomas' book: The Eden Alternative, *University of Missouri Press, 1994. Available through the Eden office.*

Selections from the
Friends of The Eden Alternative Newsletter

Blood Tests[1]

The discovery of blood tests for loneliness, helplessness and boredom would revolutionize nursing home care. Imagine the scenes that would follow. "Dr. Good, your patient has a markedly elevated serum loneliness factor, what should we do?" To which Dr. Good would have to reply, "Ummm, I don't know." The nursing home inspection process also would be changed forever. Inspector: "The blood work shows very high levels of helplessness and boredom. What are you doing about this?" What could the nursing home say? Which department will be responsible for loneliness? Who would "Take care of" boredom. How could helplessness be reduced.

The fact that tests for loneliness, helplessness and boredom remain science fiction gives us an important clue to the nature of the problem. While diabetes can be treated by measuring blood glucose levels and injecting appropriate doses of insulin, there will never be a pill for loneliness....

Non-Dependence on Others[2]

Frail people are generally denied chances to give something back to their helpers or their communities. Their offers are refused with statements like, "You don't have to do that. We'll take care of it." Helpers mean well, without realizing how urgently people in their care crave a tangible counterbalance to their dependency.

Pet Assisted Therapy and Horticulture Therapy[3]

Tioga may be[4] home to more than 5 dogs, 5 cats, 100 birds, and 2 rabbits, not because we are intent upon maximizing "pet assisted therapy," but because our residents are lonelier than they ought to be. Also, on the grounds there will be hundreds of plants and blossoms and rock, vegetable, and herb gardens, not because we advocate "horticulture therapy," but because there is a fundamental need to sense the passions of spring and fall.

The Sounds in the Old Age Home

At one point during our tour, I stopped and realized that we were surrounded by the song of birds. It wasn't just the aviary birds I was hearing — it was the birds from the residents' rooms. No television, no screaming, moaning or crying out for help, no staff complaining. Everyone seemed happy.[5]

The Confusion of Care,
Treatment and Kindness
Or
The Story of Kahlid the Kind
(A Chapter from Dr. William Thomas' Book,
The Eden Alternative)[1]

Long, long ago a lone traveler set out to cross the Sahara Desert, heading north from Timbuktu. Days passed and he made steady progress on the road to Marrakech. On the eighth day of his journey, the traveler was set upon by a ferocious sand storm. The wind lashed him without mercy and confused his sense of direction. When it was over, he was lost. Dunes of pitiless sand stretched in every direction. There was no shade and he had lost his supplies in the storm. Soon his tongue began to swell and his lips cracked, every ounce of his being cried for water. Vultures circled slowly overhead. The man wandered aimlessly until hope deserted him; he fell to his knees, ready to die.

The traveler did not know it, but just over the eastern dune lay the Oasis of Kahlid the Kind, known throughout the Sahara as the possessor of the finest, purest water and the most generous heart the desert had ever known. Kahlid the Kind regularly rode the dunes in search of the lost and the forsaken.

Just as the traveler prepared to close his eyes for the last time, the desert silence was broken by the plodding sounds of a camel. The camel and rider were soon at his side. Kahlid gathered up the prostrate traveler and rode swiftly home.

Kahlid offered the traveler water and the man drank deeply. Again and again he drank until his thirst had gone. At last the traveler spoke. "Great is my fortune to have encountered Kahlid the Kind when Death held his cold hand upon my throat."

"It was the will of God that you should live, I am but his poor servant," Kahlid responded. "Now you must drink more for truly you have not taken enough."

"I would drink more but of water I am full, now I feel weakness and a great hunger, might I have some food?"

"Food, how can you think of food? Kahlid cried. "It is water you need now. Not so long ago you were nearly dead of thirst. So drink and drink deeply."

"Kahlid, I am in your debt. But I have taken my fill of water and now I must eat."

"I think the sun has addled your brain, my fine friend. You must drink more water or Death will claim you yet."

The traveler turned his head away when Kahlid offered him the ladle. Water spilled to the ground. Convinced that his new friend was insane for refusing the water he must need, Kahlid swept him up from his resting place, and waded into the spring with the man in his arms. Again and again he dunked his new friend's head into the water. The man choked and fought for air, swallowing great gulps of fresh water. Kahlid was pleased.

When the traveler began to weaken, Kahlid redoubled his efforts, holding the man under for longer periods to ensure that he would take water. Again and again the poor man was submerged until his strength waned to nothing, and Death did take him. The traveler died in Kahlid's warm, powerful embrace.

Tears streaked the loving face of Kahlid the Kind. "If only he had drunk a little bit more, he might have lived!" The man's body was buried near the Oasis. His was not the only body laid to rest by Kahlid the Kind. "Water, they must have water," he muttered as he mounted his camel and headed out into the desert heat.

The Gerbils and Bunnies
of Kindergarten[1]

כד הוינן זוטרי לגברי
השתא דקשישנא לדרדקי
When we were young,
we were told to be mature.
Now that we are old,
we are treated like babies.
(Bava Kamma 92b)

Opening Quote (About Dogs, But Applicable to Other Animals)
When the subject of dogs in nursing homes comes up, I often hear comments like: "We had a dog once, but it just didn't work out." Or, "Sure the residents would like it if we had a dog, but they are too much work." These complaints miss the point. Nursing homes are supposed to be good at giving care — giving care is what they do. Just what is a person to think of a nursing home that cannot or will not manage the care of dogs? Should such an institution be trusted with taking care of Mother? *(Dr. William Thomas,* The Eden Alternative, *University of Missouri Press, 1994.)*

I. What The Children Have in School
Guinea pigs, hamsters, gerbils, fish, snakes, chameleons, lizards and iguanas, rabbits, caterpillars-becoming-butterflies, chicken eggs-becoming-chicks in cages, boxes and cartons, and tanks. (This partial list does not include Show and Tell, which would also include cats, dogs, parakeets, cockatiels, canaries, parrots, and other house pets.)

II. Where They Have These Animals
In the classrooms in public schools, private schools, pre-schools in the public school system, pre-schools in synagogues[2] and churches, parochial schools, including Jewish Day Schools, Summer camp.

III. My Personal Likes and Dislikes (Using the Vocabulary of Young Children
to Describe my Reactions)
1. Likes: I like cats (all sizes, up to and including tigers and lions), dogs, birds, giraffes, horses,
2. Dislikes: All rodents[3] (gross, stinky), bugs of every kind (icky), unless multi-colored sublime-looking butterflies are considered bugs...then it would be *almost* all bugs, particularly cockroaches, spiders, and scorpions, Snakes of every size and color, lethal or harmless (slimy), but not all reptiles.[4] Just snakes.

IV. Why They Have Animals in Schools — In No Particular Order

1. It teaches the children about caring.

2. It teaches the children *how* to care, including some of the difficult aspects of caring such as what kind of food, and not too much food, or not too hot or too cold, and including some of the unpleasant aspects of caring, like cleaning the cage. When they ask, "Who is going to take care of the hamster during Winter Break?" — they have learned a very important lesson.

3. It teaches them about Life itself, about things that breathe, about animation.

4. It teaches them about the needs of living things: food, water, shelter, companionship, affection, and how regularly these needs have to be met, and that The Great Rule is: *Every* living thing needs something and someone.

5. It teaches them that there are all kinds of living things in this world, and each one is different than the next, whether it be one different species than another, or a newborn in contrast to a baby or mature or old creature, or — even as a twin, triplet, quadruplet or more, the same genes do not produce the same personality or behavior.

6. It teaches them about relationships. Recalling the *Sesame Street* clips about spatial relationships: "The toy car is *inside* the box," "The flower is *behind* the car," "The book is *on top of* the table," the students can learn by comparison how important it is for children to know about tenderness, and dependency, and gentle touch, and Big Living Thing in relation to Small Living Thing, human being in relation to animals, love of parent and child, and dependability, trust, and hope.

7. It teaches them that there are such things in life as sickness and disease and that creatures suffer when they are sick.

8. It teaches them that sickness and disease can be passed from one living thing to another, but, with the appropriate care and safeguards, they can be controlled or prevented.

9. It teaches them about allergies.

10. It teaches them that the immediate surroundings of the creature can have a profound effect on the animal's wellbeing, and that accommodating to the specific needs of the specific animal — in sickness as well as in health — is the most reasonable, considerate thing to do.

11. It teaches them about the cycle of Life:

A. They see birth when the chicks hatch. They see marvelous transformation and metamorphosis when a caterpillar becomes a butterfly. Life!

B. They witness aging, diminished energy, slower reflexes, weight change, in some cases changes in fur, feather, or skin color.

C. If one of the animals dies, they learn about death and dying. Often, the children will ask, "After it dies, who will take care of it?"...a *very* great question.

12. It teaches them that living things are gifts. When the teacher says that those who have behaved well may feed the fish or pet the rabbit, it teaches a great message.

V. A Question to Consider

If there are so many things the children can learn by having animals in pre-school, kindergarten, 1st, 2nd, and 3rd grades, why don't they have animals for the 10th graders, including (meaning: *particularly*) the ones from broken and breaking homes, the anorexic and bulimic teen-agers, the ones tending toward addiction?

VI. Reasons Why Animals Shouldn't Be in the Classroom —
   In No Particular Order

1. Allergies (children, siblings stopping by, parents, teachers, principals, custodial staff, visitors).

2. Disease (from animal to human and from human to animal).

3. Bites and scratches.

4. Some people just don't like them (children, siblings stopping by, parents, teachers, principals, custodial staff, visitors). (Using the language of children: gross, dis*gust*ing, icky, *fooyeh*.)

5. Who will take care of them — feed them, make sure they don't get out, clean the cage or tank or box? Who will *remind them* to take care of them?

6. Noisy.

7. Smelly.

8. Dirty.

9. Distracting.

10. The kids are going to love the animals and then come home and ask if they can have a pet.

11. The animals get sick and die and then you have to explain to them all about sickness and death.

VII. Pets in Housing for the Elders
   (Old Age Homes and Independent Apartment Complexes):
   A Comparison to the Situation in Primary Schools —
   In No Particular Order

A. Reasons Why Elders Shouldn't Have Animals Living in Their Housing
   (Both Old Age Homes and Independent Housing for the Elders) —
   In No Particular Order

1. Allergies (residents, visiting relatives, medical staff, administrative staff, CEO's, custodial staff, visitors).

2. Disease (from animal to human and from human to animal).

3. Bites and scratches.

4. Some people just don't like them (residents, visiting relatives, medical staff, administrative staff, CEO's, custodial staff, visitors).

5. Who will take care of them — feed them, make sure they don't get out, clean the cage or tank or box? Who will *remind them* to take care of them?

6. Noisy.

7. Smelly.

8. Dirty.

9. Distracting.

10. The animals get sick and die and then you have to deal with the residents' feelings of yet another loss in their lives.

10. No time to re-engineer the policies of the housing.

11. Too much trouble to deal with.

12. What's so important about them having a bird to look at, a cat to pet, a dog to sit next to them on the couch?

13. A *visiting* pet program from the humane society is sufficient to meet the human needs of the residents.

B. Reasons Why Elders Who Live in Housing for the Elders
   (Both Old Age Homes and Independent Housing for the Elders)
   In Particular Should Have Animals in Their Housing Facilities —
   In No Particular Order

1. Allergies (residents, visiting relatives, medical staff, administrative staff, CEO's, custodial staff, visitors) are only a logistical problem. Where the animals live and how far they roam[5] is a matter of geography. It is no different from friends who are allergic coming to visit in a dog- or cat-inhabited house or apartment. Accommodations are made and Kitty and Poochie are safely put away for the duration. The host may even take additional steps to detoxify the visiting areas.

2. Disease (from animal to human and from human to animal). All the issues have been worked out. All the immunology[6] problems have been studied and rigorously documented. Call the Delta Society for articles: 1-800-869-6898 (V/TTY), fax: 206-235-1076. Logically, if some *hospitals* can have resident animals, and even cancer patients have access to them, certainly an old age home should be able to figure out a way to do it.

3. Bites and scratches. This is, indeed, a problem, but can be managed with as much care as one would take at home with a household pet. I once had an article (which by now I could never find)...it's in a box of Mitzvah articles from six or seven years ago. But the gist of it was a study done in Minnesota that stated that more injuries were caused to residents of old age homes by staff than by animals. Also, see footnote 6 about Huntington Memorial Hospital in California. I am sure they have ideas about how to keep the problem of bites and scratches under control.

4. Some people just don't like them (residents, visiting relatives, medical staff, administrative staff, CEO's, custodial staff, visitors). Liking or not liking animals is not the issue. The issue is the wellbeing, happiness, and liveliest lifestyle for residences for Elders, for both old age homes and independent housing. It seems absurd to say it, but if I (and President Bush) don't like broccoli, why would I withhold it from others who would benefit from its undisputed nutritional value? If some forms of penicillin are dangerous to me, so toxic it could cause me serious damage, would I withhold it from someone else who needs it if their own bodies do not have adverse reactions to the drug? If I don't like skiing, would I close the slopes to others? Sadly, this is often the greatest obstacle to creating a resident pet program: *someone* high enough up on

the administrative ladder either just doesn't like animals, or doesn't really care enough about them one way or another to see if they might not be of benefit to the people in his or her charge (and, I might add, whose families, insurance companies, and governments pay his or her salary).

5. Who will take care of them — feed them, make sure they don't get out, clean the cage or tank or box? Who will *remind them* to take care of them? See the opening quote in this article. In the situation of old age homes, the irony is that dozens of people are there — all around them 24 hours a day — reminding the residents to take their medications. Why couldn't they just mention, "Did you remember to feed the cat" while they are giving them Digoxin, Lasix, Zanax, or Zantac? For Elders living in independent housing complexes, one of the best things about being human is to have to remember to do things. Feeding the pet and cleaning the cage may simply be added to the daily list of "pick up the mail" and "lock the door". We should also take into account that illness — real or imagined or a combination of both — is egocentric. The Elders often spend much time and expend much effort worrying about their sore knee, the side effects of a new drug, or the slow recovery from their cataract surgery. They could put all this emotional energy to a better purpose: worrying about the welfare of someone or something else. Staying up late or half the night or all night to make sure a sick animal is recovering is better than staying up half the night groaning over one's own aches and pains. It takes the human being out of his or her own world of personal problems.

6. It gives the Elders a sense of responsibility. First, *they, the residents*, not the staff, should be taking care of the pets whenever possible. We should encourage any human activity that counteracts the feeling of weakness, helplessness, and the discomfort of being the recipient of the good will of others. This is true for people who in more active stages of their lives controlled agencies or corporations, or had the power to move things, people, money, anything...to make things happen. Taking care of pets is making something happen that *they* made happen. Ask an Elder who used to be a jogger what it feels like to be in a wheelchair and to be pushed from one place to another.

7. Noisy. True. But (a) no one complains about the same potential problem in the kindergarten through 3rd grade settings, (b) anyone who knows anything about these programs knows how to select quieter pets[7], and (c) in some homes for the Elders, visitors get very spooked by how quiet it is, eerie. It is not uncommon for a teen-ager to remark how much it sounds like a funeral home. A *little* noise is natural, and might just be the best thing that happened to many of the residents, visiting relatives, medical staff, administrative staff, CEO's, custodial staff, and visitors.

8. Smelly. This is truly a sad excuse, particularly for old age homes. The smell of disinfectants and medications is so strong in some of the places I have visited, it overpowers anyone inside the walls of the institution. Tragically, some places smell of human waste. Dr. Thomas' Eden Alternative homes have so many plants everywhere, it is the freshest air I have ever inhaled except, perhaps, when I climbed to the top of Mt. Sinai 20 years ago. As for individual apartments in independent housing for Elders — the same way

"regular people" deal with smells from the cat or birds or other animals applies in this case. Lysol, treated kitty litter, air fresheners, sachets (those little whatchamacallits of barks and herbs tied all pretty in a little bundle by a colorful ribbon), open windows, whatever.

9. The animals will run crazy all over the place. Logistics. This is merely a logistical problem, and every program that has ever had animals where Elders live has already solved it.

10. Distracting. Exactly the point. Distracting *from what*? Distraction from loneliness and boredom. The pets draw their attention to something warm, friendly, alive.

11. Something to love. Researchers, psychiatrists, veterinarians, and authors who have no expertise other than a reasonable amount of common sense have written fat and slender books on this topic. It is so obvious, there is no need even to discuss it here.

12. Something that loves them back in a non-judgmental fashion. For many people, this is often preferable to conversations with their relatives. This is not meant facetiously. An additional abundant dose of pure affection is good for everyone.

13. Companionship.[7a] This is the advantage of resident pets as opposed to visiting pets in old age homes. Say it is 2:00 a.m. and one of the Elders can't sleep. So he or she gets up, finds the puppy and spends a little time petting it or playing with it, or just sitting there with it on his or her lap, or goes over to the aquarium and watches the fish swim around, dazzled by their colors. On the benefits of aquariums in old age homes, you may speak to Brian Jacobs of Fins Aquatic Systems, Inc. of Leawood, KS, 913-338-3333. It was my good fortune to be in Kansas City when his son was celebrating his bar mitzvah. His father told me that one of his most personally satisfying projects is installing aquariums in residences for the Elders. He is very enthusiastic about his work and welcomes calls.[7b]

14. Fun. Who doesn't want people to have fun?

15. Lowers blood pressure. Hard data is available from the Delta Society or your local veterinarian or humane society: put a cat or rabbit or other gentle, furry animal on someone's lap and let him or her stroke it a while, and the result is a measurable drop in blood pressure. In the research about human-animal interrelations, this significant physical reaction is an old story. Specialists in child psychology may have made comparative studies about the calming effect of stuffed animals on children at various ages (particularly hyperactive children), but that is a different field and another issue and misses the point concerning the Elders. Our interest is the benefits of living, breathing animals and human beings who are being denied opportunities offered to the other segments of "regular" society.

16. Something beautiful to look at. A love bird or cockatiel, stretching its wings in the sunlight, is a dazzling display. Everyone who wants to should be treated to that beautiful picture as often as he or she wants.

17. Pleasant to talk to. I have been a guest in hundreds of households over the last 30-some years. I am amazed by how many so-called perfectly ra-

tional adults, some of them leaders in their fields, bosses of companies multi-national they have built with their bare hands, chiefs of this or that department, published scholars of the first magnitude...how so many of them will stand there or sit there — or even crawl around on all fours to be at eye level with the animal — and will engage in lengthy baby talk and babble with their cocker spaniel, Burmese cat, or parakeet...even their goldfish. Elders in independent housing and old age homes should be allowed to do the same. Why do we deny them that pleasure? Why would we even *want* to deny them that pleasure?

18. Pleasant to listen to. I am even more amazed at how many so-called perfectly rational adults — some of them leaders in their fields, bosses of multi-national companies they have built with their bare hands, chiefs of this or that department, published scholars of the first magnitude — will hear a chirp or meow or bark or whatever goldfish say with their voices through the water and walls of the fish tank and turn to me and explain what they said, with what passion Goldie or Midnight or Phineas said it, and how bright their animals are. Elders in independent housing and old age homes should be given the opportunity to do the same if they want to. Why do we deny them that pleasure? Why would we even *want* to deny them that pleasure?

On a recent vacation in Hawaii, I made the rounds with The Bird Woman at the Hyatt. We played with the macaws and parrots and cockatoos and listened to these magnificent birds as they went through their routine for the benefit of the tourists. Everyone took pictures with one or two of the birds perched on a suntanned arm or shoulder. The Bird Woman explained that, under the right conditions, they live 50-100 years; she told us which species were friendlier than others, and which were the best talkers. We were surprised to hear how one bird could learn the vocabulary of another, and she said that when they are put away at night, they have a fine time of it talking back and forth to each other. She emphasized that the African gray parrot has the most extensive vocabulary, and that it is capable of imitating a cat, a horse, a cow, and certainly the sound of its owner reciting the numbers on his or her credit card. A day or two later I visited an area of jungle/animal sanctuary, and through the thick stand of trees I was sure I had heard a cat. I walked toward the meow sounds, but I couldn't find the kitty. There was only a cockatoo with a knowing smile on its face and a look of "Fooled those dumb human beings again" in its eyes. It was a wonderful moment, pure Life's pleasure. Why shouldn't everyone who wants to enjoy such pleasures be allowed to do so?

Furthermore, "Wild Birds Unlimited," a pet store in upstate New York created an interesting variation of this project. They attached a transmitter to a bird feeder which they then donated to a nearby old age home. They also installed a speaker in one of the public rooms inside the building so the residents could listen to the chirping and singing of the birds as they enjoyed their seeds and suet. A brilliant, yet simple, idea.

19. For Jewish Elders — it gives them an additional opportunity to make a blessing expressing how exquisite Life is. Jewish tradition teaches that when a person acquires something new,[7c] he or she should recite the Shehecheyanu-שהחיינו blessing, which states, "Blessed are You, our God,

who has given us Life and allowed us the privilege of reaching this blessed moment." In independent housing situations, if the Elder bought the pet for his or her own apartment, it is an opportunity to bring relatives, friends, and other guests together for a celebration. In old age homes and for public rooms in independent housing buildings, *everyone* owns the pets, and it is a wonderful opportunity for a ceremony and a feeling of being connected to others.

20. It reinforces in the Elders' minds the fact that an animal's environment has a profound effect on its wellbeing, and that accommodating to the individual needs of each animal — in sickness as well as in health — is the most reasonable, considerate thing to do. The analogy to environment-and-wellbeing for the *human* beings is obvious.

21. It may lead to astonishing improvement in the human being's physical condition. (a) Having to take care of an animal is good reason to get out of bed in the morning. (b) The presence of an animal may provide the stimulus for astounding physical improvement. The story of J.S. and Serra the cockatiel[8] is just one example: As a result of a stroke, J.S., a man in his 60's, had not spoken for years. His frustration was obvious. However, within a week of receiving a bird as a present he began to say "Pretty Bird" and his own nickname "Bob". Why this happened and exactly how it happened physiologically is not as important to us as is the bare fact that it *did* happen (and *does* happen in the lives of many other people). It may not happen every day, but it *does* happen, and when we consider the heroic efforts made to save the lives of others, or the hours, days, weeks, and months of rehabilitation we offer other people, we should at least not ignore this option.[8a]

Furthermore, the Delta Society's AAT (Animal Assisted Therapy) video has a segment about the dogs that live and work in the wards of Huntington Memorial Hospital in Pasadena, CA. I have shown it 50 times at my lectures, and two scenes keep coming back to me. In the first, a man in a wheelchair is playing Fetch the Ball out on the lawn with one of the dogs. When the dog brings it back, they play tug of war, and it is obvious that the man is stretching very far in order to keep his grip. The physiotherapists must be pleased with this great flexibility. The other scene is someone in a rehabilitation session who is practicing his balance and testing his ability to walk again. Actually, he is walking one of the dogs on the leash. I wonder how many people, disheartened and depressed by the effects of their disease or accident, refuse to get out of bed and practice walking...until they were told they have to walk the dog. That inducement alone must motivate many of the patients to work harder at recovering and returning to their normal lives.

22. If one of the animals dies, it reminds them about death and dying and causes them suffering when they recall all the friends and relatives they have lost. They have endured enough tragedy in their lives. This is undoubtedly one of the difficult ones to answer. When I asked my friends the question, "Is it harder for the little children to deal with the death of the animal than it is for an old person?" there were clear and emphatic responses supporting both sides of the issue.

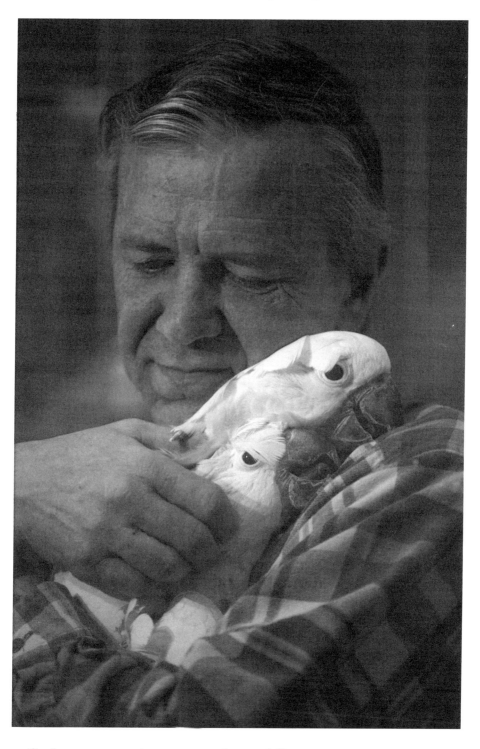

Cockatoo companions can make a difference between a lonely existence and one filled with love and affection. (Courtesy the Delta Society)

(a) The children will have a harder time because for many, it is their first encounter with death.

(b) Death is very unreal to some of the children. They watch TV and movie violence all the time. In daily life, they see and hear about it so much of it, they cannot connect it to their own sense of reality. As a result, one friend suggests, the death of the pet will also be unreal to them and won't be so traumatic.[9]

(c) Children will manage more easily because they are so active. They will move on to other things more quickly.

(d) The children will have a comparatively easier time because the death of the animal happens in a controlled situation. There is someone there to talk to and to respond to their thoughts and feelings. This is a good point, but it is also true for Elders living in communal situations. People are there for them to talk to and to respond to their sadness.

(e) The Elders will manage better because they have had many occasions to deal with loss and have had to create methods to put the loss in its proper psychological place. I would theorize that research would demonstrate that learning to deal successfully and meaningfully with loss is a significant contributing factor to greater longevity.

(f) Studies show that the many benefits to the Elders far outweigh the psychological risks that come with the loss of a pet. More important: the real-Life situations upon which the studies are based show that this is true.[10] Call the Delta Society for a review of the scientific literature.

(g) After the many conversations with friends and their children, the conclusion would seem to be that the little children and the Elders will react *differently* to the death of the animal. Individuals in either age group will have an easier or more difficult time depending on the circumstances, *but* in both cases the benefit of having animals is much greater than not having them, even if the animal dies.

23. Many of the Elders have had pets for several years or all their lives, and depriving them of pets is a particularly cruel thing to do. I remember visiting my friend Steve Vinocor, and I began to tell him what my latest Mitzvah interests were. His sister, Ms. Toby Pollack, a gerontologist and social worker, told me she used to work for many agencies that used their resources to keep Elders living independently. She told me that many of the people she visited were so poor, their living conditions horrified her. Nevertheless, they refused to be moved to the recommended subsidized housing because it would mean surrendering their pets. They just couldn't do it. If necessary, they would rather live with their dog or cat or bird or other pets in appalling circumstances than surrender their pets and live in a "better" place. Greater understanding on the part of landlords would alleviate this situation. According to Dr. Juana P. Lyon, "...subsequent studies of the effects of compliance on the part of housing owners and managers has shown little if any negative experience as a result. Pet owning tenants generally will do anything to be able to keep what is often their only living companion."[10a]

24. In many living situations, the Elders are entitled *by law* to have pets.[11] The impetus for the law may very well have been The National White House Conference on Aging held in Washington in 1981. The participants passed the following resolution:

> **Whereas,** the companionship of animal pets is a source of security, helps to keep aged persons physically active and responsible through caring for their pet, fulfills their need for giving and receiving affection, and has been proven to have measurable therapeutic effects on their physical and emotional health, and

> **Whereas,** the forced separation of older persons from their companion animals upon entering housing projects for the elderly inflicts immeasurable emotional suffering and often leads to severe psychological trauma and consequent mental and physical deterioration, including loss of will to live,

> The comfort of a companion animal is a civil right not to be denied responsible pet owners.

> The cooperation of the United States Congress, the Delegates to the 1981 White House Conference on Aging, the respective federal, state, county, and municipal agencies and the practitioners in the medical, veterinary, social service and other helping professions is hereby urged to end this senseless cruelty and to establish humane policies and regulations ensuring that the human/companion animal bond can remain intact for responsible pet owners, in federally funded housing for senior citizens and the handicapped.

> Nothing in this resolution should prevent the owner of rental housing, or the local housing authority or any other appropriate authority of the community where the housing is located from establishing reasonable rules on the number, size, kind or conduct of the pets allowed.[11a]

In 1983, the Housing and Urban Recovery Act (United States Code: 12USC §1701r-1) was passed. It covers issues of tenancy by elderly and disabled individuals in federally assisted rental housing developments. In part, section 227 (a) reads: *No owner or manager of any federally assisted rental housing for the elderly or handicapped may — (1) As a condition of tenancy or otherwise, prohibit or prevent any tenant in such housing from owning common household pets or having common household pets living in the dwelling accommodations of such tenant in such housing; or (2) Restrict or discriminate against any person in connection with admission to, or continued occupancy of, such housing by reason of the ownership of such pets by, or the presence of such pets in the dwelling accommodations of, such person.*

The law specifies what kinds of pets, what is meant by "federally subsidized," the regulations concerning immunization of the animals, how old is "elderly," how "disability" is to be defined in this case, and many other issues. The details are just that: details, issues peripheral to applying the law appropriately. It is a matter of studying the law and then enforcing it. Where the law applies, it should be followed.

I would suspect that many old age homes and independent housing complexes for the Elders[12] that are subject to this law have not made this public. It is time — high time — to bring it out into the open and demand compliance.

VIII. Teaching The Children (and Everyone Else)
  Why Gerbils and Bunnies Are in Kindergarten Classrooms

A. Unlikely Story #1

Imagine the following most unlikely scenario: A group of parents makes an appointment with the principal of the school where their children are in kindergarten, 1st, 2nd, and 3rd grades. They demand that she or he remove all the animals from the classrooms and hand him a sheet of paper listing ten sensible reasons why they should not be allowed in their school or any other school for that matter. Any hesitation or reluctance on the part of the principal is met with threats to take the issue to the school board and superintendent, even to the Health Department if necessary.

It won't happen.

It just never did and never will.

Why, then, is there such apathy and opposition when the same issue is raised concerning animals and Elders? It would appear to be a case of prejudice and discrimination against the Elders, or what is called "ageism".[13] What brought the American psyche to this unfortunately biased state of affairs? Whatever the origins and reasons for the prejudice, clearly the issue of pets for the Elders is an excellent way to teach the nature of prejudice and how to overcome the unfortunate results of prejudice, namely, by creating programs that will eliminate this injustice.

B. Unlikely Story #2

Imagine the following scenario: A visually impaired woman with a guide dog goes into a post office. As she stands in line, one of the postal workers steps our from around the counter and either gently or forcefully says, "You can't come in here with an animal." The employee takes her by the arm[14] and begins to lead her out the door.

It won't happen.

It just never did and never will.

It is perfectly legal for visually impaired people to bring their guide dogs into government buildings.[15] I choose the guide dogs for a number of reasons: (1) They have been a familiar presence in our society for decades. (2) People with disabilities and people who work in organizations that promote complete access for individuals with disabilities[16] know all too well how much preference is given to visually impaired people in the scale of priorities. It is also a well-known fact that it is easier to raise money for visually impaired people than for hearing impaired people. *Nobody* is going to take on visually impaired people and their dogs. And yet, in our case with the Elders....

C. Unlikely Story #3

Now imagine the following most unlikely scenario: The passengers have settled into their seats on a Boeing 747 for the flight from Los Angeles to Kahului, Maui. They are in a festive mood, having waited months, sometimes years, for this vacation opportunity. They are already picturing themselves on

Kaanapali Beach, pineapple juice in one hand, their bodies glistening with #30 or higher suntan lotion, a worthless spy novel in the other, and nothing of cosmic significance on their minds. They can already feel the glorious rays of the sun baking their brains; they are anticipating the taste of grilled mahi mahi and seared ahi and opakapaka in macadamia nut butter. They hear the mighty engines kick in and begin to warm up, and the adrenaline begins to flow. The flight attendant stands in the aisle and explains how to buckle the seat belt low on the body and tightly around the waist, demonstrates how the life vest inflates, and says, "In the event of an emergency, oxygen masks will come down from the compartment above your heads." She shows the passengers how to fit the mask snugly over the mouth and nose and adds, "If you are traveling with small children, first put on your own face mask, then put the mask on your children." The announcement is repeated thousands of times a day, a few moments before any plane is ready to take off.

Now imagine someone suddenly standing up and beginning to shout, "That's stupid! I'm not going to do it! I'm going to put the mask on my child first and nobody had better try to stop me!"

It won't happen.

It just never did and never will.

Distasteful and illogical as it sounds the first time a parent hears it, on second thought it makes perfect sense: (1) The child would be terrified enough in an emergency, having an unconscious parent would only compound the terror, and (2) An unconscious adult will be of absolutely no use to the child in such an emergency. Non-parents and people not traveling with small children understand the regulation, too, even though it doesn't effect them. *Everyone* gets it.

D. A Very Unusual Jewish Law the Teachers Didn't Get To
   Or Forgot to Teach Us
   When We Were in Religious School

Imagine this: The family has decided to treat itself to dinner at Moish Fong's Kosher Chinese Gourmet restaurant on a Sunday afternoon. Mom orders the garlic chicken with peanuts, Dad takes the Szechwan crispy fish, and the kids split a Peking Duck (@ $47.95 for two), after the egg rolls and soup, of course. The waiter comes out with a heavy tray laden with goodies. From the moment he opens the kitchen door to walk the 25 feet to your table, you know it's your order. You can smell it long before he starts putting the dishes down on the table. After the plates are set out and the waiter begins to head back to the kitchen, one of the kids says, "Sir, would you like some of my duck? It looks perfectly delectable."

It probably won't happen.

It certainly used to happen.

And most likely will start happening again.

Here's the curious Jewish law:

כל דבר שמביאין לפני האדם
שיש לו ריח והאדם תאב לו
צריך ליתן ממנו לשמש מיד
ומדת חסידות הוא ליתן לו מיד
מכל מין ומין

Everything that is brought to people who are having a meal
that has a particularly wonderful aroma
and thereby adds to the craving to eat the food —
those who are eating have to offer some of that food immediately
to the person serving [17] them.
Offering some of every one of the dishes
is a particularly fine way of doing this religious act.
(Shulchan Aruch, Orach Chaim 169:1)

The reason for the law is obvious. The employee is surrounded by the wonderful smells of the food, sees people either enjoying or about to enjoy the tastes, and he or she is left to suffer. I wouldn't suppose this is one of the Ten Most Earthshaking Laws in the History of Humanity, but it makes perfect sense. It is the right, the decent, the Menschlich thing to do.

In some ways, Elders in old age homes and independent housing are like the servant. They do not have the same control over their own lives as they once had. We would, therefore, be compounding their distress by withholding basic necessities and pleasures which are rightfully theirs. Why would we want to do that?

IX. Just Do It:
   How to Get Pets into Old Age Homes
   And Independent Housing for the Elders

A. Approach #1

Meet with the director and/or chairperson of the institution or agency and discuss all the logical reasons why the-people-for-whose-welfare-they-are-ultimately-responsible would benefit from having resident pets. Give the director and/or chairperson a copy of Dr. William Thomas' book, *The Eden Alternative.*[17a] (As discussed above, a visiting pet program just isn't good enough.)

B. Approach #2

Bring the young children (and their teachers) who have animals in their classrooms to meet with the director and/or chairperson of the institution or agency and discuss all the logical reasons why the-people-for-whose-welfare-they-are-ultimately-responsible would benefit from having resident pets. Their natural innocence should be enough to convince the person in charge of the justice of their request.[18] Have the children give the director and/or chairperson a copy of Dr. William Thomas' book, *The Eden Alternative.*

C. Approach #3

Meet with the director and/or chairperson of the institution or agency and present the logical argument that, if hospitals[19] — with all the potential (though non-existent) health hazards and other associated problems — can allow animals, then certainly *this* institution or agency can do the same.

D. Approach #4

In the situation of old age homes, meet with the director and/or chairperson of the institution and discuss all the financial reasons why the-people-for-whose-welfare-they-are-ultimately-responsible would benefit from having resident pets. Give the director and/or chairperson a copy of Dr. William Thomas' book, *The Eden Alternative*. Review Dr. Thomas' findings that, as part of an overall re-engineering of the tenor, atmosphere, nature, and program of the institution or agency, the costs for medications should be significantly reduced.

E. Approach #5

In the situation of old age homes, contact all insurers who are paying the medical bills and share with them your interest in introducing pets into a specific old age home. Send them copies of Dr. William Thomas' book, and tell them you suspect the costs of medications will go down significantly...less so than a total overhaul of the program, but still noticeable just by introducing pets. If they express interest in pursuing the matter, they have considerable leverage with the old age home, and they can deal directly with the appropriate administrators at the home.

F. Approach #6

Do your homework. Examine the law carefully and assess the specific situation of the home or housing project you wish to approach. Find out if the law applies to the particular home or project you want to change, and, if it does, if it is in compliance. *Then* meet with the director and/or chairperson of the institution or agency and discuss the legal reasons why the-people-for-whose-welfare-they-are-ultimately-responsible would benefit from having resident pets. Even if the facility is not required by law to allow pets, suggest that the institution or agency might want to do it anyway because of the many, many benefits to the Elders. Give the director and/or chairperson a copy of Dr. William Thomas' book, *The Eden Alternative*.

X. Summary

It would appear that the lack of pets in many old age homes and independent housing projects for Elders can be attributed to several factors, among them: lack of interest, ignorance, a lethargic approach to change or out and out apathy, ageism, insecurity (not wanting to rock the boat, not wanting to lose a job), and a dislike for pets among people in positions of power.

Whatever the cause, there are measures that can be taken to correct the situation. Be polite and pleasant, but be firm. Remind yourself — and state clearly to the people you are approaching — that you do not in any way want this program to inconvenience or threaten the wellbeing or safety of others. All concerns on those issues have been covered by the many model program around the country that have already introduced pets to their homes and apartments. All medical concerns have been covered by those models.

It is, I believe, essentially a matter of raising the issue and convincing the administrators of the merits of the program.

The rest is merely logistics.

Most of all, remember that, because you are doing the right thing, you can't lose.

The Ziv Tzedakah Fund[1] Annual Report

זיו

Ziv Tzedakah Fund, Inc.
A Non-Profit, Tax-Exempt Corporation (IRS #51-1219427)
Danny Siegel, Founder and Chairman

April 1, 1995

I.   *To All Ziv's Contributors and Friends, שלום -Shalom!**

Once again, we have had a very exciting year. The places we have worked with in the past are doing well. We are inspired by new projects we have discovered. This is the third consecutive year we have had more than $200,000 to distribute — reaching about 95 projects...all this while keeping our total overhead for the last 14 years at around 4 1/3%.

Summary of Ziv's Financial Activities[2]			
	4/13/81-3/31/94	4/1/94-3/31/95	Total to Date
Allocations	$1,555,000.00	$208,000.00	$1,763,000.00
Expenses	$68,277.49	$12,458.78	$80,736.27

If you would like to make a donation, please make the check out to "Ziv Tzedakah Fund," and mail it to:

Ziv Tzedakah Fund
c/o Gerry Eisenberger, Treasurer
384 Wyoming Ave., Millburn, NJ   07041

II.   *What We Do*

(1) People give us money; (2) in turn, we give the money to places that we have discovered that are using their funds efficiently and wisely *to make a difference*, and then (3) we report back to our contributors about our activities.
(4) We encourage people to give away more of their money and to use their time, effort, creativity, and other talents for the sake of תיקון עולם-Tikkun Olam, Fixing the World.

*See p. 103 at end of this chapter.

(5) We encourage people to visit the projects we support and to discover their own; to meet our Mitzvah heroes and to discover their own; and, most of all, to be a part of their work.

(6) We encourage people to learn more about צדקה-Tzedakah, and, of greater importance, to *perform* acts of צדקה-Tzedakah, to have an impact on the lives of others, to make the world a more just, more peaceful, more Menschlich and decent place.

Though we have a very simple program, idealistic and high-sounding, it works. We are awed by the power of Mitzvah money and how it changes the lives of many people, and we are enthused about how our work fits into the money-can-make-miracles-happen context. It is our enthusiasm that accounts for emphatic phrases like "a *must* place to visit" and "a *must* thing to do" that will appear at different places in this annual report.

To summarize: we believe that, as you read this report, you should keep in mind the words of the well-known educator, John Holt, who said, "Charismatic leaders make us think, 'Oh, if only I could do that, be like that.' True leaders make us think, 'If they can do that, then...I can, too.'" Many of the people we describe are awesome human beings. *They* are awesome because their Mitzvah work is awesome. If we were to stand back and merely admire them, we would miss the point. If they can do that, then...(to whatever extent I am able), I can, too."

The following are a few interesting examples of recent developments:
(The asterisk [*] indicates places we have supported in the past.)

*A. Bone Marrow Tests-*בדיקות נפש *($3,750)*:* Carrying on the work of the late Allison Atlas, ז״ל, and her family, Jay Feinberg and his family and friends have continued to raise funds and arrange drives to augment the number of potential donors in the two national bone marrow registries. While Jay himself has not yet found a match, many others have as a result of the Feinbergs' incredible efforts. Two of my own friends have been donors, saving the lives of individuals in desperate need of a bone marrow transplant. We encourage you to call the Feinbergs to set up a drive and to have yourself tested if you have not already done so.

We gave Friends of Jay $2,500 directly, and $500 each to George Washington University and Brown Hillel for the drives on campus initiated by students.

In addition, we gave $250 to Friends of Sergey Andreyev. Sergey, who needs a transplant, is the son of Rabbi Stuart and Ella Altshuler. To donate directly for Sergey, write to Friends of Sergey Andreyev, c/o Rabbi Stuart Altshuler, 438 Lavergne Ave., Wilmette, IL 60091, or call 708-256-0983. (Fax: 256-3225.)

[Friends of Jay Feinberg, POB 326 (W.O.B.), W. Orange, NJ 07052, 1-800-9-MARROW, fax: 201-403-8792.]

B. Leftovers from School Cafeterias — The Big Time ($107.50): Here is an excellent example of Mitzvah power....As a sixth grader, David Levitt convinced his entire school system to donate leftovers from the cafeterias to shelters and soup kitchens in Pinellas County, FL. Now, if we could only convince others to call him and launch similar projects around the country, imagine how much food would be available for hungry people! Call 813-398-1766. Our contribution was used to purchase containers to transport the food from the school to the appropriate agencies that feed hungry people in his community.

C. The Mitzvah Horses ($12,696.90)*: We are in the horse business once again. Comet, Katie, and Little John have been hard at work since the Fall at the Therapeutic Riding Club of Israel near Netanya. They join Nur, a horse we purchased a couple of years ago. Our three most recent Mighty Mitzvah Steeds were bought in New Jersey and shipped via El Al cargo. Anita and Giora Shkedi, directors of the program say they are marvelous horses and will have a long and productive life providing wonderful rehabilitation possibilities for an entire range of people: people who have had car accidents or strokes, who have been injured in wartime or terrorist attacks, people who have become disabled[3] due to disease or accident, Elders from old age homes...so many people.[4] This is a *must* place to visit when you are in Israel. After my years of experience with the Therapeutic Riding Club, I can only say that the work is miraculous. Very roughly, our investment comes to about $1.00/lesson over the course of the 10-15 years of remarkable work these horses will do.

[The Therapeutic Riding Club of Israel, POB 3168, Bet Yehoshua, Israel, Attn: Anita Shkedi, 09-697-776 or 698-289. Home: 09-967-705. Fax: 09-696-103.]

We also made a donation (**$250**) to The North American Riding for the Handicapped Association (NARHA), the umbrella organization that publicizes and encourages therapeutic horseback riding. We urge you to see it in your own community. Call 1-800-369-7433.

[NARHA, c/o Wm. J. Scebba, POB 33150, Denver, CO 80233, 1-800-369-RIDE or 303-452-1212, fax: 303-252-4610.]

D. Residences for the Elders With Half the Drugs, Half the Infections, a Natural, More Human Setting, and Longer Life Expectancy — The Revolution Has Begun: ($5,000)*: Dr. William Thomas has radically changed the living conditions in the 80-resident Chase Memorial Nursing Home in New Berlin, NY. Other nursing homes around the country, including the state-owned homes in Missouri, have put his revolutionary, yet *very* logical, ideas into action. It's known as The Eden Alternative. His book by the same name is *must* reading.

These two statistics alone should give us all good reason to be in touch with him: *(1) In the first full year of his program, he cut the cost of medications from $220,006 to $135,901, a savings of $84,105, more than 38%! (2) By the end of 2 1/2 years, the cost had been reduced by 50% from pre-Eden days.*

Knowing this, we should ask how an abundance of children, birds, cats, dogs, plants, gardens, decency, and caring make for such staggering results? If the corporate "in" phrase is "re-engineering," perhaps we should start here...re-engineering the old age homes of America based on Dr. Thomas' model.

While Dr. Thomas is no longer associated with Chase, he is developing other homes in the Eden image. He travels throughout the country encouraging *institutions* to make his vision a reality, namely: to start over again based on a *human* model, rather than on the much-outmoded *medical* model.

To give some perspective to Ziv's long-time readers and contributors: we consider our association with Dr. Thomas one of the half-dozen most important breakthroughs in our history. A most instructive example of Dr. Thomas' vision would be to mention something that happened just as we were completing final revision of this annual report. I received a significant contribution in the mail from Rabbi Lewis John Eron, Chaplain of the Jewish Geriatric Home in Cherry Hill, NJ. The attached note simply said, "A gift from our residents." While I was pleased to receive this donation, I was not the least surprised. Our question — Dr. Thomas' question — really is, "Are people who live in nursing homes a different kind of human being than we are?" It is time to reconsider our answer to that question and to act accordingly, sooner rather than later.

[The Eden Alternative, c/o Dr. William Thomas, RR 1, Box 31B4, Sherburne, NY 13460, 607-674-5232, fax: 607-674-6723.]

We also contributed **$500** to a group that is Edenizing three homes in the greater Binghamton, NY, area.

[United Health Services Foundation, 20-42 Mitchell Ave., Binghamton, NY 13903, 607-762-2449, 762-2602, Attn: Ms. April Rozboril.]

In addition, we are in touch with Ms. Batyah Joseph, Program Manager for Adopt-A-Nursing-Home, Texas Department of Human Services, Region 11. She co-ordinates volunteers in 85 nursing homes, and has accepted the offer we made in our November Update to have ten of her facilities purchase birds for the personal benefit and enjoyment of the residents. We will be reimbursing the ten homes $100.00 each in our next fiscal year. That was the limit of our offer — ten homes — and she decided to take on the entire project herself. If you would like to find out how she is doing it, call her at 512-878-3204. She will certainly share her enthusiasm with you and give you ideas about how to implement similar programs in your own community.

Those are some of the things we do. What follows is a description of all the other programs we have supported this year.

III. *Some People Who Are Doing It Absolutely Right: A Few of Our Favorites (Taken from All Areas of Tzedakah)*

A. The Shoe Woman of Denver — Ranya Kelly ($15,000)*: Ranya began with 500 pairs of brand new shoes which she found in a dumpster. To date, she has collected more than 165,000 pairs, which she has distributed to people in need. Her "collection" has expanded into many other types of merchandise — and food — that stores were throwing out,...all perfectly good items, all perfectly edible, fine food. This year, Ranya will have handled $1,500,000 worth of goods and food. Her idea is very simple: the merchandise and food is donated to The Redistribution Center (the name of her Mitzvah

Ranya Kelly poses with a teddy bear worth $550.00 that was being trashed by a local department store because its nose had some yarn hanging loose. The bear was later donated by Ranya to a hospital.

project), she then donates it to those who need it. Our contribution covers most
of her operating budget. (She takes no salary.) The ratio of goods and food to
expenses is easy to calculate: *for every penny we contributed, Ranya redis-
tributes $1.00 worth of merchandise and food.* An even more striking fact: the
$1,500,000 is the "salvage figure" used for IRS purposes. True market value
is considerably higher.

We take great pride in mentioning that the American Jewish Joint
Distribution Committee delivered a 20 cubic foot container to her warehouse.
She then filled it with $250,000 worth of goods and food which the Joint
shipped to the Former Soviet Union. Ranya's bill to the Joint was $75.00 for
the bags she used to package the goods. $1,300 of our contribution went for a
trailer, to make it easier for her to haul the massive quantities of goods from one
place to another.

Our hope is that many more Redistribution Centers will be established
throughout the country based on her example.

[Ranya Kelly, c/o The Redistribution Center, 7736 Hoyt Circle, Arvada, CO 80005,
303-431-0904, fax: 424-3368.]

**B. The Rabbanit Bracha Kapach, One of the Wonder
Women of Jerusalem ($11,219)*:** The Rabbanit Kapach provides for
nearly all of the human needs of hundreds of people in Jerusalem and the surrounding area. The individuals and families benefit in many ways. Her
Passover food program alone reaches more than 2,000 families. If they need
furniture or furnishings, she finds it. Many kids enjoy her Summer camp
(which she founded more than 20 years ago). And she is, of course, the famous Wedding Dress Woman who lends wedding dresses to brides who cannot
afford to buy or rent their own. Consider bringing one or two or five when you
travel to Israel. Many, many brides will benefit. And if you also bring gently-
used or new clothes, toys, and games, she will make certain they get to people
who need them the most.

I have known her for 20 years, and I cannot begin to calculate how
many lives are lived with greater dignity because of this one woman. On your
next trip to Israel, you might consider taking the time to meet this extraordinary
human being.

[The Rabbanit Bracha Kapach, 12 Lod St., Jerusalem, 02-249-296. She has incorpo-
rated her work as "Keren Segulat Naomi". Tax-deductible contributions (minimum of $25)
through PEF-Israel Endowment Funds, 41 E. 42 St., #607, NY, NY 10017, 212-599-1260.
Ask about PEF's other projects. They are great Mitzvah people!]

C. Yad Sara-שרה יד **— *Nothing Quite Like It In the World
($14,000)*:*** By conservative estimates, Yad Sara saved the Israeli economy
more than $220,000,000 last year. Here is the story: (1) They began as a sim-
ple project to lend medical equipment, free of charge, to anyone who needed it.
(2) They have over 70 lending stations throughout Israel, and now have more
than a dozen in the Former Soviet Union. (3) They are the largest volunteer organization in Israel, with more than 4,000 volunteers. (4) They have expanded
their program to include many projects for Elders, for individuals with disabilities, and other segments of the population whose needs were not being met.

Their founder and director, Uri Lupoliansky, a close personal friend, set the tone of Yad Sara from the very first day: everything is to be done in a Menschlich manner, with care and consideration for each individual's needs.

We purchased 50 emergency alarm systems @ $280.00 apiece so that more people could be tied into their countrywide computer system. Press the button, and Yad Sara's response is instantaneous.

You are welcome to bring new or used hearing aids to them on your next trip. They will recondition the old ones and get them to people who need them. Also needed are glucose testing machines for diabetics. (Yad Sara can use all models up to, but not including, the 1994 models.) Yes, this, too, is another *must* place to visit. You can even build a wheelchair while you are there.

[Yad Sara, c/o Uri Lupoliansky, 43 HaNevi'im St., Jerusalem, 02-244-242, fax: 244-493. Uri's home: 813-777. Tax-deductible contributions: Friends of Yad Sara, c/o Ms. Els Bendheim, Parker Plaza, Room 1450, 400 Kelly St., Ft. Lee, NJ 07024, 201-944-7920.]

If you want to start a wheelchair lending service in your synagogue, contact Rabbi Gerry Walter in Cincinnati, 513-791-1330.

We understand that some of the health services in Fair Lawn, NJ, conduct a similar program of lending medical supplies free of charge. If you would like to explore such a program for your local government, call Allan H. Glazerman at 201-796-5040. We are also looking into a project in Massachusetts called Pass-It-On, founded by Mr. George Navin, who has given himself the title "President and Truck Driver". It, too, resembles the medical equipment lending idea of Yad Sara. (They also donate equipment.) For information, call Mr. Navin at 508-477-6966.

D. Grandma and the Gangs ($2,800)*: Grandma Edie Lewis is one of those unique people who is capable of giving boundless quantities of love to young people who are considered losers or incorrigibles by society. She is also fearless. Her forté is getting gang members out of the gangs and into a dignified lifestyle filled with opportunities and hope. If you are in the Dallas area, a visit to Grandma's House is a worthwhile and uplifting experience.

[Grandma Edie Lewis, Youth Projects, Heart of Texas Foundation, POB 462205, Garland, TX 75046, 214-494-9609.]

E. Back To the Wilds ($550): Wilderness Inquiry, based in Minneapolis, takes people on adventures into the rivers and mountains and wild places of the world, but with a special twist. This is what Greg Lais, the director wrote me about their track record: "Since 1978, Wilderness Inquiry has served over 30,000 people, approximately half of whom have some sort of disability. Last year we served about 3,500 people. Again, about half of these folks have disabilities." When you order their poster of Ms. Erin Broadbent going up the side of a rock wall in her wheelchair, you will know why we have chosen to be a part of their work.

[Wilderness Inquiry, 1313 5th Ave. SE, Box 84, Minneapolis, MN 55414, 1-800-728-0719 or 612-379-3858 V/TTY, fax 612-379-5972, ATTN: Greg Lais or Sarah Toffler.]

*Grandma Edie Lewis and Koe Jones, former Blood Gang member,
striking a pose.   Koe is now a champion boxer, and a very popular
speaker in the schools...warning the students about gang life, drugs
and violence.*

F. Religious School for Hearing Impaired Children ($250):
The Board of Jewish Education of Greater Washington now has a religious school for children whose first language is American Sign Language (ASL). The program is called סימן טוב-Siman Tov, which means both "A good sign" and "A good omen". Contact the Washington people to create a similar program in your own community.

[Siman Tov, c/o Tifereth Israel, 7701 16th St., NW, Washington, DC 20012-1495, 202-882-1605, 882-1605 (TTY), 829-0635 (fax); ATTN: Janet Gordon. If you wish to speak to a satisfied parent, call Dennis Kirschbaum, 703-528-0170 (V/TTY) (h), 528-7701 (w), fax: 528-4451]

G. A New Aspect of Youth Work ($450): We are just beginning to publicize a new program for youth created by our friend, Ari Newman. We believe that youth group presidents should have a discretionary fund of $100 to be used for emergencies, the most drastic of which is when one of the members seems to be in great emotional or psychological need. This is not a substitute for professional therapy or other programs, but will, nevertheless, allow the president to respond at once: a movie, a dinner, a time away from pressures. Rabbi Daniel Syme introduced the idea at a Union of American Hebrew Congregations regional convention, and all nine congregations in his session were so enthused about the idea, they wanted to be a part of the pilot program. We provided $50.00 for each of the congregations, to be matched by them. (We have only provided seed money for Rabbi Syme's stage of the program. Local communities will, hopefully, provide the funds for their own group leaders.)

[Rabbi Daniel Syme, c/o UAHC, 838 5th Ave., NY, NY 10021, 212-565-5900. Ari Newman, 617-731-6391 or 401-861-3474.]

H. Shalva-שלוה, Jerusalem ($5,000)*: Kalman and Malky Samuels offer an incredible variety of programs — including respite care — for children with many kinds of disabilities. Shalva is just one of those magic places. The personal touch, great love, a determination to have every child develop to his or her full potential — you can feel these qualities from the moment you come by to visit.

[Kalman Samuels, c/o Shalva, 90 Shaulson St., POB 35199, Jerusalem, phone: 02-651-9120 or 651-8260; fax: 652-1578.]

IV.   *How To Find Mitzvah Heroes*

There are two excellent projects which locate giants in the field of Fixing the World. Both groups tell the stories of these Grand Human Beings and publicize their work, and both provide excellent teaching materials. They are devoting themselves to answering the question, "Just exactly who do we want to be when we grow up?" — a good question for people of all ages.

A. The Giraffe Project ($1,000)*: Giraffes are people who stick their necks out for the common good. Many of our Mitzvah heroes are Giraffes. I cannot stress enough just how useful and inspirational it is to become a member and receive their materials. They also have available a wonderful video for everyone as well as excellent curriculum materials for schools.

[The Giraffe Project, 197 Second St., POB 759, Langley, WA 98260, Attn: Ann Medlock, 360-221-7989, fax: 221-7817.]

B. The Caring Institute ($500): Besides reaching larger, general audiences, i.e., The People of the American People, The Caring Institute of Washington, DC, has certainly had an impact on legislators and others in positions of influence, hoping to have them use their power to make decisions based on their constituents' wellbeing. Four of our Mitzvah heroes have received awards from them, and this year's ceremony included an award for Dave Thomas of Wendy's fame for his work on behalf of children in need of adoption, as well as our "own" Ranya Kelly and Grandma Lewis. Subscribe to their magazine; the stories are inspirational.

[The Caring Institute, 320 A St., NE, Washington, DC 20002, ATTN: William Halamandaris, 202-547-4273, fax: 546-8968.]

V.   *The Mitzvah Menagerie*

Over the past several years we have taken note of many programs in which animals have been shown to make significant differences in people's lives. We have already mentioned The Therapeutic Riding Club of Israel (section II:C) and Dr. William Thomas' groundbreaking work in old age homes (section II:D). Additional breakthroughs are happening every day, everywhere. When I mention this idea to some of my audiences, I have often noticed a bit of hesitation by some of the attendees who know that many people are allergic to animals or may not particularly like them. I explain my position with the following analogy: I am allergic to penicillin. Nevertheless, I see the many benefits for people who need it, and as long as I take into account *their* needs, I would most certainly support the use of penicillin.

We particularly refer you to the all-important laws concerning the rights to pet ownership for elderly people and people with disabilities in federally-funded housing: Section 227(b) of the Housing and Urban Rural Recovery Act of 1983 (United States Code: 12USC §1701r-1) and the Department of Housing and Urban Development rules of 1986 in the Code of Federal Regulations, found at 24CFR, Part 243. The laws' implications are far reaching, particularly for a substantial percentage of subsidized housing projects for the Elders in Jewish communities across the country. We invite attorneys and other interested parties to read the law, see if it applies in their local communities, and then to contact us with any programs that may be established as a result.

A. Mitzvah Dogs, Part One: Guide Dogs for the Blind in Israel ($180) The Israel Guide Dog Center is a very exciting place. It is the major training center for dogs that will be given to visually impaired Israelis who find this method for more complete integration into society the most suited to their particular needs.

[Israel Guide Dog Center for the Blind, Bet Oved, 76800, Israel, ATTN: Hadas Tamir, phone: 08-408-213 or 202, Fax: 8-408-220; in the U.S., contact The Man Who Made It Happen, Norman Leventhal, 701 Easton Rd., Warrington, PA 18976 215-343-0373, fax: 343-0211.]

B. Mitzvah Dogs, Part Two, Canine Companions for Independence (CCI) ($1,454.34)*: CCI trains dogs to work with people who use wheelchairs and for hearing impaired people. (Very striking is their newfound mobility and ease of movement within the larger society.) I have known CCI for years, and have even spoken at one of the graduation ceremonies. They have matched more than 965 of these service dogs with human partners. You can (a) call them to see if someone with a CCI dog will come to your group to give a demonstration and talk, (b) get their videos and wonderful t-shirts, and (c) become a puppy raiser. Ask for details. A 1994 study by Dr. Karen Allen reported that the average annual savings for the 48 people with disabilities who participated in her work came to $13,000! There is much, much more to know about CCI. Call them.

[CCI, 4350 Occidental Rd., POB 446, Santa Rosa CA 95402, 1-800-767-BARK or 707-528-0830, fax: 528-0146, Attn: Corey Hudson, or speak to Becky Duncan or Nancy Foust in the Northwest office, 707-579-1985.]

We also commend the fine work of Dr. M.J. Willard, who trains Capuchin monkeys to work with people with disabilities. For information, contact her at 617-787-4419.

C. The Ultimate Resource — The Delta Society ($230)*: The Delta Society is the foremost authority on the benefits of animal/human interaction. They are familiar with the latest research, have directories and listings of programs all over the world, have available a fabulous video, can refer you to other videos...in short, they are the first place to call for information on any of these items.

[Linda Hines, c/o The Delta Society, 321 Burnett Ave. S., 3rd Floor, Renton, WA 98055, 1-800-869-6898 (V/TTY), fax: 206-235-1076.]

D. Dogs in the Hospitals

I had read about it, seen it on TV, then finally got the video from the Delta Society: visiting dogs and resident dogs in hospitals, for companionship, for therapy, a break from the woes of sickness and operations. We support two of the many programs that exist:

1. Huntington Hospital (Pasadena, CA) ($250): Their Pet Assisted Therapy Program (PAT) includes Chelsea and Barney, two dogs from the local humane society, who live and work at the hospital.

[Huntington Hospital, PAT Program, 100 W. California Blvd., POB 7013, Pasadena, CA 91109, ATTN: Ms. Holly Pfau, 818-397-3495, fax: 397-3623, ATTN: Ms. Pfau.]

2. Denver Children's Hospital ($180): Though animals in hospitals are intended for all patients, the benefits to children are so great, they are difficult to describe unless you have actually seen them. On a visit in November, I experienced many moving moments: happy kids — despite a multitude of IV lines, tubes, bandages, casts, loss of hair, and pain. Wonderful!

[The Denver Children's Hospital Rx Pet Program, 1056 E. 19th Ave., Denver, CO 80218, ATTN: Ms. Donna Miedema, 303-861-6286, fax: 764-8062.]

E. The Mitzvah Dolphins and Sea Turtles ($300)*: The Full Circle Program provides remarkable interaction between children with disabilities and a variety of sea creatures. These dolphins, sea turtles, and other marine animals also have disabilities. One dolphin was attacked by sharks, another has birth defects. The program has produced astounding results. To find out how and why it works, call them, or, if you are in Florida, visit and observe the program in action.

[The Full Circle Program, Clearwater Marine Science Center, 249 Windward Passage, Clearwater, FL 34630, Attn: Ms. Marianne Klingel, phone: 813-441-1790 X 21, Fax: 813-442-9466.]

F. Two Programs in Israel

1. In צפת-Safed ($750): The Everett Children's Nature Study Center has an incredible variety of animals. It is a special place, and children in psychiatric treatment make use of it as a crucial component of their therapy. Workers include people who have chronic mental health problems and prisoners sentenced to community work. Visually impaired individuals also benefit from the Petting Room. So much is happening here! (We paid for food for the animals.)

[Friends of the Everett Children's Nature Study Centre, POB 1434, Safed, Israel, 06-922-566. Attn: Dr. Lionel J. Davidson. Dr. Davidson at his office in Akko: 049-811-911, fax: 049-812-092.]

2. On the Outskirts of Jerusalem ($250): Kibbutz Tzuba has a marvelous animal nature center visited by groups from the surrounding area. The center is used for educational programs as well as being a pleasant place for a leisurely afternoon visit. We funded programs to bring special needs children and adults to benefit from this experience.

[Joël (pronounced "Yo-ayl") Dorkam, Kibbutz Palmach Tzuba, Doar Na Haray Yehuda, Israel, 02-347-871.]

G. Ziv's Golden Eagle ($240)*: Sigrid Ueblacker has been saving birds of prey for years, releasing back to the wilds those capable of living safely in Nature and keeping the others to live their lives in her care, safe and healthy. We sponsored the recovery of Windsong, a golden eagle. She is scheduled to return to her Home High Up some time later this year.

[The Birds of Prey Rehabilitation Foundation (BPRF), 2290 S. 104th St., Broomfield, CO 80020, 303-460-0674, Attn: Sigrid Ueblacker.][5]

VI.   *For People on the Economic Edge*

A. Four Projects in Israel

1. Tova's Kitchen ($1,050)*: Every Wednesday for many years, Tova Cohen has been preparing a hot meal for about 30 elderly people in Jerusalem. Though Tova's Kitchen (as it is known) is tiny, very tiny, her soup and chicken and vegetables and bread and fruit make all the difference to the people she feeds. Just stroll around in the vicinity of 11 Joseph Caro St. on an early Wednesday morning and ask for Tova. Any of the neighbors will bring you to her. (Tova finally has a phone: 822-789.)

2. The Chicken Lady of Jerusalem ($1,000)*: Clara Hammer, up in her eighties, provides Shabbat chickens for over 60 families every week (and for holidays, too)...among the many other Mitzvahs she performs. This is really *someone to meet* when you are in Jerusalem. She is American by birth, so if your Hebrew is not-yet-fluent, no problem.

[Clara Hammer, Mishmar HaGvul 4, Ramat Eshkol, Jerusalem, 02-816-164.]

3. Trudi Birger's Mitzvah Work ($2,167)*: Trudi Birger is an extraordinary human being. Her Dental Volunteers for Israel (DVI) program provides free dental care for children who have little if any access to that part of the health care system. For that program she needs volunteer dentists, donations of equipment, supplies of gloves, and, of course, money. $1,167 of our contribution was for DVI. The remaining $1,000 was given to her Keren Rehavia Family Project which provides direct support for families who just can't seem to hold on financially no matter how hard they try. Trudi keeps their lives together, with dignity.

[DVI, 29 Mekor Haim St., Jerusalem, ATTN: Trudi Birger, phone: 02-783-144; Keren Rehavia Family Fund, 2 HaMeyasdim St., Jerusalem, ATTN: Trudi Birger, phone: 02-436-628, fax: 433-623.]

4. Scholarships ($500)*: For many years we have supported the AACI Jerusalem Scholarship Fund. It pays for non-tuition necessities for students who would have missed out on crucial educational opportunities were it not for the fund. What impresses me most about AACI's program — a tribute to founders Michael Bargteil and his late wife, Hannah, ל"ז — is the personal contact and the care given to each of the individual students who receive the scholarships. I frequently get calls like, "Where can I give money for education in Israel?" *This* is a most worthy place to send your money.

[AACI Jerusalem Scholarship Fund, 6 Mane St., POB 30018, Jerusalem, ATTN: Ms. Judy Hoffman, phone: 02-617-151, fax: 661-186.]

B. Food

1. Operation Food Share: Leftover Food from Restaurants, Hotels, and Similar Businesses ($250)*: Bruce Feldman developed the idea in Dayton — have linen delivery trucks pick up leftovers from restaurants, cafeterias, and other food establishments, bring them back to their central warehouse, and, finally, have shelters and soup kitchens pick them up to feed hungry people. Since Bruce created the program, they have saved well over 200,000 pounds of food nationwide, and enabled others to save an additional 180,000 pounds for hungry people. Six cities are in full swing, with 14 more in the works. Call to find out how to start a program in your community.

[Operation Food Share, 131 N. Ludlow St., #302, Dayton, OH 45402, Attn: Don Cook, Director, 513-224-7283, fax: 513-224-8271.]

2. Ari Newman's Work ($450)*: Ari began his Mitzvah food projects by getting the Kosher food facilities at Boston University, Brandeis, and Harvard to donate their leftovers. Ari arranged for the food to be delivered *directly* to Jews in need. Now he has written a fine pamphlet explaining every step anyone needs to know on getting leftover food to hungry people. Contact him for a copy. ($100 of this contribution went to his youth discretionary fund project. See section III:G, above.)

[Ari Newman, Garin Mitzvah Network, 14 Upton Rd., Providence, RI 02906, 401-861-3474. Call his Boston number first, during the school year: 617-731-6391. Otherwise, use the 401 number (Providence).]

3. Mazon-A Jewish Response to Hunger ($180)*: Mazon is the national Jewish organization funding both Jewish and general programs worldwide that provide food for hungry people. They are also involved in larger efforts to get society to re-think and re-configure their priorities on solving the problems of hunger in America and around the world.

[MAZON, 2940 Westwood Blvd., #7, Los Angeles, CA 90064, Attn: Irving Cramer, 310-470-7769, fax: 470-6736.]

4. Holy Work in Youngstown, OH ($2,500)*: Joseph Lordi is a very gentle, saintly man. There is no charge for the food at Gleaners Food Bank, and everyone is treated with the utmost dignity.

[Youngstown Community Food Center, Inc. and Gleaners Food Bank, POB 3587, Boardman, OH 44513, Attn: Joseph Lordi, 216-746-8436 (food bank), 216-726-9591 (h).]

5. The Potato People ($1,500)*: Last year alone, Ken Horne, Ray Buchanan, and their people gathered 19,000,000 pounds of potatoes and other produce from farms and similar food-producing establishments...180,000,000 pounds since they started in 1983. They are just simple folks gleaning, trucking, re-routing food to hungry people. Our $1,500 funded an entire truckload of 45,000 pounds of produce (give or take a few pounds). About 3¢ a pound (though the Potato People anticipate it may go up to 4¢ or 5¢ in the future...) — incredibly low costs.

[Society of St. Andrew/The Potato Project, State Rt. 615, POB 329, Big Island, VA 24526, Attn: Ken Horne or Ray Buchanan, 1-800-333-4597 or 804-299-5956, fax: 804-299-5949.]

6. Jewish Food Banks: There are many Jewish food banks around the country, and many more are needed. We supported two this year. Call either one to find out how to create one in your own community.

Milwaukee Jewish Food Pantry ($180): Even though Milwaukee is a relatively small Jewish community (28,000 Jews), they have recognized a need for a Jewish food bank. Logically, larger communities should consider doing the same. Call them for information.

[Milwaukee Jewish Food Pantry, 6255 N. Santa Monica Blvd., Milwaukee, WI 53217, ATTN: Dorene Paley, 414-964-4444, fax: 964-0922. The Jewish Federation and Jewish Community Center are co-sponsors of this program.]

Boston's Family Table ($280)*: Shortly after Boston established its Jewish food bank a year and a half ago, it quickly became apparent just how great a need there was for such a service in their community. Our contribution was used for a month's supply of Challah. A quote from Marti Mirken, Administrator of Family Table says so much: "What is one of the added benefits and one of the biggest surprises is how it has brought isolated Jews back into the community as a whole."

[Family Table, c/o Jewish Family and Children's Service, POB 9125, Boston, MA 02114, Attn: Ms. Marti Mirken, 617-227-6641, fax: 227-3220.]

7. *Sunday Hot Lunches ($250)**: A Monday-through-Friday lunch program — even allowing for extra food for Shabbat — leaves many people hungry on Sunday. We supported the efforts of the Jewish Federation Association of Connecticut to provide Sunday hot lunches in the Hartford area.

[Jewish Federation Association of Connecticut, 333 Bloomfield Ave., W. Hartford, CT 06117, ATTN: Robert J. Fishman, 203-232-4483, fax: 232-5221.]

8. *Passover Food ($500)**: B'nai B'rith organizes the distribution of Passover food packages for more than a hundred Jewish residents of the Washington area. The local chapters in many other communities also conduct similar programs, called Project Hope.

[B'nai B'rith Project Hope, c/o Len Elenowitz, 8801 Post Oak Rd., Potomac, MD 20854, 301-983-1345]

C. *Jewish Free Legal Services*

1. *Bet Tzedek-*צדק בית, *Los Angeles ($180)**: Every year, Bet Tzedek reaches hundreds of people. Founded as a Jewish *pro bono* service for Jewish people in need of free legal assistance, it has grown to include many members of the general legal community and now serves the larger community as well. They have an astonishing track record.

[Bet Tzedek, 145 S. Fairfax Ave., #200, L.A., CA 90036, Attn: Ralph Gottlieb, 213-939-0506, fax: 939-1040. The new director is David Lash.]

2. *Bet Tzedek-*צדק בית, *Boston ($500)**: Joy Rothenberg took us seriously when we suggested other cities should have a Bet Tzedek. Her project is growing each year, and she would be happy to help other communities organize their own "Place Where Justice Happens." Call her at 617-277-6090. Many attorneys and paralegals are looking for this kind of meaningful work. All you need to do is give them the opportunity to do the Mitzvah.

[Bet Tzedek of Boston, 1762 Beacon St., Brookline, MA 02146, Attn: Robin Weingarten, 617-232-2428, fax: 566-6281.]

D. *Housing and Home Repair*

1. *Migrant Workers in Florida ($3,300)**: Through our connections with the inspiring Caridad Asensio, we have purchased a mobile home ($2,300) to be used as a permanent home for a family of five migrant workers. Caridad is a most extraordinary woman. The remaining $1,000 went to her medical clinic and other pressing needs of the people she reaches in the South Florida area.

[Migrant Association of South Florida, Inc., 112 SE 10th St., Delray Beach, FL 33483, Attn: Caridad Asensio, 407-274-4027 (w), 391-5327 (h), fax: 274-0077. Or call Caridad's assistant, Connie Berry, 407-368-7132.]

2. *Sukkot in April ($250):* Yachad-יחד, a Washington Jewish organization dealing with decent housing for everyone, sponsors a program of home repair whereby crews go out and, often in one day, complete a thorough fix-up. We are partners in this year's venture with two other organizations, The Kehila and the Am Kolel High Holiday Community.

[Yachad, 2027 Massachusetts Ave., NW, Washington, DC 20036, 202-667-6924, ATTN: Ms. Audrey Lyon.]

E. *The Mitzvah Crib ($250)*: The idea began at St. Joseph's Parish in Seattle — set up a crib as a container for collecting baby items for infants whose families cannot afford to buy them...even the basics such as diapers and shampoo. Many synagogues, Jewish Community Centers, and Jewish Federations now have cribs. Call Ms. Jaybush, who created the project, to find out how to do it. Then do it.

[Baby Corner, St. Joseph's Parish, 732 18th Ave. E., Seattle, WA 98112, Attn: Ms. Jeannie Jaybush, 206-726-1435, fax: 329-5698.]

F. *Medical Services in Mississippi:*

1. *Dr. (also Sister) Anne Brooks, Tutwiler ($500)*: In the neglected stretches of Mississippi, this physician and her people deliver front-line medical attention to the residents. Conditions were disastrous, nearly Third World Quality, until she arrived. Noble work.

[Dr. Anne Brooks, Tutwiler Clinic, POB 462, 205 Alma St., Tutwiler, MS 38963, 601-345-8334.]

2. *Dr. Ronald Myers, Tchula ($500)*: About 50 miles down the road from Dr. Brooks is Dr. Myers' clinic. Primarily a physician, Dr. Myers is also a Baptist minister and a jazz musician. Trying to bring the most basic health care to the residents of this part of America — so far off the beaten track it was almost forgotten — is exhausting, yet rewarding, work.

[Dr. Ronald Myers, The Myers Foundation, 114 Hwy 49 East, POB 637, Tchula, MS 39169, 601-235-4227 (o), 247-3364 (h), fax: 247-3364 (then *0).]

G. *The Ferrells of Philadelphia ($2,009.99)*: Trevor's father, Frank, has created a new program, Trevor's Endeavors, which encourages others to work on behalf of homeless people.[6] The family is exploring a number of new projects, among them a ranch-type setting in the Pennsylvania countryside which will provide programs for inner-city kids. The family's 10 years of experience working with street people allows Frank to present ideas and insights into solving the desperate problems of poor and homeless people.

[Trevor's Endeavors, Box 21 Gladwyne, PA 19035, ATTN: Frank Ferrell, 610-642-4633.]

H. *Shelter and Related Projects:*

1. *Samaritan House (Denver) ($300):* We learned about this impressive project from Ranya Kelly, the Shoe Woman. My on-site visit was a very moving experience.

[Samaritan House, 2301 Lawrence, Denver, CO 90205, ATTN: Father Michael Suchnicki, 303-294-0241.]

2. *Sister Margaret ($1,000)*: Sister Margaret has been finding food and clothing and housing and jobs for so many of Shreveport's people for many years. Her energy and faith and resilience are quite remarkable.

[Christian Service Program, POB 21, Shreveport, LA 71161, Attn: Sister Margaret, 318-221-4539.]

3. Washington, DC-I ($500)*: We have supported the Reverend Steinbruck's good work for many years. Each year we buy them something from his organization's wish list. This time we funded the purchase of a printer for their computer and software for their tutoring programs.

[Luther Place N St. Village, 1226 Vermont Ave., NW, Washington, DC 20005, 202-667-1377.]

4. Washington, DC-II ($250): The people of Mary House who work on behalf of poor Washingtonians do whatever is needed — and the needs are great — to solve the immediate and pressing problems at hand. They do it with care and with the human touch.

[Mary House, 4303 13th St., NE, Washington DC 20017, ATTN: Sally or Bill Murphy, 202-635-0534, fax: 529-5793.]

I. Free Burial ($180)*: Sadly, to complete this section, we mention that there are those who die, and (1) their relatives and friends cannot afford burial costs, or (2) there are no relatives or friends at all to perform this sacred duty. Washington's Hebrew Free Burial Society is one of many organizations throughout the country that provides the funds and services for this final act of dignity.

[Hebrew Free Burial Society of Greater Washington, 4520 East-West Highway, #520, Bethesda, MD 20814, Attn: Marty Kamerow, 301-652-6700; emergency number: 230-7200.]

VII. הידור פני זקן-*The Grandeur of the Faces Of Our Elders*

A. Dental Care-Israel ($500): We are pleased to announce our support of Professor Jaime Pietrokovski's Mobile Dental Clinic for Seniors, a recently-created and very much-needed program of care for Israel's Elders. The key to the program is in the title: *mobile*, reaching the Elders where it is most convenient. Dentists — they need equipment.

[Information and tax-deductible contributions (minimum of $25) through PEF-Israel Endowment Funds (See section III:B above for details. For information in Israel, call Joan Hooper, 02-781-140.]

B. Wellbeing and Security-Jerusalem ($1,700)*: Yitav 109 is Jerusalem's wonderful telephone reassurance program for Elders. The volunteers speak daily with hundreds of people to make sure they are doing well. We encourage synagogues to create similar programs.

[Yitav 109, c/o Shaare Tzedek Hospital, POB 1499, Jerusalem, Attn: Chaim Vigolik, 02-651-2498.]

C. Myriam's Dream ($3,600=200 X 18-חי)*: Myriam Mendilow, ז"ל, had a dream that the Elders would live productive lives, creating beautiful crafts, continuing their education, and touring and enjoying their surroundings just like their younger counterparts in society. Myriam's Dream sustains this vision with workshops (including the bookbindery in New Jersey), educational programs, intergenerational activities, and adventures into the world around them. In Israel, they have projects in Tel Aviv, Eilat, Mate Yehuda, and Afula/Givat HaMoreh, and around the world in Estonia, Ukraine, and Prague.

[Myriam's Dream, Linda Kantor, President, 52 Wellington Dr., Orange, CT 06477, 203-795-4580, fax: 795-3291. Contributions: Myriam's Dream, 1500 Palisade Ave., Ft. Lee, NJ 07024.]

D. New York-Three Exceptional Programs: Project Ezra, Dorot, and Hatzilu have superb, long-standing reputations providing a variety of services for the Elders, including holiday food supplies and celebrations, home visits and personal attention to individual needs — almost everything that is missing when people fall through America's safety net.

1. Project Ezra ($15,000)*: Working with the elderly Jews of the Lower East Side of Manhattan. Our funding particularly targeted food for their food bank and home care attendants.

[Project Ezra, 197 E. Broadway, NY, NY 10002, Attn: Misha Avramoff, 212-982-3700, Fax: 677-9134.]

2. Dorot ($3,700)*: Working with the Jews of the Upper West Side of Manhattan. Part of our contribution went toward their shelter for homeless Jews — the Homelessness Protection Program (HPP).

[Dorot: 171 W. 85th St., NY, NY 10024, Attn: Judy Ribnick, 212-769-2850, fax: 212-769-4989. HPP: 316 W. 95th St., NY, NY 10025, Attn: Sara Peller, 212-666-2000.]

3. Hatzilu ($250)*: Hatzilu has a variety of vital programs that benefit elderly Jews in Brooklyn, the Bronx, and Long Island. Menschlich people.

[Hatzilu, 1106 E. 95th St., Brooklyn, NY 11236, Attn: Al Nevins, 718-485-4142.]

E. Jerusalem-Individual Needs ($5,000)*: Dr. Martin Kieselstein works directly with hundreds of Elders, particularly those who are chronically ill. His personal attention and creative solutions to individual problems have afforded the Elders he reaches the opportunity to live richer, more dignified lives. An example of his creativity: $1,000 of our contribution was used to hire musicians from the Former Soviet Union — many of them struggling to find employment — to play in institutions for the Elders.

[HaAguda LeEzra VeIddud VeShikum Keshishim VeCholim Birushalayim and Keren Lema'an Cholim Chroni'im Birushalayim, 6 Rabbi Binyamin St., Jerusalem, Attn: Dr. Martin Kieselstein, 02-652-3471.]

VIII. *Quiet Mitzvahs ($7,060)*

Some Mitzvah situations require a quieter or quicker or more anonymous approach. We respond by appointing individuals or organizations to serve as our agents to accomplish what needs to be done with a minimum of intermediate steps. On a number of occasions in any given year, this is an essential part of our work. All of these records are on file.

IX. *Refuge and Relief for Abused Women*

We believe that there are too few specifically *Jewish* programs for Jewish battered women. There are, at most, 10 Jewish battered women's shelters in North America, four in Israel. We encourage our Ziv people to get involved, to support existing projects and create new ones where they are needed.

A. Shalva-שלוה **($250)*:** Our contact in Chicago, Ms. Sherry Berliner Dimarsky will readily assist you if you want to create a network of services for Jewish battered women.

[Shalva, 1610 W. Highland, #53, Chicago, IL 60660, ATTN: Sherry Berliner Dimarsky, 312-583-HOPE.]

B. Jerusalem ($500)*: We continue to support the Jerusalem shelter's exceptional work. We have been with them since their founding.

[Shelter for Battered Women, Jerusalem, POB 10403, Jerusalem, Attn: Ruth Rossing, 381-587 or 382-009. Checks written to "Woman to Woman" or through The New Israel Fund, 111 W. 40th St., #2600, NY, NY 10173, 212-302-0066. Indicate that you recommend the contribution be for the Shelter for Battered Women, Jerusalem.]

C. Counseling-Israel ($300): The Counseling Center for Women provides many vital services for abused women who *do not* choose to go to a shelter. In the painful world of domestic abuse, this is just one more crucial aspect of the broad range of needs that must be met.

[Counseling Center for Women, 16 Modigliani St., POB 16312, Tel Aviv, 03-696-8008; in Jerusalem: 02-651-4133. Our Jerusalem contact is Ms. Bella Savran 02-733-827.]

X. *Exceptional People/People with Special Needs*

A. ALYN-אל״ן **Orthopaedic Hospital for Children ($8,000)*:** ALYN is a most astonishing place. The children are wonderful, the staff is fabulous, the atmosphere is one of overwhelmingly love and care...all with the goal of integrating the kids into Israeli society as independent citizens. Each year we purchase equipment. This year, among other items, we bought an oxygen monitor and adjustable computer tables. Whatever our contact, Brenda Hirsch, wants for the kids (within our budget), we buy. If you want some magical, sublime moments on your next trip to Israel, go to ALYN.

If you would like to start an American Friends of ALYN in your community, call Pam Lippitt in Detroit at 810-353-9038 for details.

[ALYN, POB 9117, Olsvenger and Shmaryahu Levin Sts., Kiryat HaYovel, Jerusalem, Attn: Brenda Hirsch, phone 02-494-222, fax: 433-653 or 437-338. U.S. Contributions: American Friends of ALYN, 19 W. 44th St., #1418, NY, NY 10036, 212-869-0369.]

B. Special Spiritual Needs ($300): Rabbi Shira Joseph is creating a project called "So All May Worship," which will meet the specific needs of elementary age children with severe mental disabilities. Her point of departure is exploring the unique way the children will be able to appreciate Jewish prayer. We admire and support her creative efforts in this area.

[Rabbi Shira H. Joseph, c/o Shir Ami, 101 Richboro Rd., Newtown, PA 18940, 215-968-3400, fax: 968-3296.]

C. People with Down Syndrome

1. Hadassah Levi's Work ($7,000)*: About 17 years ago, when Hadassah Levi saw that some infants with Down Syndrome were being abandoned in the hospitals, she took them in, almost 40 of them. Her project became Ma'on LaTinok-מעון לתינוק, "A Home for Infants". Young adults now, they are under the supervision of another program, but, through Hadassah, we still subsidize specific needs for some of them. She hopes to open another home for more infants if conditions permit. She is a giant — insightful, awesome, my friend and Rebbi.

[Hadassah Levi, POB 413, Givata'im, Israel. Phone: 09-929-265. *Contributions made out to "Ma'on LaTinok"*. Hadassah is no longer associated with Jerusalem Elwyn.]

2. Adoption ($2,500)*: In 18 years, Janet Marchese has facilitated the adoption of approximately 3,400 infants and children with Down Syndrome. In any given year, she singlehandedly does more than any *agency* in the country in this area. This past year alone she facilitated the adoption of 116 infants. She receives no salary for her work. Janet is just one of those unique human beings we are sometimes blessed to meet in our lives.

[Janet Marchese, A KIDS Exchange (= Adoption, Knowledge, and Information on Down Syndrome, formerly the Down Syndrome Adoption Exchange), 56 Midchester Ave., White Plains, NY 10606, phone/fax 914-428-1236.]

D. Making a Radical Difference ($1,050)*:

Sheer, simple brilliance. Professor Jack Daly of Case Western Reserve University's School of Engineering has recruited many of his students for the purpose of designing devices that will make the lives of people with disabilities more manageable. The resourceful students have made some astounding breakthroughs, and the idea is spreading to other engineering schools around the country. We urge you to have your local school call Professor Daly's people so they can set up similar programs. We contributed toward publicizing their work at other schools and for their computer lending program.

[Case Engineering Support Group, Department of Mechanical and Aerospace Engineering, 10900 Euclid Ave., Glennan Building 416, Cleveland, OH 44106, 216-368-2943, fax: 368-6445, ATTN: Ms. Julie Grubaugh.]

E. Large Print Jewish Books ($180):

We donated funds to the Board of Jewish Education of Greater Washington's library for large print Jewish books. We feel there is a great need for such programs in many other communities.

F. Two Jerusalem Workshops

1. Chazon F'taya-חזו"ן פתייה, ($9,000)*: Simcha Ovadia, the director, prefers the term "people who have experienced a personal crisis" rather than "people who are mentally ill." Chazon's workshops provide many significant opportunities for renewed wellbeing and a more complete return to the larger society. A marvelous place. *Very* caring.

[Chazon F'taya, POB 6070, 6 Shimon Chacham St., Jerusalem, Attn: Simcha Ovadia, 02-827-826, fax: 817-117.]

2. Yad Ezrah-עזרה יד **($2,000)*:** Reb Osher Freund has created an incredible number of Mitzvah projects in Israel. We devote our efforts to the sewing workshop, a small program providing sensitive and caring surroundings for people who have experienced a personal crisis. As with Chazon, the people who come to work there have a considerably-higher-than-average rate of recovery.

[Sewing workshop: 4 Kinneret St. Yad Ezrah-main office, 9B HaRav Sorotzkin St., POB 7199, Jerusalem, Attn: Shmuel Katz, 02-386-414, fax: 386-462. For tours, speak to Shmuel's secretary. Contributions: Boston Friends of Yad Ezrah, c/o Elihu Stone, 145 Pond St., Sharon, MA 02067, 617-784-2848, fax: 722-0301. Call Elihu if you don't happen to be going to Israel, but would still like to purchase their Challah or Matzah covers.]

G. Jewish People in Institutions ($500)*: For years, members of this Jewish organization in Pittsburgh have been making visits to, and providing holiday celebrations for, Jews in institutions through the area. This is a very caring group of Mitzvah people doing the right thing.

[Western Pennsylvania Auxiliary for Exceptional People, 281 Sharon Dr., Pittsburgh, PA 15221, Attn: Arnold Lazarus, 412-271-1578.]

H. Special Education-Jerusalem ($100)*: Once again we donated money for supplies and equipment to this school for children with learning disabilities.

[Limudei HaShem-השם לימודי Center for Special Education, King George St. 39a, Jerusalem, 02-241-853. Contact: Yehuda Ovadia at Chazon F'taya, 02-827-826. He has a child in the school.]

XI. Immigrants to Israel

A. Volunteers ($10,000)*: The Yaakov Maimon Volunteers give the personal touch to resettlement in Israel. They tutor the new arrivals, provide many acculturation experiences, and, in general, foster a warm and very human element during their period of adjustment. The Maimon people reach immigrants from the Former Soviet Union, other parts of Europe, and Ethiopia. It is a fine, fine group of people.

[Joël (pronounced "Yo-ayl") Dorkam, Ya'akov Maimon Volunteers, Kibbutz Palmach Tzuba, Doar Na Haray Yehuda, Israel, 02-347-871, fax: 347-955.]

B. For Ethiopians ($1,025)*: The North American Conference on Ethiopian Jewry is engaged in many activities with Ethiopians in Israel. We contributed specifically to after-school tutoring and other programs for the children in the caravan sites.

[NACOEJ, 165 E. 56th St., NY, NY 10022, Attn: Barbara Ribakove Gordon, 212-752-6340, fax: 980-5294.]

C. Jerusalem's Ramot Neighborhood ($5,000)*: When the great waves of immigrants began arriving in Israel from the Former Soviet Union, my good friend, Rabbi Jonathan Porath, and his neighbors devoted their efforts to resettling the ones who came to their area of Jerusalem. They do it with a strong interest in each individual's needs. We donated money toward that good work. We also provided Rabbi Porath with funds for immigrants outside of their neighborhood who have emergency medical needs. In addition, through Rabbi Porath's connections, we provided scholarship money for Ethiopian children to attend Summer camp.

[Rabbi Jonathan Porath, Keren Klitat Aliya Neve Orot, Nerot Shabbat St. 623/10, Ramot Alef, Jerusalem, 02-868-757, fax: 241-382.]

D. Interest-Free Loans ($1,250)*: Dr. Eliezer Jaffe's Israel Free Loan Association (IFLA) has extended more than $5,000,000 in loans to more than 4,500 immigrants and hundreds of Israeli families struggling to make ends meet. Dr. Jaffe is our main resource person in Israel on grassroots Mitzvah projects, and, a few years ago, when we heard he was establishing this fund, we wanted to play a part in the program. Over the years we have given more than $15,000, which, of course, equals much more than $15,000 in Mitzvah power, since the money is recycled again and again.

Interest-free loans are vital in any society, particularly for immigrants. Ziv is a member of the Hebrew Free Loan Association (HFLA). If your community does not have a free loan society, contact Mark Meltzer of the Los Angeles group at 213-655-6922, who will explain what is involved in establishing such an organization.

[Our contact: Dr. Eliezer Jaffe, 37 Azza St., Jerusalem, home phone: 02-637-450. IFLA: 64 Azza St., POB 4579, 02-630-248, Fax: 02-669-504. Tax-deductible contributions through PEF-Israel Endowment Funds. See Section III:B above.]

E. A Friendly Place to Relax ($500)*: More than 100 immigrants from the Former Soviet Union meet four days a week for a subsidized hot lunch in downtown Jerusalem. It is a place to see friends, to enjoy a hot meal, and to make social, business, and employment contacts. The Luncheon Club also provides a Passover Seder, holiday parties and gift parcels, Hebrew lessons, lectures and trips. It is an all-purpose program that strives to ease the immigrants' transition into the new world.

[Idud VeAmit LaOleh, 111 Agrippas St., POB 61188, Jerusalem, Attn: Edna Karpas, 02-245-138.]

XII. Around the World

A. Survivors of The Shoah-הארוש-Holocaust ($1,800)*: Over the years, many survivors of the Shoah have found themselves in financial distress. The Blue Card supports Survivors throughout the United States. They carry out their work with the utmost sensitivity.

[The Blue Card, 2121 Broadway, NY, NY 10023, 212-873-7400, Attn: Florence Smeraldi.]

B. Support of Righteous Christians ($500)*: A number of years ago, Rabbi Harold Schulweis realized that many of those people who had risked their lives to hide and protect Jews during the Shoah had fallen on hard times. His organization has located rescuers wherever they are now living. Contributions go to direct support of these noble human beings.

Inquire about their program to honor individual rescuers.

[Jewish Foundation for Christian Rescuers/ADL, 823 United Nations Plaza, 8th Floor, NY, NY 10017, Attn: Ms. Stanlee Stahl, 212-490-2525 X 317, fax: 867-0779.]`

C. Cuba ($300): There is a new vitality in the small Jewish community in Cuba. Certain individuals from the U.S. and other countries are traveling there, bringing medical supplies, and working to get more and better food to the Jews in Havana and other communities. This Summer, there will even be a camp for the children.

[Jewish Solidarity, 5055 Collins Ave., 5-A, Miami Beach, FL 33140, Attn: Eddie Levy, 305-868-7755.]

D. Warsaw (250): The Ronald S. Lauder Foundation is funding programs to provide for the small Jewish community in Warsaw. Among other activities such as communal Shabbat and holiday celebrations, there is a school supervised by my good friend, Helise Lieberman. Our contribution paid for one of the Shabbat dinners.

[The Lauder Foundation, 767 5th Ave., #4200, NY, NY 10153, 212-572-3935, fax: 572-4329.]

E. The Italian Jewish Community in Israel ($250): There is a closely-knit group of Jews who immigrated to Israel from Italy. They have several projects in operation, and we are supporting their small Tzedakah fund for people struggling with the economic realities of Israel.

[Fondo Anita Italiani Bisogrosi, POB 61070, Jerusalem, ATTN: Audrey Scher, 02-724-807.]

F. Rwanda ($1,800): We participated in the worldwide relief efforts on behalf of the devastated Rwandan people. As has been our practice with other international relief work, we made our donation through the American Jewish Joint Distribution Committee.

[American Jewish Joint Distribution Committee, 711 3rd Ave., 10th Floor, NY, NY 10017, Attn: Debra Malki, 212-867-6200, fax: 370-5467.]

G. Bosnian Children-I ($500): Joel Weinberg and his group in Israel are involved in a number of projects concerning war-torn Bosnia. Some of the projects are within the former Yugoslavia — getting supplies of shoes and clothing, for example. They are also bringing Bosnian children to Israel for rehabilitation from their war wounds. Our contribution went for the rehabilitation program.

[World Conference on Religion and Peace/Israel section, c/o Joel Weinberg, POB 1459, Jerusalem, phone 02-810-169, fax: 259-889. For information in the U.S.: 212-687-2163, the organization's world headquarters.]

G. Bosnian Children-II ($500): Mark Grazman has made some amazing contacts with children suffering the horrors of war in Bosnia. His program links American Jewish religious school students with these children. Besides writing letters, the Americans' contributions provide vital supplies for the children in Bosnia. Educators: this is a most worthwhile program to pursue. Recently he has expanded the work into areas in Croatia. Call Mark.

[Children Helping Children, c/o Mark Grazman, 1919 16th St., #7, NW, Washington, DC 20009, 202-467-2417, fax: 728-0546.]

XIII. *People Living with HIV/AIDS*

A. Los Angeles ($360)*: The Los Angeles Jewish community has a program that includes outreach, counseling, a speakers bureau, and "Project Chicken Soup," homemade Kosher meals delivered to the individual's home. If you are interested in setting up a Jewish program in your community, the first step is to call this group. Our contribution went to the meals project.

[Los Angeles Jewish AIDS Services, 6505 Wilshire Blvd., #608, Los Angeles, CA 90048, 213-653-8313.]

B. Israel ($180)*: Besides providing counseling and other services for people living with AIDS/HIV, the Israel AIDS Task Force co-ordinates the difficult job of educating the Israeli public about AIDS.

[Israel AIDS Task Force, POB 867, 128 Allenby St., Tel Aviv, Attn: Ms. Sue (Shoshana) Newman, 03-566-1639, fax: 560-2316. In Jerusalem, you may speak with Mikey Goldstein, 02-734-548.]

C. New York ($280)*: God's Love We Deliver prepares and delivers hundreds of meals a day to people living with AIDS who are unable to prepare their own food. The person delivering the food provides the all-important human touch.

[God's Love We Deliver, 895 Amsterdam Ave., NY, NY 10025, ATTN: Ms. Kathy Spahn, 212-865-4800, fax: 865-4901.]

D. Denver-I ($360): Hearts & Voices was established to provide live entertainment for persons living with HIV/AIDS in hospice/hospital situations. The volunteer performers come from various areas of the entertainment world.

[Hearts & Voices, 1544 Race St., Denver, CO 80206, Attn: Doug Rosen, 303-329-0839.]

E. Denver-II ($360): The AIDS/HIV Interfaith Network of Colorado provides spiritual support for people with AIDS/HIV. They also sponsor educational forums. The participants represent the full range of religions, and the program fosters an element of unity on this critical problem in America.

[AIDS/HIV Interfaith Network of Colorado, 1280 Vine St., Denver, CO 80206, Attn: Rev. Laurene Lafontaine, 303-377-3595, fax: 333-0512.]

XIV. *A Variety of Projects*

A. *Relatively Small, Personalized Tzedakah Funds*

1. Denver ($180)*: After admiring their work for years, I finally had the opportunity to personally meet the people at Friends of Man. Last year they distributed $300,000 in Tzedakah money, *with no overhead*. They are a very devoted, grassroots group of people meeting many kinds of personal needs from prostheses to food to clothing...the gutsy part of Mitzvah work.

[Friends of Man, POB 2919, Littleton, CO 80161, Attn: Stuart or Ellen Witkin, 303-337-4377.]

2. Boston ($360)*: The name "Yad Chessed-יד חסד" means "The Gracious, Compassionate Hand". This relatively small, mighty fund, administered by my friend, Bob Housman, works every day to meet front-line human needs compassionately and graciously.

[Yad Chessed, 46 Columbia St., Brookline, MA 02146, Attn: Robert Housman, 617-738-8449.]

We also bring to your attention the many years of Mitzvah work of Stan and Betty Mayersohn's Tzedakah Fund, Inc. in Scottsdale, AZ. If the concept of a small Tzedakah fund appeals to you, contact them at 602-945-5354. They will give you details about how it works.

B. Mitzvah Projects on Campus ($500)*: We support Brandeis University Hillel's efforts to encourage their students to engage in Mitzvah projects. Their program is called G-D-C, Giving-Doing-Caring. We recommend parents who have children in college contact Brandeis Hillel for details about how a college student can balance academic requirements with the need for Mitzvah work.

[Hillel at Brandeis, 133/148 Usdan Student Center, Brandeis U., Waltham, MA 02254, Attn: Rabbi Albert Axelrad or Ora Gladstone, 617-736-3570, fax: 736-3577.]

We also highly recommend speaking with Rabbi Alan Flam at Brown University Hillel (401-863-2805, fax: 863-1090.) Brown has a very impressive array of Mitzvah options for its students. Ultimately, we hope the National Hillel organization will include in their catalogue listings for Tzedakah opportunities.

C. The Roof-גג לחייל המשוחרר ($1,000)*: Yehudit Harris is like a mother to many demobilized Israel soldiers, some of whom had nowhere to go after they finished their army service. She gives them a home, good חברה-friends, and educational and other life-saving opportunities. The Roof is one of those lovely, warm, inspirational places to visit.

[Gag LaChayyal HaMeshuchrar, Shivat Tzion St. 83, POB 1311, Haifa, Attn: Yehudit Harris, 04-669-414. Contributions through PEF-Israel Endowment Funds. See section III:B, above, for details.]

D. Interest-Free Loans in Jerusalem ($1,500)*: Dr. David Weiss's Gomel L'ish Chessed-גומל לאיש חסד free-loan society is a paradigm of fine Mitzvah work. Freely translated, the name means, "Doing the appropriate gracious and compassionate act for the benefit of others." My translation is cumbersome, but it expresses well how this fund operates.

[Gomel L'Ish Chessed, 56 Ben Maimon St., Jerusalem, Attn: Dr. David Weiss, 02-669-363.]

E. The Right Connections ($250)*: Alan Teperow's position as Executive Director of the Synagogue Council of Massachusetts allows him great creativity in his Tzedakah work. This year we contributed toward a Simchat Torah celebration for New Americans and an access ramp at Congregation Kehillath Israel in Brookline. Call him for Mitzvah project ideas.

[Alan Teperow, c/o Synagogue Council of Massachusetts, 1320 Centre St., Newton Centre, MA 02159, 617-244-6506, fax: 964-7055.]

C. Our Tree ($10)*: Every year I plant a tree in Israel in honor of Ziv's contributors.[7] When Ziv is 100 years old, we'll have our own forest in Israel where we can sit in the shade, sip a Coke-קוקה קולה, and plan our next round of Mitzvah projects.

XV. *Ziv's Agent in Israel and Ziv Interns*

A. David Morris, Our Man in Israel ($7,200)*: David serves as our agent, educator, researcher, and guide in Israel during the course of the year. Since I am there only in the Summertime, his work is vital to us in many ways. Many of the projects on this report are a result of David's work on our behalf. We wish him a יישר כח-Yasher Koach for his efforts. To contact David: POB 77164, Jerusalem. Phone/fax: 02-715-753.

We will be allocating $7,400 for our agent next year. *As in the past, no funds for our agent are taken from our general account. Only contributions specifically recommended for our agent will be applied to this part of Ziv's program. If you would like to contribute toward this part of our work, please write "Agent" on the bottom left of your check.*

B. Summer Interns ($5,191.37)*:[8] Last Summer I had three marvelous interns working with me in Israel: Neal Gold, Jenny Sherling, and Ari Newman. We shared six weeks of intensive Tzedakah work and Torah study, and all three did extraordinarily well. I wish them all a יישר כח-Yasher Koach, and many more years of such good work.

XVI. *Notices, Announcements, General Information*
(In No Particular Order of Importance)

A. We make our annual, respectfully-stated reminder: *Ziv is not taking requests for new programs to fund.* New entries that appear on the annual report are people and places we have located by our own efforts. It is a logistical matter: Ziv is just myself, our Administrator, the treasurer, our small board, Pam Lippitt-our mailing list person, a couple of education consultants, our *pro bono* accountants, and a few others who lend a hand on special projects. We appreciate your enthusiasm, but the requests overwhelm us.

B. We were pleased with the response to our November announcement that we are willing to consult on Tzedakah investments of $10,000, $25,000, $100,000 or more. We received three or four calls — including some attorneys who were interpreting the language of wills — and hopefully we gave them some useful guidance. If you have large sums of Mitzvah money available, we are willing to suggest possible places where the money will have great impact. Naturally, there is no charge, for this service. It's what we like to do — make money perform miracles.

C. Please note: quite often the money given to our people and projects does not represent a single grant. More likely, we have spread out the contributions as the year goes on, adding later to our initial donations, depending on how much money has been sent to us in the meantime, and what additional needs may have come up for that particular project.

D. We want to announce that Sheda Braunhut (Tel Aviv) has expanded her service customizing computer software and hardware for children with disabilities. She is now also using her creativity in the area of computers for Elders. For information, write her at 6 Yerushalmi St., Tel Aviv, or call 03-546-1989.

E. If you would like to know how to get leftover food (*both* cafeteria and home-brought lunches) from day schools to hungry people, contact Marilyn Moses, 617-598-4331.

F. If you would like information about Late Onset Tay-Sachs Disease, please call Gary and Judy Kaplan in Lynn, MA, 617-592-3305.

G. The address of Life Line for the Old-יד לקשיש is 14 Shivtei Yisrael St., Jerusalem. Phone number: 02-287-831.

I personally would like to wish a יישר כוחכם to Pam Lippitt, our mailing list person, and to the firm of Snyder, Kamerow of Bethesda, MD. For years, their accountants have filed our tax returns without accepting payment. All the more strength to all of them.

Most of all, a יישר כח-Yasher Koach to Naomi Eisenberger, the Administrator of our fund. Since she began working on our behalf, we have moved much farther and more quickly toward our Tzedakah goals. She is a whiz, and we appreciate all the long, long hours she puts in on our behalf.

One word of Torah before closing:

אשרי משכיל אל דל....
אמר ר' יונה אשרי משכיל ונותן אל דל
מהו משכיל שמסתכל וחושב עליו היאך להחיותו

Happy is the person who is משכיל-Maskil
in relation to the person in need. *(Psalm 41:2)*
Rabbi Yona said, "Happy is the person who is משכיל-Maskil
i.e., using his or her talents,
[and discovering new ones in the Mitzvah process]
when giving to those in need."
What does משכיל-Maskil really mean in this verse?
That the person-doing-Tzedakah takes an intense look
at the Mitzvah situation at hand
and considers the very best way to give back to the other person
his or her decent and dignified Life. *(Midrash on Psalms 41:3)*

I am personally grateful for the many exquisite moments you have allowed me to enjoy doing this work as your שליח-Mitzvah Messenger. We have done well. You, the Ziv partners, have moved Heaven and earth this year. So may it be for many years to come.

Danny Siegel, Chairman

We have reprinted copies of the Ziv Tzedakah Fund Annual Report in large print. For copies, contact Naomi Eisenberger, 201-763-9396.

Why People Who are Blind Should Own Their Own Cars Or: How To Think Mitzvahs

I. Cars for Blind People

First, we must begin with microwave ovens for blind people.

Blind people might benefit from having microwave ovens because:

1. They are safer.

2. They go "bing" when the cooking, baking, defrosting, or reheating is finished and the popcorn or soup or casserole or baked apple is ready.

3. Everyone else has microwave ovens.

4. Many new microwavable foods are coming out which allow for a wider range of nutritional benefits.

5. *Everyone* has microwave ovens.

6. It is easy to put Braille on the keyboard.

7. If you have a microwave oven, you don't have to plan meals so far ahead of time, and why should blind people — just because they cannot see — have to plan their meals differently than people who can see?

8. There are probably 15 other good reasons why, which anyone can figure out if he or she just sits down and thinks about it or sits down with a friend and talks about it.

Solved by:

John Fling, Mitzvah hero, Columbia, SC, who tries to make sure his many blind friends have microwave ovens.

Who would have thought of it?
All of us.

Now, to the cars. Here are some reasons why blind people might want to own cars:

1. Everyone else has one.

2. They might need to go somewhere, and a friend or neighbor who usually drives them to that somewhere might have his or her own car tied up at that moment, and if the blind person didn't have a car, he or she couldn't get to the right place at the right time. The most common example would be the friend's teen-age kid used the car to pick up his or her date or for an outing with friends down at the bowling alley, malt shoppe, or miniature golf course. This is by no means uncommon.

3. In case of emergency, there *has to be* an available car. It is life-saving, an issue of פִּיקוּחַ נֶפֶשׁ-Pikuach Nefesh.

4. The car owner, who happens to be blind, can lend the car out to someone else who needs it, just like everyone else does in similar situations.

The right to lend is a matter of כבוד-Kavod-human dignity. The only difference is that one car owner can see and the other cannot.

5. Once, when I was giving a talk, one of the people in the audience once mentioned that this is a matter of personal property protection: when someone goes away on a week's vacation, he or she cancels the newspaper or asks the neighbors to take it off the lawn so a potential burglar won't come by and take out the TV, VCR, computer, and jewelry. If some disreputable persons cruise the neighborhood looking for a likely candidate for a break-in, if they see a car in the driveway of every house except for the one where the blind person lives, it makes the blind person a much more likely victim.

Solved by:

John Fling, Mitzvah hero, Columbia, SC.[1] He bought a car for his blind friend, Emily McKinsey (she could not afford one for herself), so she could do errands, go to the store, the movies, a picnic, anywhere she needed to go, without having to ask the neighbors to drive her around in *their* cars. It so happens he got there first, but —

Who would have ever thought of it?
Anyone of us.

II. Introduction, i.e., Conclusion

The answer to the question,

"Who would have thought of it?"

is not,
"Mr. Mitzvah Hero X or Ms. Mitzvah Hero Y."
That is too easy an answer.
The correct answer is always,

"*I* would have thought of it."

All of us could have thought of these things, these grand Mitzvah schemes, these solutions to problems, if we would only spend some time using our minds, imaginations, and talents thinking about them.

And once we *think* of these new ways to do some תיקון עולם-Tikkun Olam, the next step — the critical one — is to *do* it, to make these imaginative breakthroughs happen in real life.

This article comes as a result of (1) spending time with people who think Mitzvahs and act on those Mitzvah thoughts, (2) mentioning these topics in my lectures, and (3) getting spontaneous responses from the audiences.

Read on, and see how it works.

III. *Body Casts and Heart Attacks*

The problem:

1. Someone, somewhere, sometime, somehow has an accident, falls, and breaks a bone in his or her back. It happens.

2. Prescribed therapy: a body cast.

3. Let's say the patient also has a bad heart.

4. And let's say that three weeks later the person has a heart attack.

5. And let's say that the average time needed to remove a body cast so that the emergency medical team can begin pounding the heart back to life or shooting epinephrine right into the heart muscle or using a defibrillator to give it the life-saving charge is 4 minutes and 29 seconds.

6. The result of the brain being deprived of oxygen for 4 minutes and 29 seconds: brain damage.

The solution:

1. Design a body cast that lets an emergency team get to a troubled heart in 15 seconds.

2. Train emergency room staff to use these special casts so they can get to a troubled heart in 15 seconds just like you train people to bake extra-rich chocolate chip cookies or play clarinet or learn to become proficient at Microsoft Word 5.1 on the computer.

The result:

People who would have become brain damaged for the wrong reason, or who would have died for the wrong reason, would not have become brain damaged or died for the wrong reason. It didn't have to happen. People with brain damage and deceased human beings should be much fewer in number than the way things are in reality: namely, too high a percentage of people become brain damaged or die for the wrong reason, like being wrapped in the wrong body cast. The sentences are complex and convoluted, but the idea is simple — let's do all we can to prevent tragedy from happening, and let's start with simple solutions.

Solved by:

Dr. Jesse Lipnick, Rosemont, PA, Resident in Rehabilitative Medicine, who designed exactly what the patients needed: a body cast that allows the emergency team to get to a troubled heard in 15 seconds.[2]

Who would have thought of it?
Anyone of us.

(One would allow a certain kind of expertise on the details, but the broad strokes, the general picture — all of us could have figured this one out. In retrospect, it's so obvious.)

IV. The Mitzvah Menagerie
(Once you start on this one, there's no end.)

The Problem:
Finding ways to use animals to make the lives of human beings happier and healthier, and more fun, plus a few other ways to do some עולם תיקון-Tikkun Olam with our furry, feathery, and finny friends.

Bunches of Solutions:
1. Getting animals into residences for elderly people, either as part of a visiting or resident pet program. It is happening already in many old age homes.

The best of the best: An old age home in New Berlin, NY, that has more than 100 birds, 2 dogs, 4 cats, 2 rabbits, 1 rooster, many hens, plus hundreds of plants to take care of, plus an abundance of visiting kids of all ages, plus a summer camp for kids *on the grounds of the home.* This is where Dr. William Thomas established his first Eden Alternative program, an experiment in Menschlich living for Elders in old age homes. *Of ultimate significance — and to be remembered when everything else in this article is forgotten: in less than 2 1/2 years, this home cut the quantity and cost of medications in half.* Any statistician or social scientist who would want to do a rigorous study of the re-lationship of pets, plants, children, etc. to a reduction of medication in old age homes is invited to start with the concept of The Eden Alternative. Call Dr. Thomas at 607-674-5232 and ask him how he did it.

2. Getting animals into hospitals —

A. Visiting pets: Cindy Niemetz, 818-574-7194.[3]

B. A Pet Room, i.e., having a special room set aside so family members and friends can bring in *the patient's own pet.* (E. g., Beverly Hospital on Boston's North Shore; Dr. David Schwartz, 617-631-2540).[4]

3. Getting birds to lonely people (e.g., 317-630-3063, Carol Hutton).[5]

4. Getting videos of animal shows (*National Geographic, PBS specials, commercial movies on video*) to lonely individuals who love animals but (a) aren't well enough to care for them, or (b) are allergic to them. Bring popcorn, friends, the video, and make an afternoon or evening of it.

5. Training animals to assist individuals with disabilities —

A. Dogs (e.g., Canine Companions for Independence, 708-528-0830 (V/TTY), Corey Hudson).[6]

B. Monkeys (Helping Hands, 617-787-4419, Dr. M.J. Willard).[7]

C. Horses (in Israel: The Therapeutic Riding Club of Israel, 08-967-705;[8] in the United States and Canada, NARHA [North American Riding for the Handicapped Association], 1-800-369-7433).[9]

D. Dolphins (Clearwater, Florida).[10]

6. Giraffes, i.e., finding Good People doing good things in this world, and who take risks while doing these good things for the benefit of others,

designating them as Giraffes for sticking their necks out, and publicizing their work (The Giraffe Project, 360-221-7989).[11]

7. Saving injured birds of prey (e.g., The Birds of Prey Rehabilitation Foundation, 303-460-0674, Sigrid Ueblacker).[12]

8. Saving all kinds of endangered species (call any animal shelter, any veterinarian, any wildlife foundation).

Solved By:

Many people whose lives and work we might want to study: Lis Hartel founder of modern therapeutic horseback riding), Dr. Bonnie Bergin (founder of Canine Companions for Independence), Ann Medlock (founder of The Giraffe Project), and a few of the others listed above.

But we must remember, these programs had to start somewhere, some-time, had to get their first push into reality by

Some One.
Now, who would have thought of these things?
Any One of us.

V. *Wheelchairs on the Beach*

The problem:

Getting on to the beach — all the way to the water's edge — in a wheelchair.

The solution:

Make a wheelchair with giant, balloon-sized wheels that roll easily on sand. (And eventually refine the design with easy-to-change wheels for a regular wheelchair, and refine it another way so that, if, the person in the wheelchair doesn't want to be pushed by someone else, there will be a mechanism so the person in the chair can manage the oversized wheels by himself or by herself.)

Solved by:

Someone already. I have a picture of such a balloon-wheel wheelchair, a sun-flooded picture from one of the beaches on the Maryland shore.[13] Whoever did it simply got there before we did. But —

Who in his or her wildest imagination
could have thought of it?
Anyone of us.

VI. *Leftover Food from School Lunches*

The problem:

1. The kid comes to school with a sandwich, a bag of pretzels, another with carrots and celery and other healthy munchies, and a big orange.

2. The kid loves the sandwich and snarfs it down, goes for the carrots and celery and orange, but decides not to eat the pretzels.

3. The kid throws out the bag of pretzels.

The solution:

1. A collection box in the cafeteria.

2. One person takes the leftovers at the end of the school day to a local shelter or soup kitchen.

The results:

1. Less food is wasted.

2. Many hungry people are less hungry or not hungry at all.

3. Money used by shelters and soup kitchens for food can be used for other things like job training, social workers working to find new living arrangements, computer equipment for re-training residents of the shelters, cars for transportation for people (whether or not they can see) who need to get to their new jobs.

Solved by:

In a Jewish day school — four 5th graders at a Solomon Schechter Day School in Baltimore.[14]

In the public schools — David Levitt, a 6th grader from Pinellas County, FL, did it. From an article I read, it appears that it took less than six weeks from the time David wrote to the Superintendent of Schools until the time the decision was made to change the school policy.[15] Call him (813-398-1766) if you want to find out how to do it in your own community.

Who in his or her right mind would have thought of it?
They did.
But *anyone of us* could have.

Everyone is talking and writing about right brain/left brain performance. Perhaps it is time to talk about and write about The Right Mind and The Other Mind. The Other Mind is the one that deals with our everyday, familiar goings on. The Right Mind is the Mitzvah Mind.

Follow-up:

Once you get started with leftovers, the possibilities are everywhere...bakeries, grocery stores; the White House,[16] Congress, and Supreme Court, the State Department, Treasury Department, and Pentagon dining facilities; the governor's office, the mayor's office, the city council dining room; stadiums[17] and arenas; pizza parlors, greasy spoons and burger joints; university cafeterias and university Kosher eating clubs;[18] hotels, motels, and resorts (we could get in an extra Mitzvah while we are on vacation); catering halls; airlines, AMTRAK, and charter boat companies; art museum cafeterias, symphony hall cafeterias; corporate headquarters cafeterias; overnight camps, day camps, retreat and conference centers, and anywhere else there might be food and a likelihood of leftovers.

VII. Interlude: Some Historical Perspective

1. *Someone* had to be the first person to "invent" fire for heating and cooking. Now all of us take fire for granted.

2. *Someone* had to be the first person to invent a wheel. We take wheels for granted. Wheels — how could we live without wheels?

3. Along the way, Louise Braille (1809?-1852) took a previously-known system of raised dots, adapted it, and developed a method that enabled blind people to read. Braille — we take it for granted....That's just the way many blind people read. And nobody flinches when he or she sees hearing impaired people when they use sign language to carry on a simple or complex conversation. *Someone* had to invent it. Nowadays, it's just one of those "regular things" in life, just one of the ways things are.

4. Somewhere along the way someone figured that dogs could be trained to lead blind people. No one stares or flinches when a guide dog walks by with its blind owner.

5. Microchips. It's the same story as fire, the wheel, Braille, and the guide dog for the blind person. By using brain power, insight, imagination, people keep coming up with these astonishing breakthroughs.

6. Take, for instance, the story of Dr. Ignaz Semmelweis (1818-1865) in Vienna in the late 1840's.[19] Childbed fever was killing mothers at a frightening rate in the hospital where he worked. Indeed, it was happening everywhere. The joy of giving birth was being destroyed by the tragedy of the mother's death, again and again and yet again. Semmelweis urged the doctors to wash their hands. The number of deaths from childbed fever went down dramatically. Some members of the hospital staff listened to him, and some didn't. Semmelweis spent years fighting to prove his theory. He eventually died in a mental institution, driven mad by the resistance to this incredibly simple idea.

To wash their hands! What doctor in his or her right mind nowadays, what doctor who wants to keep his or her license would ever begin any medical procedure or examination without washing his or her hands?

Such a simple thing.

VIII. The Little Shampoos

The problem:

1. In any given town of 50,000 people or more, there are lying around the house at least 47,983 little shampoo bottles, hair conditioner bottles, soaps, sewing kits, shoeshine rags, shower caps, hand lotion bottles, and other tiny useful items people pick up at hotels.

2. They are just sitting there in the closet or medicine chest or in a cute little display on the sink in the bathroom.

The solution:

1. Gather all these items.

2. Distribute them to individuals on limited income through food banks, shelters, and soup kitchens.

3. Save them thousands of dollars, which can be used for all kinds of other, more important things. (See VI: The results, 3 above.)

Solved by: Elana Erdstein, Detroit, MI, age 12-13,[20] but —

Who would have thought of it?
Anyone of us.

IX. *The Chilean Children*

The problem:

In Chile in the 1950's, for every 1,000 live births, more than 130 infants died before their first birthday.

In Chile in the 1950's, more than two-thirds of Chile's children age six and under were undernourished and, as a result, suffered some mental damage.

The solution:

Set up nutrition centers and intensive children's treatment programs throughout the country to solve this one very specific problem.

The results:

By 1992, the infant mortality rate had fallen to less than 16 deaths per 1,000 live births.

By 1992, less than 8% of Chile's children were undernourished, and the children now growing up in Chile are virtually free of mental disabilities caused by the deprivations of hunger and undernourishment.

The average height of Chilean children is six inches greater than it was in the 1960's.

Solved by:

Dr. Fernando Monckeberg and the thousands who joined him in his work. (The headline of the article[21] about Dr. Monckeberg runs, "One Man Widely Credited with Saving Chile's Children".)

Without even asking the question,

"Who would have...?"

we know that

anyone of us

could have thought of the solution. And — once we thought of the solution — we could have solved the problem ourselves, if we had the time, the energy, the guts, and the persistence to make it happen.

X. *Mitzvah Clowning*

The problem:
Unhappy kids, sad kids, kids whose hair has fallen out because of cancer therapy, unhappy adults, sad adults, adults whose hair has fallen out because of cancer therapy, all kinds of other sad and unhappy people in hospitals and institutions.

The solution:
Learn clowning, dress up as a clown, and go into the hospitals and institutions and make people happy.

Solved By:
Many, many clowns, including Debbie Friedmann, 301-365-4140.[22]

Solution #2:
Teach clowning in the religious school. Have the graduates go into hospitals and institutions to make people happy.

Solved by:
Sweet Pea and Buttercup, 201-376-2885.[23]

Follow-up:
1. Make a study of accelerated recovery rates.

2. Calculate the millions of dollars saved because of earlier discharge from the hospital, savings in cost of medications no longer needed, reduction of hospital staff, and all other related costs.

3. Get reduced insurance rates for people, hospitals, and institutions who have clowns on staff.

4. From there, it is one easy step to solving all the medical problems in the world. Dig in: pick another area of health care and solve it, then another, then another, until health care is solved around the world and you can then move on to some other piece of עולם תיקון-Tikkun Olam.

XI. *The Elbow Brace:*

The problem:
Someone with cerebral palsy has a problem with one of her arms. It tends to lock up against her body. Whatever is going wrong neurologically, it is interfering with this woman's daily activities and is damaging to her present and future welfare. And it is most certainly detrimental to her sense of כבוד-human dignity.

The solution:

1. Get an engineer or work groups of engineers together to talk to the woman, to take into account her human needs, and to work on the mechanical problem.

2. Figure it out and do it, do it right, and do it inexpensively.

3. Let the person with cerebral palsy go her merry way living an easier, more pleasant, and more dignified life.

4. Just out of curiosity, submit the project for bids to commercial firms that develop and manufacture these devices for profit.

5. Publicize the results to make a good point about

Who would have thought of it?

Solved by:

Some graduate of Case Western Reserve University's School of Engineering, a member of the Case Engineering Support Group, founded by one Professor Jack Daly (216-368-6045).[24] The purpose of the group is to solve problems exactly like the elbow brace, or, in our terms, to do some Tikkun Olam-תיקון עולם — World Fixing.

1. The elbow brace designed by the Case group member cost $16.

2. The commercial firm put in a bid for $8,000 to design and produce a device similar to the one made by the Case graduate students.

Now, who would have thought of it?
Anyone

with a good eye for mechanics,
some training in engineering,
a fine and fine-tuned human heart,
and a little time, insight, will, good will, and will power
to make it happen.

Follow-up:

1. Think of ways to use the other $7,984 for Tzedakah.

2. Have the engineering graduate teach the commercial firm how to do it the right way: simply and cheaply.

3. Electrical engineering students at the University of Massachusetts-Lowell are doing similar Mitzvah work: using their talents to design devices that will be of benefit to individuals with disabilities.[25]

4. Volunteer Medical Engineering, a national non-profit organization, provides technical assistance to individuals with disabilities.

5. Apple Computer provides information about hardware and software (as well as technical support) for people with disabilities. Call 1-800-600-7808 and 1-800-755-0601 (TTY).

6. "Handy technology" (or "universal design") is a rapidly-growing line of products. Bathroom scales with large numbers for visually impaired people is one solution to one problem. Another is a bathtub with a door in its side, so the person doesn't have to climb over the side if his or her mobility is limited.

A third example is a pill bottle that has a cap that records the time the medication was taken.[26]

Surely, we could ask,

"Who Would have thought of these things?"

Obviously, many people are thinking of these things., and it would be good to meet some of them and learn from them.

XII. Interlude #2: The Optometry of Mitzvahs

1. We should train ourselves to look at any given object and think, "Aha! This is how it can be used for Mitzvahs."

A. They may be real or imagined objects, including strange looking things that just pop into our heads. They may be big or small, ugly or beautiful, normal or weird: airplanes, candy bars, erasers, trees, parking lots, inner tubes, tubes of toothpaste, the human face, old tires, bread crumbs, movie houses, gum wrappers, Karate uniforms in the closet, spatulas, balls of string, rubber bands lying around in a drawer, toothpicks and umbrellas, to name a few, each one with Mitzvah potential. Dollar bills, $50 bills, pennies and quarters are also among those objects, of course.

B. We should exercise our Mitzvah imaginations by taking any given object and juxtaposing it with any person or any situation and seeing what this proximity might yield in the way of new Mitzvahs. A particularly juicy example would be: Mitzvah Manicures, i.e., getting manicurists to donate their time, come down to the synagogue, and donate all proceeds of the event to Tzedakah. (Call Ethel Shull, 813-960-1321.)[27]

2. We should look at any given human situation and think, "Is this, can this be, or can it become, a Mitzvah situation, an opportunity for some act of צדקה-Tzedakah-Justice to occur?"

3. We should take any moment, beginning with Now, on to One Moment From Now, all the way to Way Into The Future, and think about the possibilities for Mitzvahs that could happen at any of those times.

4. Consider, for example, all the human hours used to solve higher theoretical math problems. If we asked 21 mathematicians to take 9-17% of the time they spend thinking math and to transfer it to solving Mitzvah problems, we'd be ahead — we, all of us, the human population, the earth itself, Life. Or, for one more example: if we took 3-12% of the time we spend on crossword puzzles, board games, or tinkering with our many toys, and used that 3-12% of our time to apply Mitzvah principles to human situations....Or think of what we might come up with just .639 of 1% of the time spent on watching TV...if we did some Mitzvah thinking and planning and acting instead.

5. The end result will be a new and astonishingly impressive sum of Mitzvahs, and, without a doubt, a staggering number of Mitzvah breakthroughs: new ways to fix up the world no less significantly than when life

changed when the light bulb was invented, or the internal combustion engine, or the telephone.

6. In another context, the ערוך שלחן-Shulchan Aruch Code of Jewish Law says that giving away less than 10% of our income to Tzedakah is considered "רעה עין-Ayin Ra'ah," which may be translated as "weak eyesight". Using our eyes to consider objects, time, and human situations as possibilities for Mitzvah work would help us overcome that same visual problem, and it would most certainly save us many hours filling out the medical insurance forms when we visit the Mitzvah optometrist in our neighborhood.

XIII. A Bunch of Miscellaneous Items (In No Order of Importance)

Problem #1:
Integrating individuals with Down Syndrome into the army.

Solved By:
צה"ל-Tzahal, The Israeli Army. Thirty young people, in uniform, work on army bases once a week.[28]

Who would have...?
Any one of us.

Problem #2:
Using an enormous amount of paper in our business uses up too many trees.

The Solution:
Plant trees to replace the paper the company uses.

Solved by:
Working Assets, 1-800-788-8588. They do it figuring a ratio of 17 trees/ton of paper.[29]

Who would...?
Any one...

Problem #3:
What to do with prom dresses the day after the prom.

The Solution:
1. Get people to donate them.

2. Open a second-hand prom dress store for next year's proms, with discounts, and a portion of the profits donated to Tzedakah.

3. Call it Project Promise or whatever you like, but have a catchy phrase to advertise the project, like "A second chance at the dance."

Solved by:

Ellen Barth, high school junior, Howard County, MD.[30]

Who...?
Any...

Problem #4:

How to inform the Jewish and general community about which facilities and services are available to individuals with disabilities.

Solution:

Hold a Disabilities Faire (they spelled it that way in LA), with displays, booths, programs, and speakers to inform, teach, and publicize the services and facilities.

Solved By:

The Commission on Jews with Disabilities of the Council on Jewish Life of the Jewish Federation Council of Greater Los Angeles. (Call Elaine Albert, 213-476-0512.)[31]

...?
...us/we/I/me.

Problem #5:

Channukah presents.

The Solution:

Mitzvah Mall or, How to give Mitzvah Channukah Presents Instead of Silly or Useless Toys — e. g., Shabbat dinners for people who are unable to leave their homes, inoculations for children in danger of the most common diseases, shares of a cow on a Kibbutz, food for guide dogs, etc. The Mitzvah Mall is connected to a group called The Committee for the Prevention of the Purchase of Tchatchkas.

Solved By:

Sharon Halper, 914-723-7727.[32]

...?
...any ONE...

Problem #6:

The high cost of catering Mitzvah meals.

The Solution:

Set up a co-op of families to do the catering themselves.

Solved By:
A certain Marilyn Moses and her friends, 617-598-4331.[33]

?

!

XIV. Pre-conclusion.

And now we say, "It's so obvious."

The Torah lesson would then be: let us do some cosmically and universally astounding things with our lives that will have students and observors think — "How obvious! Now, why didn't I think of that?"

To which we can reply —

"Who would have thought of it?
Anyone of us."

And, if someone wanted to, she or he could do some of this professionally, becoming:

1. Lawyers doing a nice percentage of free (*pro bono*) work, or

2. Ombudspersons for a variety of institutions or agencies, to cut through bureaucracy and snarled-up communications lines, or

3. Radio, TV, newspaper, or magazine "Action Lines" — the reporters and columnists who get complaints that "Merchant Ploni sold me a faulty blender and wouldn't refund the money when I brought it back to the store." Or worse: The medical team refuses to allow X, Y, or Z. Or, less seriously, "I went to Melbourne, FL, but my suitcase went to Melbourne, Australia, and the airline says it'll take 6 days to get them back to me," or

4. Employees of Better Business Bureaus or watchdog organizations that keep tabs on anything from crooked government contracts to the honesty of charitable organizations or the fair labeling of food and drugs.

And this is just to mention a few possibilities of how to be a full-time מתקן עולם-Tikkun Olamnik. And, of course, you could bring some refreshing creativity to the job, using your Right Mind all the time you are on the job.

XV. Introduction, i.e., Conclusion

The answer to the question,

"Who would have thought of it?"

is not, "Mr. Mitzvah Hero X or Ms. Heroic Person Y."

That answer is too easy, and much too costly for all of us.
The correct answer is always,

"I would have thought of it."

All of us could have thought of these things, these grand Mitzvah schemes, these solutions to problems, if we would only spend some time using our minds, imaginations, and talents thinking about them.

There are many pieces of reality that are beyond are powers to change. So let's:

1. Determine which ones they are (e.g.,....Well, I can't think of any at the moment.)

2. Take on one of those we thought was beyond us, and sit with some friends and solve that one problem.

3. And after the first one is laid to rest, solved, done, and the solution is out there in reality doing wonders, let's pick another, and then another.

4. After three of them, take a week-end up in the mountains or down at the shore. Have fun, nothing but fun.

5. Then come back and start all over again, now that we know that the answer to the question,

"Who would have thought of it?"

is,

"Anyone of us."

If The Plaza Hotel
Can Donate Leftover Food
(Without Fear of Being Sued),
Why Couldn't Every Place Else Do It, Too?

The Plaza Hotel's Leftovers

The Plaza Hotel donates leftovers.

Call the Plaza people and ask them how they do it: 212-759-3000. Actually, *how* they do it is explained a few paragraphs down. Call them and ask them *why* they do it, meaning, why the liability issue is not so much of a problem it keeps them from donating the leftovers. If *the Plaza* has worked it out, fancy-schmancy place that it is, certainly other places could do it.

The 21 Club donates leftovers.

Call them and ask them not *how* they do it, but *why* they do it. Their phone number is 212-582-7200.

And the very chic Union Square Café donates leftovers. The number is 212-243-4020.

Only let's not hear any more excuses that they can't do it from synagogues or churches, small-time or huge catering establishments, public schools and Jewish day schools, Mom-and-Pop bakeries and enormous multi-national bakeries. (Mrs. Fields does it. Call 801-463-2000 in Salt Lake City. Afterwards, you can call 800-344-2447 to order a boxful or tinful of your favorite cholesterol-raising variety by mail.)

It's passé, *very* bad form in 1995 to use that excuse. It's all been very carefully worked out. Just call them, any one of them.

It's also not very Jewish to throw out perfectly edible food. It's what Jewish tradition calls בל תשחית, which means "the willful destruction of anything still usable". It is considered, as it were, a slap in God's Face, a denial of God's blessings, an act of ingratitude for Divine gifts.

How the Plaza Hotel Donates Its Leftovers

How the Plaza donates is only a mechanical problem. In this particular case, the key is City Harvest, an organization that picks up food from restaurants, caterers, special events, and other places and occasions where food is in abundance. For twelve years they have been picking the food up and getting it to agencies and groups that feed hungry people.

I called them today because I knew they were the main connection for Ramaz Yeshiva's food donation program. (See next section.) Talking to one of the staff members was like catching up with an old friend. I had spoken about City Harvest in the past, written about their awesome Mitzvah accomplishments in previous books, but had fallen out of touch. It was like old times, and these were the new facts I was given: on average, they handle 17,000 pounds of food a day, at a cost of approximately 39¢ a pound, using about 15 drivers, and covering all five of New York's boroughs. (This is *food* food, restaurant-type food, not canned or boxed items.) They even got Donald Trump's wedding cake, which went to a senior center in Brooklyn. (Those who enjoyed the feast still talk about it.)

They are very taken by the Ramaz kids. It even appears that public schools want to get involved in donating leftovers, and City Harvest has referred some of them to Ramaz to learn how to do it best. Some of the Ramaz kids even come to City Harvest board meetings.

When I asked the staff member who some of the classy donors were...you know the answers: The Plaza Hotel (and too many others to list)!

Which is *exactly* the point: if the Plaza Hotel can do it, why can't every other place that has food do it?

Whether or not your community has a City Harvest-type pick-up service — and City Harvest has regulations (they won't pick up small amounts of food, for example — something can be worked out. If we only set our minds and talents and hands to doing it.

Call City Harvest. They know *everything* you need to know. 212-463-0456, fax: 727-2439.

This was going to be a footnote. It was too important to stick at the end of the book. I didn't want anyone to miss it.

Ramaz Yeshiva's Lower School, New York City

Part of a letter dated April 22, 1994, from Ms. Vicki Ginsberg, 5th grade teacher and Faculty Advisor for the City Harvest Program:

....Every day our students donate and collect the food from their lunches which would otherwise be thrown away. They collect, wrap, box and pack for the daily pick-up by City Harvest. So far this year, a total of 7,000 lbs. of food has been saved.

Simple, direct, effective. Call Ms. Ginsberg for details: 212-427-1000 X 228.

Cohen-Hillel Academy, Marblehead, MA

The Cohen Hillel Academy donates leftover food both from its hot lunch program and also from the lunches the children bring to school. My friend, Marilyn Moses, is in charge of the hot lunch program. The following is part of a letter she sent me reviewing the school's program . For more information, you may call her at school: 617-639-2880, or at home: 617-598-4331.

....Here's a number of ways to prevent wasting of extra food with the leftovers from our Kosher hot lunch program.

1. I am able to encourage volunteers to help us serve food twice a week. During the time we work together, I am able to recognize when someone is in need. All our volunteers are invited to take home "goody bags". In order to re-

spect their Kavod [dignity], I let them know that they will be able to save time later in the day and not have to worry about what to prepare for dinner for their family. When I am certain I have discovered someone in need, I additionally encourage them to take home larger portions of leftovers.

2. Whenever I see anyone — student, volunteer or staff person without a lunch for any reason, I make certain they enjoy one of our lunches. Again, to protect their Kavod, I let them know anyone can forget a lunch — even me sometimes.

3. I know a staff person who has a large number of grandchildren. He truly appreciates our gifts of leftovers because we prepare kid-friendly foods.

4. I offer an exchange program. If a parent is available to help serve lunch, they are offered lunch as well as any siblings (not enrolled in the school) who come along to help.

These first four ways have been in place for the five years I have managed the hot lunch program. Here are some news ways being worked out.

5. A number of our 7th grade students are organizing a Mitzvah or Tzedakah project with leftover food — both items they bring from home and items left over from our lunch program. These items must be self-enclosed in wrapping — natural or otherwise. For example: oranges, tangerines, apples, yogurts, puddings, cookies, chips, etc. These children have decorated cardboard boxes and we present them in our lunch room and encourage everyone to contribute. These children have contacted Jewish Family Services and other needy agencies in the area. The children arrange with agreeable adults how to transport these donations. One of the agencies in our area is a soup kitchen called My Brother's Table. There also are shelters: Inn Transition, A Haven from Hunger, H.A.W.C. or Help for Abused Women and Children.

If your school (Jewish, public, or secular/private) is not yet donating leftovers perhaps a call to Marilyn would be of use. I have yet to meet children or adults who are not appalled by the waste from school lunches...both from the cafeteria and from home-brought food. Perhaps it is time to act. Now.

Feeding Hungry Jews
By Ari Newman[1]

...All great projects start by those
who see no limitations...

If I were ever confronted with a problem that required heavy duty
Mitzvah thinking, I'd skip past the professors, the rocket scientists, the Nobel
Laureates, the CEOs, the great men and women of our day, and go first to those
under the age of Bar/Bat Mitzvah. Then, depending on the complexity of the
problem, I would approach high school students, and then college students.
The reason for this hierarchy? All great projects start by those who see no limitations.

Who are these people? **The children.**[2]

So I took French II twice in high school and was rejected by my first
choice college. If anyone had told me then, four years ago, that I would be the
one to whom Jewish communal professionals would turn for help in solving the
hunger crisis in the Jewish community, I certainly would have doubted them.
Yet, at the end of my Junior year at Boston University, I have been asked to
prepare a "how to" manual by many leaders in Jewish communities throughout
North America.

Please use this Sourcebook as your starting point. There are experts in
your community who can assist and influence you. Seek their advice and use it.

A final note before we begin. I want to thank several people who have
taken me under their wing, taught me, and enabled me to grow in my Mitzvah
work: Bob Housman, Marti Mirken, Alan Teperow, Jules Gutin, Joyce Juda,
Alan Hassenfeld, Elie Wiesel, Louise Cohen, Josh Blumenthal, Rabbi Daniel
Liben, Rabbi Alvan and Marcia Kaunfer, the Family Table Board, and Danny
Siegel. As always, a special thank you to Mom, Dad, Erica, and the rest of the
gang from Providence.

One additional thank-you to Charlotte Bloomberg and her family who
established an award at Hebrew College which I recently received and which
will help defray the costs of producing this manual.

...poor Jews...

It's a good thing I do not work for a Jewish community agency, because many Jewish agency professionals do not like to see those two words together. My response: I don't care.

Although I am not a meteorologist or a statistician, I feel confident saying that Winter 1994 in Boston was colder than usual. In fact, (and I know this
to be true) more snow fell in Boston this past Winter than ever before. So one
night in mid January, I dropped everything when a friend called to tell me there

was a homeless Jewish family living on the streets several blocks from my Brookline apartment. I had to investigate.

The report was accurate. A mother, father, and daughter were living on Commonwealth Avenue. For those not familiar with Boston geography, the Charles River divides Boston from Cambridge, and Commonwealth Avenue runs parallel to the Charles only one block away. I point this out because the most frigid areas during the Winter are those closest to the river The wind runs from the ocean and up the river, bringing the wind chill factor well below zero. So not only was the family living on the streets, they were on Boston's coldest streets.

Allow me to add by saying that in all fairness to the established Jewish agencies in Boston, this family's problems were not just financial, but emotional and mental as well.

This particular family is just one of the many living on the economic edge. They are simply an example. There are many other stories I could have told. The bottom line is that we should not be afraid to call Jews living under such conditions "poor Jews". If we can't say the words, how can we possibly begin to solve the problems? Lesson: Jews can be poor too.

Let me take this one step further. There are over twenty soup kitchens in the greater Boston area and any poor Jew can walk into one of these places and receive a good meal. Problem: what if the person wants a Kosher meal? What if the person wants Hamantaschen for Purim? What if the person wants matzah for Passover?

Many might say (although in my experience, children almost never do) that the poor individual should be happy that he/she is eating at all. They shouldn't be greedy and ask for matzah. My students at the Temple Reyim religious school in Newton love to eat candy, and they would never make such a comment. If they were starting a food bank, they would make sure it had plenty of candy and ice cream and soda and cake and all the good stuff. They're not interested in beans and peas. Why? Because my sixth graders understand, probably better than most adults, what the Rambam meant when he said, "Whatever I want for myself, I want the same for that other person." If my students want candy, then they want the food bank to have candy. If Hershey Kisses make my students smile, then they are not going to insist that the children at a soup kitchen eat only beans and rice.

The starting principle is that the problem of Jewish poverty needs to be dealt with by the Jewish community. How else can a poor Jew eat chocolate Hanukah gelt on Hanukah? To say they're poor isn't enough; we must take the next step. We must also say that they are Jews and help them Jewishly. If we don't, we're denying them their dignity — and the ability to connect with their religion and tradition.

I might even go so far as to suggest that not calling them 'poor Jews' is degrading. (Many Jewish agency staff argue the opposite.) By refusing to call them "poor Jews," we are making a statement that Jewish poverty doesn't exist. Yet, several blocks from my apartment, a Jewish family spent Winter 1994 on the streets. Imagine if someone told them there were no poor Jews in Boston. Their very existence would be denied. They would feel abandoned.

A brief sales pitch: The Montreal Jewish community has a 13-minute video that profiles five examples of Jewish poverty within their city. It is a must when teaching about Jewish poverty. Call Jennifer Roskies-Fefferman at the Federation CJA (514-735-3541) to find out how you can get a copy of the video ($18 contribution). The statistics are: one of every five Jews in Montreal lives below the poverty line. The good news: the Montreal Jewish Community is on the cutting edge with regard to front line Mitzvah projects, and has an ambitious program to solve some of their poverty problems.

I spent Sukkot 1993 with Danny Siegel and Louise Cohen (of the Combined Jewish Philanthropies of Boston) at Brandeis University. After each meal, the Jewish students in the Sukkah would dump their chicken bones and whatever else was left on their plates onto the paper table cloth. The plastic forks, knives, spoons, cups, and plastic plates were then collected for recycling. The table cloth full of bones and leftovers was rolled up and thrown away. The Mitzvah of recycling had just occurred in a manner that was foreign and even humorous to Danny, Louise, and myself. The process looked a little goofy and was not especially esthetically pleasing for my friends or adults to watch. However, the students took obvious pride in telling us that they, and not the administration, were taking the initiative so that the plastic would be properly recycled and not pile up in some already overloaded landfill.

The experience caused the three of us to think about the following: If we're going to invest time in recycling the paper to save the trees and the environment, shouldn't we also make sure the leftovers from the kitchen are salvaged to save the people?

This Sourcebook will cover the following:
1) Starting a Jewish Food Bank
2) Starting a Kosher Food Leftover Program
3) Salvaging leftovers from restaurants, schools, government buildings, etc.

...food bank...

STEP 1 — Forming a Committee
Those interested in establishing a food bank must join forces. Food banks are complicated and will involve several different agencies in the Jewish Community if they are to succeed. A committee should representing various agencies should be formed. It will be a "working committee," and various tasks should be assigned to specific organizations or individuals depending on their strengths and the resources they represent.

The following is a list of key agencies and the role they may play in the establishment and operation of a food bank:

Jewish Family Service: They are already involved in providing assistance to Jews in need. Their social workers will be the primary link between the food bank and those in need. Use their expertise. In fact, they may already be involved in some type of supplemental food program and may be eager to expand their services.

Synagogues: (The Congregations are the primary source of food.) Without their involvement, volunteers will be difficult to find and food will not be donated as frequently. The best way to reach them is through regional offices of the United Synagogue, the Union of American Hebrew Congregations, and Orthodox groups such as Young Israel. If there is a unified synagogue agency (like the Synagogue Council of Massachusetts in Boston) or a Board of Rabbis, this may be the best route for soliciting congregational assistance. If not, the local Federation will be able to provide guidance.

Federations: In addition to funding, the Federation can generally offer a great deal of support in establishing a food bank. The Young Leadership Division may be interested in volunteering. Many Federations have a volunteer services coordinator who can identify potential volunteers. The Community Relations Council may want to take on this type of project as well. The structure and size of the Federation will determine the commitment they will be able to make.

Schools, Youth Groups, Hillels: As already stated, children can be the key to great Mitzvah projects. Schools can conduct food drives and incorporate Mitzvah work into a Tzedakah education program. Youth groups are into social action — get them involved. They'll help with food drives, *shlepping*, and they're great at coordinating. Hillel students can also be a big help, although, due to academics, they may only be available for limited amounts of time. However, they can still have an impact. Example: The Brandeis gang organized a soap and shampoo drive during Parents' Weekend. The parents were all staying in hotels and donated hundreds of little soaps and bottles of shampoo rather than have them collect dust in a basket in the bathroom.

STEP 2 — Planning a Strategy

In Boston we did the following: We planned to start in October following the High Holidays. I recommend doing the same — it's much easier because many people are interested in new projects in the Fall, and it is much easier to reach people through the media and synagogue bulletins around the High Holidays.

In Boston, twelve synagogues are assigned various items to collect on a regular basis. Then they deliver the food on the third Sunday of every month to the collection site. Volunteers from one of the congregations prepare the packages of food and deliver them to the recipients. The twelve synagogues rotate so that each only does home deliveries once a year. (At the end of the manual there is a two-page information sheet about Family Table [Greater Boston's Jewish Food Pantry]. Please read it and if you have any questions, write to Family Table, P.O. Box 9125, Boston, MA 02214-9125.)

Regarding your strategy:

A.   First you need to decide if you want to be a "Kosher Food Bank" or a "Jewish Food Bank". What is the difference?

A "Kosher Food Bank" is a Food Bank whose items all meet a certain level of Kashrut. However, the recipients do not necessarily need to observe Kashrut.

A "Jewish Food Bank" is a Jewish response to hunger; however, the food is not necessarily Kosher, and the recipients do not necessarily need to observe Kashrut.

A "Jewish Food Bank" has some advantages over a "Kosher Food Bank" if you are requesting the assistance of Congregations representing all the movements; no one is excluded, neither recipients nor donors. Many people who do not keep Kashrut may still want to participate in the "Jewish Food Bank".

Although a line must be drawn either way, "Jewish" and not "Kosher" provides somewhat greater flexibility. Not all Jews observe Kashrut and we should not turn any Jew away, or send him or her back to the regular food bank. At the same time, we need to gather as much Kosher food as possible, because Jews who observe Kashrut often cannot find Kosher food [at food banks].

B.   I recommend having kick-off day in the Fall. Promoting the food bank amongst congregations is easiest around High Holiday time.

C.   Preparing a menu: In the United States, many of the families you will be servicing already receive FEMA money. However, this is often not enough. (In Canada, the situation is similar in that the money provided by the government is not enough.) Therefore, your service will want to intervene when these people are most needy. This time is generally the end of the month, since FEMA money arrives at the beginning of the month and may run out by the third or fourth week. This is especially critical when servicing areas in the north, where food money may go toward the heating bill.

Using the following guide provided by a nutritionist, you may decide on the items and quantities to collect. The number of days you wish to provide food as well as the size and composition of the family must also be factored in.

Sample Four Day Food Menu - *Family of Four**

(12) 16-OUNCE CANS VEGETABLES
(8) 16-OUNCE CANS FRUIT
(3) LOAVES BREAD
(1) BOX CEREAL
(3) lbs. RICE AND PASTA
(2) 16-OUNCE CANS BEANS

(2) 16-OUNCE CANS BAKED BEANS
(4) 6-OUNCE CANS TUNA
(l) lb. PEANUT BUTTER
(8) QUARTS ENVELOPES NON-FAT DRY MILK
(2) CANS SOUP
(l) lb. MARGARINE

*I recommend contacting a nutritionist in your community for advice. The list above is to provide some idea of foods which are appropriate for a food bank. Speak with an expert and plan out a four day menu.

I also recommend that you add "extras," such as Shabbat candles, Challahs, holiday food (i.e., Purim, Hanukkah, Passover), and finally the "goodies (i.e. cake, cookies, candy).

Also — Food Stamps do not cover the cost of toiletries — shampoo, tooth-paste, toilet paper, etc., or household cleaners. These items are necessary both for good health as well as human dignity. They should, therefore, be included with food. (Imagine going to a job interview without brushing your teeth or washing your hair.)

D.   Collecting the food. If you are going to have several synagogues and agencies collect food, it is best to assign specific times for each collection site. The food is then brought to a central location and distributed from there. Make sure that each collection site has a big sign giving all the details.

E.   Decide if you will offer home delivery or if the recipients will come to your pantry. The decision should be based on several things:

Volunteers — home delivery requires more volunteers.

Transportation — recipients without automobiles have difficulty getting to the food bank, or may be able to carry only limited quantities.

Food bank — your food bank may only be a storage facility and may not be able to accommodate people as if it were a supermarket.

If you decided to do home delivery, the system we created in Boston at Family Table could certainly be followed. This involves a great deal of planning, including providing directions to all volunteers, educating the volunteers about sensitivity (something that should be done by a social worker), and co-ordinating a drop off time with the recipients. Note: One of the great advantages of home delivery is that it can serve as an educational experience for the children.

If you decide to open the doors of your pantry, you will have to create a system whereby individuals are entitled to a certain quantity of food. You may want to use vouchers or some similar system.

F.   Recipients should be required to meet certain guidelines as agreed upon by the committee.[3] A sample referral form from the American Red Cross is provided at the end of the manual, as well as a suggested set of guidelines which determine eligibility for food services.

STEP 3 — Opening Day

Media attention is important. They are your ticket to more food donors and more volunteers. Contact the Jewish Press as well as the community papers.

Follow-up:

1. Evaluation is important: The volunteers, the recipients, the donors, etc.
2. Nailing down the details: whatever went wrong should be fixed.

Many people hesitate to become involved with food distributions because they are under the erroneous impression that there are insurmountable and almost punitive "health code" rules to restrict them. This is generally not true. Although you would not want any recipient to become sick, you are protected under the Good Samaritan Law if you have non-profit corporation status. I understand that a similar law protects the donor in Canada, and I therefore encourage Canadians to consult an attorney.

...Kosher leftover program...

Taught to me by Danny Siegel[4], the Key to beginning a Kosher leftover redistribution program is:

> *...anything worth doing,*
> *is worth doing poorly...*

This is so, because unless you own a refrigerated truck, you will never get started.

My story begins during my freshman year at Boston University. I soon realized that a great deal of food was being thrown away, not just at B.U.'s Kosher eating club, but at other colleges in Boston as well.

Danny had me contact Louise Cohen (Combined Jewish Philanthropies and his right hand Mitzvah resource person in Boston) who suggested I call Bob Housman (who runs Yad Chessed, a fund helping Jews in Boston who are living on the economic edge). I asked if there were Jewish families living in Boston who could use the food. He said, "Yes." So I made arrangements to pick up the food and drop it off at these people's homes. Today, we get leftovers from schools, restaurants, synagogues, organizations, stores, etc.

This project is simple. In every community there is somebody who knows how to find the poor Jews. It may be the Family Service agencies, but just as likely it's the Rabbi or someone like a "Bob Housman". The trick is to find the person who can match you up. Often, this only takes several phone calls.

Then go to your food sources. Ask them to become involved and show them a copy of the Law.[5] Generally, they will be more than happy to participate as long as they are not already donating. If they are donating to a non-Jewish shelter, then you simply explain that the Kosher food should be directed to the Kosher people. Generally, they understand. Make arrangements to pick up the food and then drop it off at people's homes.

It is important to call the recipients before you knock at the door. In addition, please make sure that the families understand that leftover food is not a guaranteed thing — if it is available, you'll try to donate it.

"...anything worth doing, is worth doing poorly..." teaches us the following: The lesson is not to adhere too strictly to the guidelines if you have any intention of getting started. My idea took several phone calls to execute. Had I listened to one agency and then another, I would have spent the next ten years worrying about trucks and other irrelevant matters. It is not that the points being made by the experts weren't valid, because they were. However, just as when I go shopping to buy meat I don't use a refrigerated car, so too when I deliver leftovers, such a vehicle is not needed. The key is common sense.

Even though health is number one, the Good Samaritan Law also applies here.[6] (I have attached a copy of the Massachusetts law. The law is similar in all 50 states as well as the District of Columbia. In addition, a similar law applies in Canada. However, I suggest you obtain a copy of the Law which pertains to you in your own state.) The only "but" is that in order not to be liable, one must have non-profit status. The solution in most cases is to attach your work to a synagogue, etc. If all else fails, my organization, Garin Mitzvah, has non-profit status and you can be in touch with me if you need to temporarily work under our name. You must be in touch first, though, and receive permission in writing.[7]

After you start, simply get the word out, recruit more volunteers, and expand your list of donors and recipients. Always be in contact with the Jewish Family agencies to get names; they screen the people and should be the backbone of your work.

Start small and remember, "...anything worth doing, is worth doing poorly...".

At the conclusion of this manual, I have attached two pages describing the leftover food program in Boston.

...going to battle against the restaurants, schools, and the government, etc...

The basic principle is that you, whether you are a fifth grader or a professor, will win against Pizza Hut, the School Board, and the Governor. Why? Because if they are not donating their leftover food, they're wrong and you're right — it's that simple.

(202) 456-1414 is the number I called. I was experimenting. After several rings, "White House, how may I help you?"

"Yes, can you please connect me with the kitchen?"...after being connected, "Yes, I'd like to know what the White House does with its leftovers." That was the beginning of my lengthy conversation with the head chef. The truth is that the White House does not donate and the reason is one of security.[8]

Several weeks later I called back and tried again. This time I made some progress. I spoke to a man who works in the Old Executive Building who personally makes sure that the leftovers go to the homeless. There is no organized system; he just delivers what is left over on his own.

Anyone can approach anyone about leftovers. There are just two details which the organizer must consider before s/he is to start.

1.   Make sure you are connected with a non-profit group (i.e., synagogue, youth group, Federation). If you're stuck, contact me as I mentioned before. This way you can show them a copy of the law when they give you a lame excuse like "we can't be responsible...it's too much risk, etc."

2.   Make sure you know where the food is going. Work out the details with the local soup kitchen.

Naturally, if the School Board, the CEO, or the Governor do not agree, then you contact Channel 5. They'll love the story. Don't worry. You'll win. (Please send me a copy of the video if it comes to this.)

Conclusion

"Charismatic leaders make us think,
'Oh, if only I could do that, be like that.'
True leaders make us think,
'If they can do that, then...I can too.'"
(John Holt, noted educator)

Using our skills, talents, charisma, mind, heart and soul, we can begin to fix some of the problems and make a difference in people's lives.

Massachusetts[9]

*Donation of Food to Nonprofit Corporation; Liability of Donor
and Nonprofit Corporation; Exceptions.*

No person who donates food, including open-dated food whose date has passed, to a nonprofit corporation for distribution or serving by such non-profit corporation without charge or at a charge sufficient only to cover the cost of handling such food, shall be liable for civil damages for any injury arising out of the condition of such food; provided, however, that at the time of dona-tion such food is not misbranded and is not adulterated and has not been manu-factured, processed, prepared, handled or stored in violation of applicable regu-lations of the department of public health; and provided, further, that such in-jury is not the result of gross negligence, recklessness or intentional misconduct of the donor or any person employed by or under the control of the donor.

No nonprofit corporation shall distribute or serve food from any estab-lishment unless that corporation has been inspected and is in compliance with all inspection or permit requirements of the department and board of health in the city or town in which food is to be distributed or serve; provided, however, that no fee shall be charged for any such permit issued to such corporation.

No nonprofit corporation which distributes or serves food without charge or at a charge sufficient only to cover the cost of handling such food, including open-dated food whose date has passed, shall be liable for civil dam-ages for any injury arising out of the condition of such food; provided, how-ever, that at the time of distribution or serving such food is not misbranded or adulterated or has not been manufactured, processed, prepared, handled or stored in violation of applicable regulations of the department of public health, and provided, further, that such injury is not the result of gross negligence, recklessness or intentional misconduct of the nonprofit corporation or any per-son employed by or under the control of the nonprofit corporation.[10]

The preparation of food in private homes for the donation to a nonprofit corporation for distributing or serving by such corporation without charge or at a charge sufficient to cover the cost of handling such food shall not be subject to licensure or regulation. The department of public health shall provide advisory guidelines and interpretations for the safe and sanitary preparation of such food.

Additional Legal Protection[11]

In an article called "Risk-Free Food Donations" in Meetings and Conventions Magazine[12], Mr. Jonathan Howe of the Chicago law firm Howe & Hutton Ltd, composed a written agreement between the donor organization and the recipient charity. It offers a greater element of protection (and peace of mind) to the donor. This is the text of his proposed agreement, reproduced by permission of Mr. Howe:

INDEMNIFICATION AGREEMENT
AGREEMENT
Agreement, entered into this ___ day of _____, 199_, by and between [insert name and address of event sponsor, which is the ORGANIZATION] and [insert name and address of charity or food recipient, which is the CHARITY].

RECITALS
ORGANIZATION desires to donate food and non-alcoholic beverages not utilized at its meetings and other gatherings to CHARITY.

CHARITY desires to receive donations of food and non-alcoholic beverages not utilized by ORGANIZATION for distribution to CHARITY.

IT IS AGREED:
In consideration of the donation of food and non-alcoholic beverages made to it by ORGANIZATION, CHARITY, shall, to the extent not otherwise provided by the law of the States, indemnify, defend, and hold harmless ORGANIZATION, its officers, directors, employees, agents, and members, and each of them, from and against any and all loss, damage, claim, liability, injury, illness or death, including costs of defense, caused by or arising from ORGANIZATION's donation of food and non-alcoholic beverages to CHARITY.

[Insert name of ORGANIZATION]
By _____
Its _____

[Insert name of CHARITY]
By _____
Its _____

IF WE'RE GOING TO RECYCLE THE PAPER
TO PRESERVE THE TREES

AND WE'RE GOING TO RECYCLE THE BOTTLES
TO PROTECT THE ENVIRONMENT

**DON'T YOU THINK WE SHOULD SAVE
THE FOOD
TO SAVE THE PEOPLE**

BOSTON'S KOSHER FOOD REDISTRIBUTION PROJECT

HELP GET LEFTOVER FOOD DIRECTLY TO
HUNGRY JEWS

For information contact:
**The Garin Mitzvah Network
14 Upton Rd.
Providence, RI   02906
401-861-3474**[13]

Garin Mitzvah Network, Inc.
14 Upton Rd.
Providence, RI 02906
401-861-3474

KOSHER FOOD REDISTRIBUTION PROGRAM
OPERATING PROCEDURES

1. This program is operated under the auspices of the Garin Mitzvah Network, a non-profit tax-exempt corporation headquartered at: 14 Upton Rd., Providence, RI 02906/Tel. 401-861-3474.
2. This program is designed to redistribute <u>Kosher</u> leftover food to the needy in the Boston area.
3. The food is collected from schools, organizations, synagogues, etc...
4. All food must be Kosher.
5. Prepared food as well as canned goods are accepted.
6. All recipients are contacted with the assistance of Jewish Family and Children's Services.
7. All food is picked up and dropped off on Sunday.

PICK-UP/DROP-OFF PROCEDURES

1. Any institution interested in donating leftover food must call 617-536-2488 on Sunday by 10:00 a.m. to make arrangements. In addition, if there are leftovers following a Saturday night event, please feel free to call the number on Saturday night to make arrangements for Sunday. (If there is no answer, please leave a message on the machine.)
2. Generally, all food is picked up between 10:00 a.m.-2:00 p.m. on Sunday.
3. All drivers will be "on call" for a certain amount of time on Sunday between 10:00 a.m.-3:00 p.m. During this "on call" period of time, they <u>may</u> receive a phone call providing pick-up and drop-off information. ("On call" times will be arranged the week before.)

American Red Cross
of Massachusetts Bay

Greater Boston Headquarters
61 Medford St.
Somerville, MA 02143-3435
617-623-0033

To qualify for the Boston Food Pantry of the American Red Cross of Mass. Bay and be eligible to receive an emergency three day supply of food up to once each month for a year:

1. There must be an emergency or unusual circumstances in the household which creates a need for food assistance and a letter to that effect must be provided by a caseworker or other human service organization (see below for definitions of emergency and unusual circumstances and details of what the letter must include).

2. Picture I.D. for the head of household must be provided.

3. Identification for all other household members (social security cards, birth certificates, school I.D., drivers license, etc.) must be provided.

4. Proof of address (utility bill, phone bill, print-out for Welfare or Social Security, etc. dated within the last two months) must be provided.

5. Verification of income must be provided (pay-check stub, unemployment check stub or copy, print-out from Welfare or Social Security).

The terms **"emergency or unusual circumstances"** apply to but are not limited to the following situations:

— dramatic decrease in income, for example: loss of job, loss of AFDC, EAEDC, unemployment or other benefits; or other decrease in income.

— dramatic increase in expenses, e.g., major medical expenses not covered by insurance, increased rent due to loss of subsidized housing;

— chronic lack of disposable income, e.g., cost of housing and utilities comprise the majority of the household's income and the remaining amount is insufficient to cover necessary expenses (this is especially applicable to those on fixed incomes paying rent at private market rates rather than subsidized housing).

American Red Cross

Location: The Boston Food Pantry
140 Clarendon Street
Boston, MA   02116

Mailing Address: The Red Cross
61 Medford St.
Somerville, MA   02143
617-623-0033 ex. 210

Open: Tuesday and Saturday
      9:00 a.m. - 12:00 p.m.

REFERRAL FORM

Date: _____

To the Boston Food Pantry:

This is to inform you that the household listed below is experiencing an emergency or unusual circumstances requiring food assistance. (Please fill out all information in ink and have the client present the form with an original signature.)

Full name of head of household: _____

Number of people living in household: _____

Complete residential address of household: _____
_____

Nature of emergency or unusual circumstance: _____
_____
_____

Please mark one of the following:

_____ This is a temporary situation requiring food assistance for one time only.

_____ This situation requires food assistance for ___ months once a month.

_____ This situation requires food assistance for once a month for the next year.

I can be reached at the following agency and phone number:

Name   Agency   Phone

Sincerely,

Signature   Please Print Name

Family Table
Great Boston's Jewish Food Bank
Post Office Box 9125, Boston, MA 02114-9125

Family Table was established in the Fall of 1993 as a unified, communal response to the rising number of Jewish families with children who simply cannot afford the basic necessities of life. A coalition of Jewish communal organizations and synagogues has come together to respond to this growing problem effecting families of our urban and suburban communities.

Under the direction of the Family Table partnership, the program operates through a network of collection sites to which specific items, personal hygiene items and paper goods are brought monthly. Each participating synagogue or organization has assigned items, based upon an appropriate mix of foods determined by a consulting nutritionist. Collection site coordinators arrange for the monthly supply of products to be brought to Family Table's distribution center at Temple Ohabei Shalom in Brookline. Challah and Shabbat candles will be delivered every month and special foods and other ritual items will be included in deliveries that correlate with the various Jewish holidays throughout the year.

In addition to being a collection site, each Family Table participant is responsible for providing volunteers to go to the Temple Ohabei Shalom distribution center to bag and deliver food to Family Table recipients for one month during the year. On that Sunday afternoon, volunteers receive an orientation and sensitivity training session, prepare packages and make deliveries. Collections are ongoing; deliveries are made monthly.

The families who benefit from Family Table are referred by social workers, rabbis or other community leaders and by the families themselves. Eligibility for the program is determined by the professional staff at Jewish Family and Children's Service of Greater Boston. Telephone inquiries by potential Family Table recipients are welcome on Tuesdays and Wednesdays from 1 to 4 p.m. at 617-227-6641. Applications can be obtained at any participating collection sites. Eligibility is based upon a family's current financial situation, other assistance received and available resources. Since Family Table is limited in the number of families it can serve, applications are reviewed according to need. All information to Family Table remains confidential.

Family Table is about Jewish community groups working together toward a common goal — reaching out to our own at a difficult time. The success of this unique program depends upon the generosity, willingness and commitment of individuals, congregations and organizations. There are many ways to be a part of this exciting mitzvah.

❤ Whether or not your congregation is a collection site, make a food assignment a standard item on your shopping list and bring it to a site each month. Talk about the project with friends, neighbors and relatives who can also contribute.

❤ Volunteers will be needed every month for a variety of tasks including: sorting and delivering food; restocking supply shelves; answering emergency phone calls on delivery Sundays; helping to orient and train new volunteers.

❤ Monetary donations are gratefully accepted to enable Family Table to directly meet special or unexpected needs for food or household-related items that recipients may have. Contributions can be sent to: Family Table, P.O. Box 9125, Boston, MA 02114-9125.

ITEMS NEEDED FOR FAMILY TABLE
*All food items indicated with an * must be labeled U, K (kosher) or P (parve).*

breakfast cereal
canned fruit juice (no fruit punch)
meatless tomato sauce* or crushed tomatoes
meatless soup*
canned fruit
canned vegetables
pasta
peanut butter*
rice
tuna fish*
vegetarian baked beans*
toothpaste
shampoo
toilet paper
paper towels

A Partnership of
Jewish Family and Children's Service of Greater Boston,
Synagogue Council of Massachusetts, Hillel Council of Greater Boston,
Congregation Eitz Chayim, Jewish Community Relations Council, Garin,
Temple Ohabei Shalom

Revelations

I. General Reflections on Revelations

Revelations, breakthroughs, earth-shaking insights — call them what you want.

They happen.

They come in all forms, at any time day or night or time of year or time of Life.

They change us, and, as a result, they change the world around us. The literature on the subject is vast: Biblical prophecy, scientific discoveries, artistic turning points — from the lofty to the not-so-sublime. Just talk to people who have taken off 45 pounds of flab. Ask how they arrived at the decision at long last to shape up.

These are a few personal reflections on the nature of revelations such as these, specifically in the context of my 20 years of Tzedakah work:

1. There doesn't seem to be a necessary connection between revelatory insights and IQ. Nor do breakthroughs depend on age or education.

2. Studying the lives of people who have made these breakthroughs may make it easier for us to achieve greater insight when it comes to changing the world and lives of human beings through Tzedakah. Einstein is a perfect example. When I was a kid, when my parents and my friends' parents wanted to brag about how smart their kids were, they would say, "He/she is a little Einstein." And yet, he attributed some of his most important insights to quite a different, unexpected frame of reference. This is what he wrote about his breakthroughs: "When I ask myself how it happened that I in particular discovered the Relativity Theory, it seemed to lie in the following circumstance. The normal adult never bothers his head about space-time problems. Everything there is to be thought about, in his opinion, has already been done in early childhood. I, on the contrary, developed so slowly that I only began to wonder about space and time when I was already grown up. In consequence, I probed deeper into the problem than an ordinary child would have done."

3. "How did he/she do it?" is not such a difficult question. Take the classic case of Kimberly Cook. At the age of 9, she invented the beeper with Braille numbers. How did she do it? I know how she did it. She put two and two together: Her father has a beeper. She has seen many blind people in her 9 years. She figured, putting two and two together, that many blind people need beepers. *Exactly* how she did it is another matter. The headline of the article I read refers to her as a "tinkerer".[1] That explains it, but asking *exactly* how she did it misses the point. That's only a matter of mechanics, just like in other tales of earth-shaking breakthroughs strategy or logistics. The point is: she did it because she was thinking about those kinds of things to do, which is exactly what we should be doing. We might want to recite each morning, after a few

sips of cappuccino, "When I grow up, I want to be just like Kimberly Cook."

4. Another Kimberly Cook-like Classic is the story of one Michael Rotjan, a junior high school student from Pomona, NY. I was speaking at a week-end at his synagogue, and during one of the breaks, he came up to me and said he wanted *to do something*. We talked for a while, and I suggested he figure out what he likes to do best, what he is good at, to read through my long-and-boring list of 116 Practical Mitzvah Suggestions, and then to be back in touch with me. A week or two later I got a package of brochures from him. He had formed "The Simcha Ensemble," a string quartet formed for the sake of playing at old age residences and wherever else people might just want a little more music and happiness in their lives. Now, how did he do it? We know the answer already: his mind and soul were ready for it. He was (forgive the pun) tuned into Mitzvahs and was ready to make the connection. Again, *exactly* how he did it is just a matter of logistics. As it happens, there are a lot of violas, cellos, and violins around the house. Mom plays in the Rockland County Symphony, and the kids all play stringed instruments. They probably already played some pieces together just for fun or for a recital or performance. He just made the connection, printed the brochures, and started publicizing the project. *That* was simple.

5. The source of the revelation may be great or small. I suppose the greatest one of all was Moses on Mt. Sinai. One of the lesser ones would be something off-hand like when I asked my Mom (now age 80), "How about if we go to tea at one of the fancy hotels?" This began about six weeks ago, about once a week or every other week. As we say to each other in Yiddish, "We'll get all *farpitzt* [trans.: *very* dressed up] and have ourselves a lovely time of it." I hate getting into suits when it isn't Shabbat or some holiday or I'm not giving a lecture, but once I saw what a delight this was for Mom, for me, and for Mom-and-me, I saw we were on to Something Big (and caloric and cholesterol-laden). It has now become one of my Tzedakah "kicks": it is time to spread the word on the intergenerational Mitzvah network that there are many, many people who don't get out as much as they used to who would really, <u>really</u>, <u>really</u> love to go out for High Tea.

6. Every person has different rhythms and methods for receiving Mitzvah revelations. Some do it best at the point of exhaustion; others by tinkering or goofing off or hugging an infant or reading a newspaper or (yes) eating Chinese food or listening carefully to the Torah reading in synagogue or the sermon; still others (such as myself) by drifting back and forth into the subconscious through well-placed and well-timed naps, or in the shower, or taking a walk, or swimming. I believe what is needed is for each person to take careful note of his or her own best patterns for Seeing the Mitzvah Light, and then to actively set up situations where the revelations are most likely to happen. If a vacation in London or Bali is the best place *you* in particular get your mind-and-soul flowing with ideas and insights on the order of Kimberly Cook, then take more vacations, and recognize that part of the vacationing is this glorious interlude to get to the very best of things, i.e., new Mitzvah ideas just waiting to be put into action. If you're doing your Mitzvah homework, you never have to apologize

to your boss or friends for 10 days in Bali. Instead of the masochistic approach of depriving yourself and viewing Mitzvah work as a sacrifice,... quite to the contrary, the revelations come more quickly if you spend time asking what you *really, really, really* like to do, and then just take the short hop over the line to using those likes, intense likes, and loves, for the sake of others.

7. Sometimes (but don't count on it) these things just happen, and don't fight it if it does. Sometimes you did nothing to prime yourself for a revelation and you were totally out of your pattern and rhythms of openness to break-throughs when — wham! — it happens. Why it happened? What do you care? You've added to the sum-total of Mitzvah ideas and projects, and that is the critical point. If you still want to study why these things happen the way they do, I would not discourage you. But don't lose the impact of *the fact* of what happened in the flurry of research about *how* it happens. I am particularly em-phatic about this since last December when I was at the awards ceremony for the Caring Institute of Washington.[2] Two of my nominees had won: Ranya Kelly, the Shoe Woman of Denver, and Grandma Edie Lewis who gets kids out of gangs and gets their lives back together and I was invited to attend the event. In all, ten people were being honored. Besides Ranya and Grandma Lewis, I only recognized one other person, Dave Thomas of Wendy's fame. He was be-ing honored for his work on behalf of children in need of adoption. There was also another couple I had read about in a newspaper article, people who deliver thousands of hot meals a month to hungry kids in Houston. All together, they were a *very* impressive group of human beings, and I listened carefully to each one's story. The Life story that applies to this article is the one about Children of the Night in Van Nuys, CA. Dr. Lois Lee is a sociologist who wanted to study prostitution and pornography. It didn't take her very long to discover how much of those two worlds is inhabited by teen-agers and even younger children. And apparently it didn't take her very long to stop being only a social scientist and to start *doing* something about it. She took the kids in, made a place in Life and in her life for them, let the kids know she could be trusted, and showed them someone cared. Dr. Lee's papers and studies were important. No doubt they have had an impact on many others trying to change this part of society. But something would have been missing if all that came of her work was an article or book or dissertation.

And she knew it, and she did something about it.

And she is still doing something about it.

8. The last issue really is, "How often does it happen? How many times a year, times in a Life do these revelations reach the human soul?" I have no answer for that. For some people, maybe once in a Lifetime. For others, it seems like every other day. I can't say much more than this: I have a sense that, if people would get themselves more attuned to revelatory Mitzvah mo-ments, it would probably happen much more frequently in their lives than it does at present. It's only a theory. Anyone who would like to try to study it more scientifically is welcome to do so.

II. Biblical Reflections on Revelations

Life's wonders are everywhere.
Torah is one of the guides to finding those wonders.

גַּל־עֵינַי וְאַבִּיטָה נִפְלָאוֹת מִתּוֹרָתֶךָ:

Open my eyes so that I may see
the wondrous things in Your Torah. (Psalm 119:18)

We ask God to give us insight,[3] to open our eyes, so we can discover the great wonders. If we search with an open mind and a willing heart, we will surely discover them.

In another Biblical passage, we are all our ancestor Jacob:

וַיַּחֲלֹם וְהִנֵּה סֻלָּם מֻצָּב אַרְצָה
וְרֹאשׁוֹ מַגִּיעַ הַשָּׁמָיְמָה
וְהִנֵּה מַלְאֲכֵי אֱלֹהִים עֹלִים וְיֹרְדִים בּוֹ:

He had a dream; a ladder[4] was set on the ground and its top reached to the Heavens! God's angels were going up and down the ladder![5] (Genesis 28:12)

When he awoke this is what happened:

וַיִּיקַץ יַעֲקֹב מִשְּׁנָתוֹ וַיֹּאמֶר
אָכֵן יֵשׁ יְהוָֹה בַּמָּקוֹם הַזֶּה וְאָנֹכִי לֹא יָדָעְתִּי:
וַיִּירָא וַיֹּאמַר מַה־נּוֹרָא הַמָּקוֹם הַזֶּה
אֵין זֶה כִּי אִם־בֵּית אֱלֹהִים וְזֶה שַׁעַר הַשָּׁמָיִם:

Jacob awoke from his sleep and said,
"God is most certainly in this place,
<u>*and I did not even know it.*</u>*"[5a]*
Shaken, overwhelmed, he said,
"How awesome is this place!
This is most certainly God's House,
and this is the Gateway to Heaven!" (Genesis 28:16-17)

Jacob's dream is prophetic, a message directly from God and a message for us, his descendants. As the Talmud teaches:

חלום אחד משׁשׁים לנבואה

Dreams are 1/60[6] of prophecy. (Shabbat 57b)

The message is: God's House is everywhere.
The Gateway to Heaven is everywhere.

We may not find the House and The Gateway everywhere because we are dreaming the wrong dreams. All we need to do is dream of The Ladder that joins earth to Heaven and Heaven to earth.

Mitzvah heroes are dreamers. They must be dreaming the right dreams. They take the hands of the angels and follow them to Heaven, see the glorious possibilities of Life, then follow the angels back down to earth. They let go of the angels' hands, but remember the Divine, Angelic Touch and the Vision, and use their own human eyes and hands to bring what is Heavenly into Life on earth.

God's House is everywhere.

Tzedakah: Tree of Life

דצדקה אילנא דחיי הוא....

Tzedakah is the Tree of Life. (Zohar, Leviticus 111a)

Before a tree becomes a symbol[1] for grandeur or growth or strength or longevity, it is a tree as real as anything in Life could possibly be. Recall a moment of childhood when you ran your hand over the bark of a maple or pine. If you can feel the grain of the bark now, years later, that is how real the act of Tzedakah was then, and how real the memory of that Mitzvah is now, many years later.

Trees give shade. If you have ever been in Israel in the Summer, you know the difference, the stark and comforting difference in degrees of discomfort between being caught in the high, blazing sun of 1:00 in the afternoon. Tzedakah is cool to the soul troubled by doubt, by worry, by ache.

Trees are shelter against the wind and the cold and the rain.

Trees provide wood for fires in the icy wind, the cold and the rain.

Trees are rooted to the rich soil. Some roots spread for hundreds of feet; others go deep, so deep, no wind can tear down the tree, no bulldozer can tear it out of the ground. Mere humans give up and walk away from any attempt to remove it from its proper place. Tzedakah anchors the soul firmly to its purpose: a life of giving, a life engaged in better things and the bettering of Life for all people.

We have it on film: the hurricane comes, some trees bend, their tops parallel to the ground. The hurricane passes (all such storms pass), the tree is firm, slowly rights itself to full stature.[2]

What would Israel be now, without the millions and millions of trees planted by loving hands in the last century, to hold the soil in its place? Instead of a sterile waste, the land flourishes.[3]

Trees hold the soil in place, the rich, life-giving soil, should waters and floods try to wash it away. Erosion fails. Life flourishes. So, too, with Tzedakah: destruction and destructiveness know better than to challenge the Tree of Tzedakah.

Trees in bloom dazzle and delight the eye, the fragrance of their flowers catch our attention as we walk by, stunning us. One need not be a trained artist to enjoy their forms and shapes against the horizon. A grove of palms at sunset is difficult to describe, so varied are the lines, weights, and balances of the scene. Tzedakah is all of these: the senses are flooded. Blood rushes through our system, enlivened by the Moment of Mitzvah. Not just the soul, but the body moves in full rhythm from doing Tzedakah, no less than the tree breathes with greater ease with the onset of the first drops of the cool rain of Fall after a long, dry Summer.

Trees are beautiful. No one asks, "Why are they beautiful?"
They just are.

Seeds fly on the wind; new trees spring up far away from their source. Scientists who know better than me say birds carry seeds on their wings, migrate thousands of miles, and there, halfway around the world, the new tree begins its cycle of life. There is no end to the reach of a Tzedakah act.

Once, while I was in Kings Canyon National Park in California, the park ranger explained why the sequoias live so long. "They don't die," she said. Only if some accident happens — the soil at the roots washes away, and there is nothing for the tree to hold on to — it might topple over. Even if fire rages in the forest, it protects itself. Even if so much of its base is destroyed, it does not have enough nutrients to sustain every inch of its massive totality, it lets the very top of itself die, and where the dead part ends, so high up we have to bend our necks in unnatural ways to see — the tree sends out a new branch, and from there, from that point, the life of the tree goes on.

Some sequoias were born in ancient California before Hillel and Shammai taught their students Torah two thousand years ago.

The fruit is our food: the apple, the peach, the orange, the mango. Tzedakah is nourishment for our well-being; our bodies as well as our souls thrive on Mitzvahs. Think of someone you know, weak, weakened by ravaging disease, living one more season, one more year, because there was so much to be done, so many Mitzvahs left to do.

The doctors could not explain it, had no evidence in the studies.

Students of Torah know why.

We all know why.

אילנא דמותא

The tree of Death. (Zohar, Leviticus 111a)

The tree of Death has no power over the one who tends the tree of Life: Tzedakah. Tzedakah is the Life-force, the opposite of dying, of giving up, of Death.

We need only think again of people we might know, weak, weakened by ravaging disease, their bodies wearing down because of the medications whose side effects make them nauseous and make their hair fall out, yet they live one more year, one more season, to the next Passover, because there is so much left to be done, so many Mitzvahs to do.

The doctors cannot really explain it with diagnoses and numbers. There is little hard and fast scientific evidence of such a phenomenon in their studies or journals.

But students of Torah know why.

We all know why.

Just think — most of all — how those miraculous trees give us human beings all that oxygen we so desperately need to live and to live well the Life of Mitzvahs.

וּצְדָקָה תַּצִּיל מִמָּוֶת

Tzedakah saves from death. (Proverbs 10:2)

Tzedakah: Beyond the Merely Human

Tzedakah shares something with the Heavenly. There are moments in the process of doing Mitzvahs that are so sublime, we say (for lack of more descriptive human language) that they are awesome or magic, Divine, Heavenly. We grope for words, though we *know* something beyond the ordinary has taken place in Life as human beings know it and experience it, something intense, and intimate, and ultimately immediate.

There seems to be built into the human being's nature a need to strive for higher things, for grandeur and majesty. Our common English phrase, "rise above the mundane" expresses it well: we don't want to be tied to this earth. We have a need to reach for Heavenly moments. For centuries, mystics from many cultures and religions have written and spoken of their experiences, as they reached for something beyond, something above, something exquisitely glorious. Artists work at it through their music, their painting and sculpture and dance, their photographs, through any means they can use to try to force the wondrous and awesome into a form that makes some sense to the human eye or ear or fingers or legs. Poets try to make words express the ineffable: moments, scenes, and things which are inexpressible in words.

Jewish tradition gives abundant examples of the basic principle:

זֶה אֵלִי וְאַנְוֵהוּ

This is my God; I will glorify God. (Exodus 15:2)

אבא שאול אומר ואנוהו הוי דומה לו
מה הוא חנון ורחום
אף אתה היה חנון ורחום

Abba Shaul says:
"This is my God; I will glorify God"—
Just as God is caring and kind,
so, too, should you be caring and kind. (Shabbat 133b)

That is the general principle.

The broadest statement I have been able to discover is to be found in a passage in the Talmud:

אמר רבה
כי מיפטרי רבנן מהדדי בפומבדיתא אמרי הכי
מחיה חיים
יתן לך חיים ארוכים וטובים ומתוקנין

Rabbah said,
When the Torah students in Pumpeditha would part from each other,
they would say,
"May God, Who gives Life to the living,
give you a long and good and stable life." (Yoma 71a)

The more familiar phrase to the Jew is God as מחיה מתים — Who gives life to those who have died, referring to the Resurrection of the Dead at some future time. Rabbah teaches us that another phrase was current centuries ago: that God gives Life to those who are alive. The meaning would seem to be that there are some people who breathe and walk and talk and go about their daily lives, but they merely exist.[1] God is able to bring them to a life where they are *really* living, where moments have significance, where there is a true, deep attachment to others and to Life itself. According to this astonishing phrase, we, too, are to do the same: to enliven, to revivify, to bring others to the joy of sublime moments and lasting connections with others and with Life itself.

Looking again at Rabbah's quote, it is possible to extend the meaning a little further. By changing the last word slightly from ומתוקנין to ומתקנין, the meaning would be "a life of making תיקון-Tikkun," i.e., fixing things, repairing what is wrong in Life and in the lives of others, a most sublime human task, and the meaning of Tzedakah.

On the surface, both texts are very audacious statements, almost arrogant....That human beings would dare to try to take on God's work! And yet, Jewish tradition teaches that this is, indeed, what God would want of us:

מַלְוֵה יְהוָה חוֹנֵן דָּל וּגְמֻלוֹ יְשַׁלֶּם־לוֹ:

One who is generous to the poor makes a loan to God;
God will repay what is due. (Proverbs 19:17)

נֹתֵן לֶחֶם לְכָל־בָּשָׂר

[God] gives food to all flesh,..." (Psalm 136:25)

מלוה יי״י חונן דל
אמ׳ ר׳ לעזר כת׳ נותן לחם לכל בשר
ובא זה וחטף את המצוה
אמ׳ הקב״ה עלי לשלם לו גמולו
הה״ד וגמולו ישלם לו

"One who is generous to the poor makes a loan to God..."
Rabbi Le'azar said,
"[God] gives food to all flesh,..."
and this person rushed to do this Mitzvah
[and fed the person before I did].
The Holy One said,
"I must repay this good, caring act"...
which is the meaning of the verse,
"God will repay what is due." (Leviticus Rabbah 34:2 [Margoliot])

So often this happens when one studies Jewish texts: a statement is recorded from hundreds of years ago, and the student must stop, close his or her eyes, and pause for a long time to take it in. Imagine! Our teachers tell us God not only wants us as partners in this glorious work of fixing the world, when we get there first, moving ever-so-quickly to respond to human need,

God is grateful to us! The need to hurry, to be aggressively seeking out Mitzvah situations, is expressed in the statement:

זריזין מקדימין למצות

Great Mitzvah People hurry to do their Mitzvah work. (Pesachim 4a)

Still, the principles are too general, as is making a comparison when we see God referred to as צדיק-Tzaddik, Ultimately Righteous, Good, and Just. By the general principles, we, too, should be striving to be a צדיק-Tzaddik, i.e., one who lives the Life of Tzedakah. Jewish tradition does get more specific about imitating God's ways, but the list should be expanded even more.

Here is one example:

וַיִּטַּע יְהוָה אֱלֹהִים גַּן־בְּעֵדֶן

God planted a garden in Eden,... (Genesis 2:8)

וְכִי־תָבֹאוּ אֶל־הָאָרֶץ וּנְטַעְתֶּם כָּל־עֵץ מַאֲכָל

When you arrive in the Land,
plant all kinds of fruit trees. (Leviticus 19:23)

ר' יהודה בר' סימון פתח...
מתחילת ברייתו שלעולם
לא נתעסק אלא במטע תחילה
הה"ד ויטע י"י אלהים גן בעדן
אף אתם כשאתם נכנסין לארץ ישראל
לא תתעסקון אלא במטע תחילה
כי תבאו אל הארץ ונטעתם כל עץ מאכל

Rabbi Yehuda the son of Rabbi Simon
gave a sermon...
Just as, at the beginning of Creation,
God took time to plant, as the verse states,
"God planted a garden in Eden,"...
So, too, with yourselves:
When you enter the Land of Israel,
you should start right away by planting,
"When you arrive in the Land,
plant all kinds of fruit trees." (Leviticus Rabbah 25:3 [Margoliot])

Jewish tradition says that something as mundane as planting trees has a divine aspect to it. In the act of dirtying our fingers, moving the soil around to make room for the seed or the seedling, we can feel in our hands that something beyond the mundane is taking place, something majestic, Heavenly.

Here is another text that gets very specific:

הָרֹפֵא לִשְׁבוּרֵי לֵב וּמְחַבֵּשׁ לְעַצְּבוֹתָם

God cures the brokenhearted,
and bandages their wounds. (Psalm 147:3)

If we are to be so daring as to reach for the sublime in Life, then one of the things we are to do is cure broken hearts, by whatever human means it takes to bring about a cure: soothing, comforting, holding a trembling hand, riding a horse on a sunny day through an open field, dancing. And if it is sometimes as messy as cleaning up a physical wound before applying the gauze and tape, we must do that, also. Sometimes the glory is to be found in a very prosaic form, without thunder, without the high winds and lightning we have seen in the movies.

A particularly rich passage is found in the prayers of the morning service. There is a long list of God's accomplishments:

פועל גבורות, עושה חדשות,....
זורע צדקות, מצמיח ישועות,
בורא רפואות,....אדון הנפלאות,
המחדש בכל-יום תמיד מעשה בראשית

God does mighty deeds,...
does things entirely new,
spreads the seeds of צדקות *- good-and-just acts,*
thereby causing life-saving awesome acts to flourish,
creates new cures,...
works wonders,
makes Creation happen every day.

Our occupation in Life would then be to set ourselves to accomplish mighty deeds; to do Tzedakah in ways so new people will say, "Nothing like this has ever been done before!"; to spread the seeds of Tzedakah everywhere, so that, even long afterwards and even in the most unlikely of places, lives will be saved; to find cures, cures never heard of in history anywhere in the world, cures and therapies that will restore people to their full strength and self-image; to work wonders, and to make our actions change the world so much it will seem we are back in the earliest moments of Creation when everything was in harmony and Life was like a garden.

Just a little further on in the service, there are more descriptions of God's works:

ומגביה שפלים,
מוציא אסירים, ופודה ענוים, ועוזר דלים,
ועונה לעמו בעת שועם אליו

God raises those who feel low;
frees those who are captive;
redeems the humbled;
does what it necessary to remove the misery of poverty
from the lives of people who are poor,
and answers The People when they cry out in pain.

We, too, then must find ways to lift up those who view themselves as lowly creatures, who have lost their dignity, and who are abandoned in the eyes of society; fight for the freedom of all who are in physical and psychological prisons; take those beaten down by Life's circumstances and raise them up to hope and belief in goodness and justice; rid the world of poverty, and poverty of the mind — ignorance, fear, and hate, and attune ourselves to hear all outcries, whether they are screams or whispers...and then act — ever so quickly — to remove those ugly sounds from the world's more appropriate music: pleasant, peaceful melodies, soothing to the soul.

There are more ways to reach and to rise above our mere human selves. The texts are everywhere, general ones and specific ones. We need but continue to make the list, review the specific items again and again, and do what we have to do to make God's Intimate Presence an everyday occurrence. The sublime will be everywhere, grandeur, majesty, and magnificence will be the rule of the day.

Very bold. Yes, it is audacious thinking,...and very Jewish.

Jewish Jewish Leadership:
The Elements of Mitzvah Work
And Tzedakah[1]

Introduction: The Theme

The topic is basic, vital. It is being explored in our day more and more, as we, Annie Sullivan/Helen Keller-like, try to locate new leaders — and to educate and train them for the needs of the modern Jewish community.

The questions are: (1) Realizing that there are many talents needed to be a Jewish leader, are the elements of Mitzvah work and Tzedakah merely an additional element, desirable, but no more critical, than administrative skills? (2) If, in fact, Mitzvah work and Tzedakah are critical components, how do the other skills of the Jewish leader interact with these specific all-important elements? (3) If Mitzvah work and Tzedakah are strong unifying forces in the Jewish community, would it not be that much more important to look for those qualities in Jewish leadership — now? (4) Can the Jewish community afford to put in positions of power people whose talents could be applied just as easily to raising funds for a university or re-structuring the staff of a lobbying organization...as if there were no difference in the purpose of their leadership? (5) If there is a distinctly Jewish component — Tzedakah and Mitzvah work — how do we get the powers-that-be to change the priorities in their hiring practices and in the way they choose their lay leadership?

No exhaustive study has been done on this topic of Mitzvah work and Tzedakah in the Jewish leader's résumé[2] nor is this article anything more than an attempt to throw a little more light on what Jewish elements make for a Jewish leader. It is not about a specific candidate's *curriculum vitae*, degrees, IQ, or communications skills. It is simply an attempt, somewhat fragmented, to re-order the priorities of what we, the Jews, are looking for — or should be looking for — in a Jewish leader. The basis for this study is Jewish text. More study is needed, much more.[3]

1. The Ultimate Purpose of the Jewish Leader:
Doing Good for Others

Rabbi Levi said,
whoever thinks to himself or herself
before going to sleep at night
"When I wake up tomorrow,
I will do good things for So-and-So."
That person will ultimately share great joy
with The Good People in the Future, in the Next World,
as the verse states,
"....For those who plan good, there is joy." (Proverbs 12:20)
(Midrash Mishlay [Proverbs] 12:1)[4]

וְלִיעֲצֵי שָׁלוֹם שִׂמְחָה... ...

א"ר לוי....

כל מי שהוא ישן על מיטתו בלילה ומתחשב בלבו ואומ'

למחר אני משכים ועושה טובה עם פלוני

עתיד לשמח עם הצדיקים בגן עדן לעתיד לבא

שנאמר

וְלִיעֲצֵי שָׁלוֹם שִׂמְחָה

Comments:

It sounds like Mom or Dad speaking. "Do good, my child." We catch a glimpse of this kind of person — the one who constantly plans new and more Mitzvahs to do — in a brief phrase from the Jerusalem Talmud (Terumot 8:5):

חד איתתא הוות רחמא מצוותא סגיא

"There was a certain woman who loved
the Mitzvah of Tzedakah very much...."[5]

To be in love with the Mitzvah of Tzedakah! That is the beginning of *Jewish* Jewish leadership.

But if more and more individuals would do as the text says, planning the night before for the next day's activities of doing good for others, we will have moved that much closer to a more wonderfully Menschlich world and Jewish world. Whatever the crises that arise, whatever other skills the leader has, will all be harnessed to that goal.

2. Everyone *Counts;* Doing *Good*

Our teachers have said:
Once, while Moses, our Teacher,
was tending [his father-in-law] Yitro's sheep,
one of the sheep ran away.
Moses ran after it until it reached a small, shaded place.
There, the lamb came across a pool and began to drink.
As Moses approached the lamb, he said,
"I did not know you ran away because you were thirsty.
You are so exhausted!"
He then put the lamb on his shoulders and carried him back.
The Holy One said,
"Since you tend the sheep of human beings
with such overwhelming love —
by your life, I swear
you shall be the shepherd of My sheep, Israel."
(Exodus Rabba 2:2, [1:129])[6]

אמרו רבותינו
כשהיה מרע"ה רועה צאנו של יתרו במדבר
ברח ממנו גדי ורץ אחריו עד שהגיע לחסית
כיון שהגיע לחסית
נזדמנה לו בריכה של מים ועמד הגדי לשתות
כיון שהגיע משה אצלו אמר
אני לא הייתי יודע שרץ היית מפני צמא עיף אתה
הרכיבו על כתיפו והיה מהלך
אמר הקב"ה יש לך רחמים לנהוג צאנו של בשר ודם
כך חייך אתה תרעה צאני ישראל

Comments:

1. Moses is living with Yitro in Midian because he is a wanted man. While the Children of Israel were enslaved in Egypt, he had killed an Egyptian taskmaster who was beating a fellow Jew. With a price on his head, Moses fled to distant lands, eventually losing his status as Prince of Egypt and becoming a shepherd for this man named Yitro. He eventually married the boss's daughter, Tzipporah.

2. Rather than curse the one stray sheep that is making his work more difficult, he values it, pursuing it into the wilderness. In many communities, the single stray sheep today include: Jews with disabilities and challenges, battered Jewish spouses, poor Jews, Jews with AIDS, and a host of other categories of people who are far from the center of Jewish activity.

3. Finding the thirsty sheep at the pool of water, Moses does not curse the stray sheep. Rather, he humbly admits his own shortcomings, admitting that he was not aware that this individual sheep had particular needs beyond that of the rest of the flock.

4. God takes note of Moses's sense of compassion (רחמים). But compassion can be a relatively cheap emotion if it remains just an emotional response to a Mitzvah-situation. It is the fact that Moses *carried the sheep back to the flock*, that he *did* something *to act* on his emotional response to the situation that convinced God that this was the true future leader of the Jewish people.

5. Consider the situation in Montreal. After a demographic study, the Jewish community discovered there were 18,000 of its 90,000 Jews living in poverty. After their initial astonishment at the magnitude of the human needs, the members of the Jewish community immediately put enormous effort and talents toward finding solutions to this devastating situation.[7] No one blamed the victims, the poor Jews, no one recited the standard list of woes, "We are already overwhelmed with work" or "Where shall we find the resources?" Foremost in the minds of the leaders in Montreal was the benefit of their poor Jewish brothers and sisters.

6. On the negative side, sadly: at the Chase Memorial Nursing Home in New Berlin, NY, a Dr. William Thomas has created an extraordinarily human environment for the residents. The actual results are quite staggering, these being just two of them: (1) they have cut the medications in half in the first two-and-a-half years of their program (called *The Eden Alternative"*) and, (2) in

comparison to the residents of a similar home nearby, the Eden residents have experienced half the infections the others have suffered. One would think, with such staggering statistics that Jewish nursing homes around the country would jump to call Dr. Thomas at 607-674-8210. At least to ask how he does it, and possibly to go see the Eden Alternative in action. Not so. The suggestion is rarely taken up, not even a thank-you from one director who received Dr. Thomas' book as a present. Imagine, cutting the quantity and costs of medication in half — a solution to all the laments about rising medical costs in nursing homes. How would one explain it?

Time to review texts #1 and #2.

7. In sum, it is how we *act*, not how we think, that defines us as Jews and as human beings.

3 and 4. Juggling One's Emotions

[While Moses was tending Yitro's flocks,
God took note of Moses's concern
for the anguish of the Children of Israel suffering in Egypt.]
....The Holy One said:
Since Moses is so disheartened and distraught
by the woes of Israel in Egypt,
he is worthy to be their shepherd.*(Exodus Rabba 2:6, [1:130])*

...אמר הקב"ה סר וזעף הוא זה
לראות בצערן של ישראל במצרים
לפיכך ראוי הוא להיות רועה עליהן

4. When the Jews are in trouble, no one should say,
"I will go home, eat, drink, and be at peace with myself." *(Ta'anit 11a, [1:131])*

בזמן שהצבור שרוי בצער אל יאמר אדם
אלך לביתי ואוכל ואשתה ושלום עליך נפשי

Comments:

Many North American Jews are living quite comfortably. Why in the world would they want to disturb their peace of mind and comfort by being "disheartened and distraught by the woes of Israel"?

Because it is the Jewish thing to do.

How does one juggle the need to be distressed with the happiness of a well-to-do life?

How do these people function "normally"?[8]

How do they define "normal"?

It would make a wonderful topic for a psychological/psychiatric study.

5. *The Jewish Leader as Tzaddik*-צדיק

A story is told of Binyamin HaTzaddik,
who was the supervisor of the community's Tzedakah fund.
Once, when there was little food to be had,
a woman came to him and said, "Rabbi, feed me!"
He answered, " I swear that there is nothing left in the Tzedakah fund."
She said, "If you do not feed me,
a woman and her seven children will die."
So he fed her from his own money. *(Bava Batra 11a)*

אמרו עליו על בנימין הצדיק
שהיה ממונה על קופה של צדקה
פעם אחת באתה אשה לפניו בשני בצורת
אמרה לו רבי פרנסני
אמר לה העבודה שאין בקופה של צדקה כלום
אמרה לו רבי
אם אין אתה מפרנסני
הרי אשה ושבעה בניה מתים
עמד ופרנסה משלו

Comments:

1. The model for Jewish leaders should be the Tzaddik-צדיק., before the successful businessperson, attorney, or organizational whiz.

2. In our literature, "Tzaddik-צדיק" often means, "a good person, a Mensch, *a guter Yid*". We should not be frightened by the term, thinking it means only "Righteous One." Few attain true righteousness; all would benefit by striving toward it. The well-known educator, John Holt, expresses this idea with extraordinary clarity, "Charismatic leaders make us think, 'Oh, if only I could do that, be like that.' True leaders make us think, 'If they can do that, then...I can, too.'" *Jewish* Jewish leaders should foster the *Jewish* Jewish leadership skills we are discussing, and which are already present in every-one....These Mitzvahs are just waiting to emerge and it is one of the leader's roles to recognize these skills and to draw them out into the daily reality of Jewish life.

3. The Talmudic tale of Binyamin HaTzaddik proves the principle: When nothing else can be done, something can *still* be done. In this story, when the resources of the community were not sufficient to solve an immediate problem, the leader took it upon himself to solve it.

4. An interesting example from the newspapers: In one particular year, a former mayor of New York City gave $125 of his $123,500 salary to (as the *Times* put it) "charity". By virtue of his position, this man capable of bringing relief to the sufferings of millions of people...and some human happiness to millions of others. No doubt he did much of that, but he failed in his personal commitment. His minister also failed as a Person of the Cloth by not impress-

ing on him that an individual's personal resources are no less important than those of the community.

6. *Where the Leaders Are; How Many There Are*

"And those who bring the people to do the right thing
shall be as the stars, eternal."....
Just as one sees the light of the stars
from one end of the world to the other,
so, too, one sees the light of The Good People
from one end of the world to the other.
Just as the stars are sometimes visible
and at other times hidden,
so, too, with The Good People.
And just as the clusters of stars
are so numerous they cannot be counted,
so, too, are the groups of Good People innumerable.
(Sifre Devarim, Ekev 11, 47; Daniel 12:3)

וּמַצְדִּיקֵי הָרַבִּים כַּכּוֹכָבִים לְעוֹלָם וָעֶד....
ומה כוכבים רואים אורם מסוף העולם ועד סופו.
כך צדיקים רואים אורם מסוף העולם ועד סופו.
מה כוכבים פעמים נגלים פעמים נכסים. כך הצדיקים
ומה כוכבים כתות כתות שאין להם מנין
כך צדיקים כתות כתות שאין להם מנין.

Comments:

    1. The leaders are everywhere, and they are too many to count.

    2. Some of them wish to remain anonymous, doing their work quietly, behind the scenes.

    3. We need to find them, to learn from them, to apply their insights into solving the problems at hand.

7. *How Much Power*

Rabbi Yehuda used to say:
Ten strong things were created in the world —
A mountain is strong, but iron cuts through it.
Iron is strong, but fire can make it bubble.
Fire is strong, but water puts it out.
Water is strong, but clouds contain it.
Clouds are strong, but the wind (רוח-Ruach) can scatter them.
Breath (רוח-Ruach) is strong, but the body holds it in.
The body is strong, but fear breaks it.

Fear is strong, but wine dissipates its effects.
Wine is strong, but sleep overcomes its power.
Death is stronger than all of them.
But Tzedakah saves from death, as it is written,
"And Tzedakah saves from death." *(Bava Batra 10a, Proverbs 10:2, [1:52])*

הוא היה אומר
עשרה דברים קשים נבראו בעולם
הר קשה ברזל מחתכו
ברזל קשה אור מפעפעו
אור קשה מים מכבין אותו
מים קשים עבים סובלים אותן
עבים קשים רוח מפזרתן
רוח קשה גוף סובלו
גוף קשה פחד שוברו
פחד קשה יין מפיגו
יין קשה שינה מפכחתו
ומיתה קשה מכולם
[וצדקה מצלת מן המיתה] דכתיב
וּצְדָקָה תַּצִּיל מִמָּוֶת

Comments:

1. Tzedakah — the good, just work being done for the benefit of others
— saves people from dying for all the wrong reasons. A society built on
Tzedakah will guarantee that no one is lost for lack of food, clothing, shelter,
medical attention, companionship, self esteem, and Meaning in Life.

2. Tzedakah saves the person doing the Mitzvah from merely existing,
i.e., being alive but not really living. Living is doing for others.

3. The benefits of Tzedakah endure long after the person doing
Mitzvahs has passed on. Eternity is achievable during the span of a human lifetime.

4. The power of life and death is an awesome responsibility, and a
source of great uplift, or what is known in the Talmud as שמחה של מצוה-The
Joy of Doing Mitzvahs.

5. For Jewish educators: It would be good and wise to communicate to
the children early on that they have this power, and that it gives true and lasting
meaning to Life. For example: every time a child brings in a can or box of food
to the synagogue food container, pasta or tuna fish that will be taken to a food
bank or soup kitchen — that child is involved in life saving Mitzvah work. For
example: every time a child takes a sweater from the drawer and donates it, or a
stuffed teddy bear or tiger, that child is involved in life saving Mitzvah work.
Through their own personal Mitzvah acts and through the gathering of stories of
Mitzvah heroes young as they are, they will know from earliest childhood that
they are capable of making an awesome difference in the lives of others.

8. The Great Paradox

Rabbi Yehuda Nesiah and the Rabbis had a disagreement.
One said:
According to the leader, so the generation.
The others said:
According to the generation, so the leader. *(Arachin 17a, Psalms 24:6 [3:140])*

זה דור דורשיו מבקשי פניך יעקב סלה
פליגי בה רבי יהודה ורבנן
חד אמר דור לפי פרנס
וחד אמר פרנס לפי דורו

Comments:

    1. This selection is a great topic of discussion in leadership seminars.
    2. Which is true, or are they both true, one more prevalent than the other — depending on the Times and the Leaders?

*9 and 10. "Schver Tzu Zein a Yid-*שווער צו זיין א ייד*" —*
It Is Difficult Enough Being a Jew.
It Is That Much Harder Being a Jewish Leader

9. When the members of his community
wanted to appoint Rabbi Akiva their leader,
he said,
"Let me discuss it with my household."
They followed him home and overheard them saying,
"If you take the position,
know that they will curse you
and they will despise you."
(Jerusalem Talmud, Pe'ah 8:6, [2:169])

ר"ע בעין ממניתיה פרנס
א"ל נמלך גו בייתא
הלכון בתריה שמעון קליה דימור
על מנת מקל על מנת מבזייא

10. Even though Rabbi Elazar ben Azariah assumed a position
of distinguished leadership in the community,
nevertheless,
he lived a long life.
(Jerusalem Talmud, Berachot 1:6, [2:170])

...אע"פ שנכנס לגדולה האריך ימים

Comments:

1. Rabbi Akiva was the pre-eminent sage, hero, and leader of his generation, a generation of spiritual, Jewish, and human giants.

2. Two interpretations have been offered by my students when they study the tale of Rabbi Akiva: (1) It is the nature of the job — if you are a Jewish leader, you will be mistreated, abused, misinterpreted, beaten down by criticism, no matter how hard you try to be faithful to the task. (2) The story only relates to Rabbi Akiva and some, but not all, Jewish leaders. It happens, and it happens frequently, but it does not *necessarily* have to happen. Surrounding oneself with caring colleagues whose ultimate concern is the dignity and wellbeing of others is one of many safeguards. It would be worthwhile to conduct leadership seminars covering this topic: how to respond to mistreatment and abuse, how to respond *Jewishly*.

3. The story of Rabbi Elazar ben Azariah (related, I believe, with a little Talmudic humor) would seem to indicate that one cannot only survive the trials of Jewish leadership, but thrive, and live long and well.

11. Arrogance: Unacceptable

There are four kinds of people no one can stand:...
[One of them is]
a communal leader who is arrogant toward his people
for no good reason. *(Pesachim 113b [3:142])*

ארבעה אין הדעת סובלתן אלו הן...
ופרנס מתגאה על הציבור בחנם

Comments:

1. Many Jewish leaders believe that anything (or *nearly* anything) accomplished for the good of the Jewish people by arrogance and high-handedness can be accomplished at least as effectively by kindness and sweetness, gentleness and humility.

2. According to the Torah, Moses was the most humble person on earth והאיש משה ענו מאד מכל האדם אשר על פני האדמה. (Numbers 12:3) We have already seen one example of his humility when he admitted that he was not aware of the runaway sheep's thirst for water.

3. Arrogance implies a lack of כבוד-Kavod/respect for the human dignity of one's constituents and other human beings, all created in God's image.

4. Jewish literature is so distressed by the societal dysfunctionality caused by this personality disorder, the Rabbis had to use a number of words to describe the many types of arrogance. Among the roots and phrases they use are: עזות פנים, חוצפת פנים, חוצפה, זחות הדעת, גסות הרוח, יהרה, גאוה and עזות מצח. So, too, with terms for humiliation and embarrassment. Among them the roots: בזה, זלל, קלל, בוש and the nouns: כלימה, בושה and חרפה.

12 and 13. Torah and Leadership

12. When Rabbi Chaggai would appoint communal leaders,
he would teach them Torah,
explaining to them that all authority is given by virtue of its Torah-source —
"Through me [the Torah] rulers reign...
Through me, sovereigns rule..."
(Jerusalem Talmud, Pe'ah 8:6, Proverbs 8:15-16 [3:141])

רבי חגיי כד הוה מקים פרנסין
הוה מטעין לון אורייתא
לומר שכל שררה שניתנה בתורה ניתנה
בִּי מְלָכִים יִמְלֹכוּ...
בִּי שָׂרִים יָשֹׂרוּ...

13. Rabbi Yehoshua ben Levi said,
I once learned eighty laws
concerning graves that had been plowed over
from Yehuda ben Pedaya,
but, because I was so involved in community affairs,
I forgot them all. *(Ecclesiastes Rabba 7:7, 1 [2:173])*

אמר ריב"ל
פ' הלכות למדתי מיהודה בן פדיה בחרישת הקבר
וע"י שהייתי עסוק בצרכי רבים שכחתים

Comments:

   1. According to text #12, the source of *Jewish* authority, the very reason for Jewish leadership is to be a partner in working out God's plan for a decent, Menschlich world.
   2. The source of *Jewish* values which allow for leadership to work in a Jewish fashion is the Torah.
   3. Text #13 reminds us that, sometimes under the stresses of leadership, and because of the demanding hours, the Torah that has already been studied is forgotten. So much the more do leaders need to concentrate their efforts on Torah study: to retain what was once learned and to continually gain new insights. Without the Jewish text/Jewish values element, there would be no difference between the employee or board member of a Jewish community agency and the director of a hospital or the president of a university.

14. Brains and Talent, Life and Privilege

Happy is the person who is מַשְׂכִּיל in relation to the person in need.
(Psalm 41:2)

אַשְׁרֵי מַשְׂכִּיל אֶל-דָּל

Comments:

Rabbinic literature records three[9] variants of a statement by Rabbi Yona on this verse in Psalms. They play on the word "משכיל-Maskil," from the familiar Hebrew/Yiddish root "שכל-Sechel," meaning, "insight, common sense, intelligence." Each of the three texts offers specific ideas about the way Jewish leaders should think.

A. Rabbi Yona said, "Happy is the one who *gives* to the person in need"
is not what the verse says, but rather, "Happy is the one who is משכיל-Maskil
in relation to the person in need," namely,
one must examine the Tzedakah situation thoroughly
in order to find the best way possible to perform the Mitzvah.
(Jerusalem Talmud, Pe'ah 8:8 [3:33a])

א"ר יונה

אשרי נותן לדל אין כתיב כאן

אלא אשרי משכיל אל דל

הדא דמסתכל במצוה היאך לעשותה

1. Since Jewish leadership is a matter of examining Tzedakah situations, i.e., places where injustice and inequity exist and things need to be returned to proper balance, this text is a reminder that the leader must use heart, mind, hands, talents, creativity, personality, all God's gifts, to make this happen.
2. One example: providing access to people with special needs.
3. Another example would be Jewish special education. Indeed, the basic principle of special education applies to all Mitzvah situations: first, see *exactly* what that specific individual needs, then bring to bear all forces to meet those needs.

B. Happy is the person who is משכיל-Maskil
in relation to the person in need. *(Psalm 41:2)*
Rabbi Yona said,
"Happy is the one who is משכיל-Maskil
i.e., using one's talents,
[and discovering new talents in the Mitzvah process]
when giving to those in need."
What does משכיל-Maskil mean in this case?
That the person-doing-Tzedakah takes an intense look
at the Mitzvah situation at hand
and considers the best way
to give the other person back
his or her decent and dignified Life. *(Midrash on Psalms 41:3)*

....אשרי משכיל אל דל

אמר ר' יונה

אשרי משכיל ונותן אל דל

מהו משכיל שמסתכל וחושב עליו היאך להחיותו

1. The Hebrew for "to revive" is להחיותו. It can mean, "to give life back to someone," "to revivify someone," "to bring one back to life." All of these mean that the Jewish leader, by the power of Tzedakah, can give people who have lost their vitality and hope a chance to begin again.

2. A variety of means are at the disposal of the Jewish leader to accomplish this: money, political power, a circle of colleagues devoted to the wellbeing of others.

3. It would appear that a responsible Jewish leader would also keep abreast of new projects, some of which might be deemed radical at first glance. One need only recall that, in the early days, Chicago's incredibly effective array of services for the Jewish poor — The Ark — was opposed and kept on the fringes of the Jewish establishment. Now we are all students of The Ark. One need only recall that when the first Bet Tzedek *Jewish* pro bono legal service was established in Los Angeles, it was not immediately accepted in the mainstream of that community's Jewish life. (Even today, there are no more than one or two other Batai Tzedek, Boston being the only other I know of.) One need only consider how few *Jewish* battered women's shelters there are in North America, and how few *Jewish* programs for Jewish substance abusers. Or presently, one need only consider how few Jewish nursing homes have resident pets: birds, cat, and dogs, and aquariums, despite the ever-growing published statistics on the benefits of the presence of pets in the lives of our Elders.

4. The creative Mitzvah person will make use of these methods without hesitation, but it takes creativity, which is Rabbi Yona's point. I often consider: if all Jewish creative artists would take only 10% of their talent for painting or sculpture or poetry or music and apply that same talent to Mitzvah creativity — I wonder how much closer we would be to the Menschlich society.

C. Rabbi Yona said,
"Happy is the person who *gives to* the person in need"
is not what the verse says, but rather,
"Happy is the one who is משכיל in relation to the person in need,"
meaning,
Look at the situation carefully,
and keep in mind how great a privilege it is
to do the Mitzvah through that person.
(Leviticus Rabba 34:1; Margoliot 4:773)

אמ' ר' יונה
אשרי נותן אל דל אין כת' כן
אלא אשרי משכיל אל דל
הוי מסתכל בו היאך לזכות בו

1. According to Rabbi Yona, one of the glories of life is doing the Mitzvah of Tzedakah. It is what makes us human. To use his term, it is a זכות, a privilege to be afforded this opportunity.

2. Whatever the burdens and trials of being a Jewish leader, if the Jewish leader remembers that this is one of the great treasures we have been given, i.e., the opportunity to spend our days fixing those things broken in life (broken people and broken hearts among them), then the labors of leadership will become a source of great meaning, joy, and peace.

Tzedakah as Radiance

I. Naming

A few years ago, I wrote some children's books about Tzedakah. Since then, I have devoted part of my talks with the kids to the issue of animals such as Mitzvah dogs and Mitzvah dolphins and sea turtles and Mitzvah horses. To get the attention of the Little Ones of Our People, I often ask the assembly at the school, "Do any of you have a pet with a silly name?" Hands go up everywhere, and I hear everything from "Bowser" (Great Dane/Poodle mix) to the standard "Muffy" (alley cat saved from Death Row at the shelter) to "Slim" and "Jim" (goldfish won at the Purim carnival). I tell them my friend Allan Gould once had a cat named "Dog," and that the Goulds had a sign on the lawn that said, "Beware of Dog," and no one ever tried to rob their house. The kids love it, and once I calm them down, we proceed with the real-live Mitzvah projects that will show them how much power they have: a stuffed animal drive, making sure they gather leftover food from the cafeteria and donate it to hungry people, going to observe therapeutic horseback riding classes in their community.

But *naming* a Tzedakah project isn't like that.

Anyone who has seen "Gone with the Wind" or who has driven through the South knows that they named their mansions and plantations. "Tara" — whatever that means — is the most famous.

In the medieval epics they even named their swords...and, of course, their horses. Nowadays, all you have to do is catch the hyperactive announcer reporting the last few seconds of the 6th race at Pimlico, and you realize people will name their horses *anything*.

But naming a Tzedakah fund is nothing like that, either.

America (as in how my grandfather, the immigrant from Russia, would have said it, "God bless America") has one or two of the stranger customs, particularly in the building industry. It seems that every new housing development has to have the name "Brook" or "Glen" or "Oaks" in it. That's all right with me, but I have to draw the line at the weird street names like "Lisa" and "Marcia". I used to wonder about them, until I found out these were the names of the developer's daughters.

Most certainly naming a Tzedakah project is nothing at all like that. It isn't even like naming a child, though there may be a few similarities.

In 1975, my friends began to give me money to give away to appropriate people and projects. Every six months or year, I would send them a report detailing how the money was distributed. By the early 1980's, it became clear I had to make it an official, legal entity, otherwise the Internal Revenue Service would wonder why $12,000 and more a year was going through my hands without stringent bookkeeping procedures. More and more often, the joke was popping up that I would have to change my address to Leavenworth.

I had to have a name for it, an official name, for check-writing purposes, for the accountants and tax people, for too many administrative reasons to recount. And it had to be a name that no one else had come up with before.

After five or six years of observing the power of Tzedakah money in action, I already knew what I wanted: Ziv, Ziv Tzedakah Fund, Inc. (in the United States), Ziv Tzedakah Foundation, Ltd. (Canada).

Ziv-זיו means "radiance," and over the first few years of my work I had observed two kinds of radiance: (1) There were moments during the very act of Tzedakah that radiated a certain warmth and sublimity, and (2) many of the founders or leaders of the projects I worked with, and many of the so-called "nobodies," just normal people doing great things — the people I have come to call Mitzvah heroes — had a certain aura about them. Their human radiance impressed me and moved me.

Now it is finally time to see how the word "Ziv-זיו" and related terms and concepts for light were understood and used in Jewish tradition.

The following is a very small portion of what I learned.

II. Adam

In those wondrous moments in the Garden of Eden, in that brief period of great innocence and beauty, things were different. The first humans were supposed to live forever, the fruits of the soil and the trees of the garden yielded their produce with no human labor. In addition, Adam had a facial radiance, a Ziv-זיו, that signified a unique place in God's vision of Life. All human beings throughout history were to be endowed with this quality.

But when the humans upset the Divine plan, God took away Adam and Eve's immortality, the land had to be worked, and worked hard, to bring forth its food, and the Ziv-זיו was taken away.

רבי יודן בשם רבי אבין אמר...
ו' דברים שנטלו מאדם הראשון
ואלו הן זיוו חייו...ופרי הארץ ופירות האילן ומאורות
זיוו מנין שנאמר
מְשַׁנֶּה פָּנָיו וַתְּשַׁלְּחֵהוּ

Rabbi Yudan said in the name of Rabbi Avin,
"....Six things were taken away from Adam, namely:
his radiance,
his immortality,...
the extraordinary ease with which he reaped the fruits of the earth
and the fruits of trees,
and the wondrous lights of Early Creation.
How do we know his radiance was taken away from him?
The verse states,
"You alter his face and send him away." (Job 14:20)
(Genesis Rabbah 12:6)

And there was another unique kind of radiance in the earliest days of the world — before the sun was created — the First Light of Creation. It, too, remained in existence even after the sun had been created...but only until Adam and Eve changed the ultimate course of history:

אמר רבי יהודה בי רבי סימון
אותו אורה שנברא ביום הראשון
היה אדם צופה ומביט מסוף העולם ועד סופו

Rabbi Yehuda the son of Rabbi Simon said:
By that very same light
that was created on the First Day of Creation —
Adam could see from one end of the world to the other.
(Pesikta Rabbati 23:14)

We wonder at how awesome that light must have been. To be able to see from one end of the world to the other means to grasp all of Life, to see and understand and know the ultimate meanings of things, to see beyond everyday trivia to the great visions of God's Plan.

וכיון שראה הקב"ה מעשה דור אנוש
מעשה דור המבול מעשה דור הפלגה
עמד וגנזו והתקינו לצדיקים לעתיד לבא שנאמר
וְאֹרַח צַדִּיקִים כְּאוֹר נֹגַהּ

Once God [looked into the future] and foresaw
the [evil] deeds of the generations of Enosh
and the Flood and the Tower of Babel,
God hid that unique light,
and set it aside for The Good People
in the Time of the Future,
as the verse states,
"The path of Good People is like radiant sunlight." (Proverbs 4:18)
(Pesikta Rabbati 23:14)

How sad it must have been to our first ancestors to experience the disappearance of that light, worse than the onset of glaucoma or macular degeneration, worse than whatever dims the light of the human eye as we know it today. Rabbi Yehuda the son of Rabbi Simon must have been very distressed by that image. Drawing on other traditions he had known, he must have felt the need to conclude that, sometime in the Future, that light would return.

Another text concludes that Adam also rejoiced. All was not lost:

אמר רבי יהודה בי רבי סימון
וכיון שראה אור שהוא גנוז לצדיקים שמח שנאמר
אוֹר־צַדִּיקִים יִשְׂמָח

Rabbi Yehuda the son of Rabbi Simon said:
....Once Adam saw that the Light was stored away
for The Good People,
he rejoiced,
as the verse states,
"He rejoices about the light for Good People." (Proverbs 13:9)
(Genesis Rabbah 12:6)

     "Sometime in the Future" no doubt meant to some of the sages either after death or at the time of the Messiah's reign. It is possible, though, that human beings may capture moments of that Great Light, the light of more innocent times, the light of the First Paradise, at moments when an act of Tzedakah floods the Good Person with a sense of warmth, of meaning, of a sense of ultimate purpose. This would, of course, also account for that certain Ziv-זיו, the aura and radiance. And we might understand Adam's joy as a metaphor for one aspect of human genetics. People are not born neutral, nor with a tendency to do all the bad things in Life we see people doing all around us. Rather, this Joy of Adam and Eve *to want* to do Mitzvahs and to bring justice and decency and dignity to Life, is in the genes of all their descendants. That would seem to be the true nature of the human being, a built-in urge-to-Mitzvah-action which produces what is known as שמחה של מצוה-The Joy of Doing Mitzvahs.

     A Talmudic text expresses this idea exquisitely:

דרש רבי שמלאי

למה הולד דומה במעי אמו....

ונר דלוק לו על ראשו

וצופה ומביט מסוף העולם ועד סופו...

ומלמדין אותו כל התורה כולה....

וכיון שבא לאויר העולם

בא מלאך וסטרו על פיו

ומשכחו כל התורה כולה....

ואינו יוצא משם עד שמשביעין אות.....

ומה היא השבועה שמשביעין אותו

תהי צדיק ואל תהי רשע

Rabbi Simla'i gave the following sermon:
What is the fetus like in its mother's womb?...
It is taught the entire Torah....
A candle burns over its head,
and by the light of this candle,
it sees from one end of the world to the other....
Just as it emerges into This World,
an angel comes and slaps it on its mouth
and makes it forget all the Torah it learned.....
It does not leave the womb until it is made to swear an oath.
And what is that oath?
"Be a Good Person, and do not be a bad person." (Niddah 30b)

The phrase is the same for Adam and for the fetus: Both were capable by this certain, unique light of seeing "from one end of the world to the other," i.e., grasping the entirety of Life's purpose. And, in both situations, it would appear that living up to God's expectations as a Good Person would allow for a return — even briefly — of that light.

Furthermore, many Biblical passages hint at these moments of illumination and enlightenment, through the special light in the world that comes from acts of Tzedakah: the Ziv-זיו, the radiance of the act itself and the people doing the Tzedakah deeds. For example:

וְהַמַּשְׂכִּלִים יַזְהִרוּ כְּזֹהַר הָרָקִיעַ

"And the ones who use their שכל-insight-for-Mitzvahs
will be radiant like the bright expanse of sky." (Daniel 12:3)

הָעָם הַהֹלְכִים בַּחֹשֶׁךְ רָאוּ אוֹר גָּדוֹל
יֹשְׁבֵי בְּאֶרֶץ צַלְמָוֶת אוֹר נָגַהּ עֲלֵיהֶם:

The people that walked in darkness have seen a brilliant light;
Light has dawned on those who dwelt in a land of gloom. (Isaiah 9:1)

זָרַח בַּחֹשֶׁךְ אוֹר לַיְשָׁרִים חַנּוּן וְרַחוּם וְצַדִּיק:

A light shines in the darkness for upright people;
The Good Person is gracious, compassionate, and generous. (Psalm 112:4)

One other passage from Jewish tradition extends the image of radiance, even beyond the very striking Biblical passages just cited:

כשהצדיק בעיר הוא זיוה והוא הודה והוא הדרה

When The Good Person is in a community,
that person is its radiance, its glory, and its brilliance. (Ruth Rabbah 2:12)

Beyond Ziv-זיו-radiance are הדר and הוד, two momentous Hebrew words. They mean "splendor" and "majesty" and "glory," all the exalted and awesome possibilities in human descriptive language. הדר and הוד usually refer to God rather than to human beings, but here, The Good Person, personifying the finest human qualities, is entitled to these words. People can be "majestic" and "glorious," "splendid,"...magnificent, awesome, grand. That is what we are supposed to be, or supposed *to try* to be. That is the message of our tradition, all the way back to the very first moment in time, until this very day, and long into the future.

III. Moses

After he had seen the Children of Israel worshipping the Golden Calf, Moses smashed the first set of the Ten Commandments. Then, after the people were punished for their disobedience, Moses returned to Mount Sinai, where

God gave him a second set of the Two Tablets. The Book of Exodus then records a most significant fact — Moses's face was radiant.

וַיְהִי בְּרֶדֶת מֹשֶׁה מֵהַר סִינַי
וּשְׁנֵי לֻחֹת הָעֵדֻת בְּיַד־מֹשֶׁה בְּרִדְתּוֹ מִן־הָהָר
וּמֹשֶׁה לֹא־יָדַע כִּי קָרַן עוֹר פָּנָיו בְּדַבְּרוֹ אִתּוֹ:
וַיַּרְא אַהֲרֹן וְכָל־בְּנֵי יִשְׂרָאֵל אֶת־מֹשֶׁה
וְהִנֵּה קָרַן עוֹר פָּנָיו

And as Moses came down from the mountain
bearing the two tablets of the Pact,
Moses was not aware that the skin of his face was radiant,
since he had spoken with God.
Aaron and all the Children of Israel saw Moses.
His face was radiant! (Exodus 34:29-30)

Rabbi Shmuel bar Nachman, one of the Talmudic sages makes an interesting comment on this passage:

ור' שמואל בר נחמן אמ'
זיו הפנים נטל משה מן הלוחות
עם שנתן לו את הלוחות מכפים לכפים
משם נטל זיו הפנים

Moses took his facial radiance from the Tablets.
Since the Tablets were given to him Hand to hand,...
that is the source of his facial radiance.
(Deuteronomy Rabbah [Lieberman] 1:31)

What a daring statement — "given Hand to hand". We naturally think of Michelangelo's image of the Hand of God extended toward Adam's, almost touching, the touch that will instill Life into the first human being. In the Rabbinic mind, something as potent as receiving the tablets Hand to hand had to manifest itself in some physical way. For Moses, it was a facial radiance. At the moment of such intimacy with God,[1] not just the soul, but also the body responds. I believe Rabbi Shmuel bar Nachman is saying that we could be Moses-like, if we can get ourselves close enough to the words of Torah. In fact, there is another Rabbinic text that shows us that the Ziv-זיו-radiance is not reserved only for the leaders and the Mighty Ones of the People. Commenting on the passage in Exodus 24:7 that describes the people's enthusiastic response to God's having spoken to them —

וַיֹּאמְרוּ כֹּל אֲשֶׁר־דִּבֶּר יְהוָה נַעֲשֶׂה וְנִשְׁמָע:

And they [the Children of Israel] said,
"All that God has spoken, we will do and we will listen" —

meaning, we are willing to follow God's commandments even before we understand them completely — Rabbi Zakkai (who had studied Torah with Rabbi Shmuel bar Nachman) said:

בשעה שעמדו ישראל על הר סיני ואמרו נעשה ונשמע
באותה השעה ניתן להם זיו מזיו שכינה של מעלה

When Israel stood at Mount Sinai and said,
"We will do, and we will hear"...
at that very moment they were given
some of the radiance of God's Intimate Presence. (Pesikta Rabbati 21:5)

All the people had — at least for that moment — the radiance. *Everyone* is capable of achieving moments of Divine Radiance. Earlier in this article it was shown that the Ziv-זיו-radiance was attainable through acts of Tzedakah. Here, it is through Torah. A verse in Psalms says it very eloquently:

פָּנֶיךָ הָאֵר בְּעַבְדֶּךָ וְלַמְּדֵנִי אֶת־חֻקֶּיךָ:

Show the light of Your Face to Your servant,
and teach me Your laws. (Psalm 119:135)

The Talmud also records a similar sentiment:

כי הוו מפטרי רבנן מבי רבי אמי ואמרי לה מבי רבי חנינא
אמרי ליה הכי
עולמך תראה בחייך...
עיניך יאירו במאור תורה ופניך יזהירו כזוהר הרקיע
שפתותיך יביעו דעת וכליותיך תעלוזנה מישרים
ופעמיך ירוצו לשמוע דברי עתיק יומין

When the Torah study session was finished
in Rabbi Ammi's (and some say Rabbi Chanina's) school,
they would say to each other:
May you see your world in your lifetime....
May your eyes sparkle with the light of Torah
and your face be radiant as the radiance of the Heavens.
May you speak words of great Torah-insight,
and may your entire being be joyous
with those things that are right and just in Life.
And may your feet hurry to hear the words of the One
Who is Ancient, Older than Time Itself. (Brachot 17a)

"...and may your face be radiant". It is a wonderful blessing. It means the same thing as "May you see your world in your lifetime," i.e., may you have sublime moments of Torah-and-Tzedakah whereby all the world, all Life, is seen as an aspect of the Divine. The Ziv-זיו-radiance shows us those moments.

IV. In Sum

The starting point it this:

אוֹדְךָ עַל כִּי נוֹרָאוֹת נִפְלֵיתִי נִפְלָאִים מַעֲשֶׂיךָ וְנַפְשִׁי יֹדַעַת מְאֹד:

I praise You, for I am awesomely, wondrously made;
Your work is astonishing;
I am profoundly, immediately, and constantly aware of it. (Psalm 139:14)

The late Professor Abraham Joshua Heschel wrote books and books on awe, on wonder, on amazement that penetrates into the deepest soul of human beings. We are awesome creations in God's eyes, so unique, comparisons between the human and the Divine appear in many places in Biblical and Rabbinic literature. Sometimes they are so close, it is difficult to tell if the reference is to a human being or God. It would appear that the following verse, therefore, allows for my interpolation in the translation:

גְּדֹלִים מַעֲשֵׂי יְהוָה...
הוֹד־וְהָדָר פָּעֳלוֹ וְצִדְקָתוֹ עֹמֶדֶת לָעַד:

God's deeds are great
[and, thus, the deeds of people doing God's work...]
God's works are magnificent and glorious
[and, thus, we human beings, are capable of magnificent and glorious acts];
eternal are God's just-and-right deeds
[and, this, we are capable of just-and-right deeds
that have an eternal aspect to them]. (Psalm 111:2-3)

Finally, a description of one of the Talmudic Rabbis, one that combines all the elements about which I have written:

מעשה היה בר' מתיא בר חרש
שהיה עשיר וירא שמים ובעל מדות טובות
ורודף מצוה וצדקה ומהנה תלמידי חכמים מנכסיו
והיו יתומים ואלמנות מצויין על שלחנו תמיד
וכל ארחותיו ביושר וכל ימיו עוסק בתורה כר' מאיר רבו
והיה זיו פניו מבהיק כזוהר השמש...

A story is told of Rabbi Mattiah ben Cheresh
who was wealthy, God-fearing, had a fine personality,
ran to do Mitzvahs — and Tzedakah in particular —
provided generously from all he owned
for the benefit of The Sages,
always had widows and orphans eating at his table,
all his dealings with other people were honest,
all his life he was involved in Torah study like his teacher, Rabbi Meir,
and the radiance of his face shone
as brightly as the brilliance of sunlight...(Midrash Tanchuma) [2]

Everything comes together: Tzedakah, Torah, a fine human being, and the Ziv-זיו, the Radiance.

The Radiance is ours for the taking.

DNA Analysts

"The average height of young Chileans
has increased by 6 inches in the past 30 years."
(Dr. Fernando Monckeberg)
The Toronto Star, March 21, 1992

וַיֹּאמֶר מֹשֶׁה אֶל־יְהוָה בִּי אֲדֹנָי
לֹא אִישׁ דְּבָרִים אָנֹכִי גַּם מִתְּמוֹל גַּם מִשִּׁלְשֹׁם
גַּם מֵאָז דַּבֶּרְךָ אֶל־עַבְדֶּךָ
כִּי כְבַד־פֶּה וּכְבַד לָשׁוֹן אָנֹכִי:

But Moses said to God,
"Please, O God, I have never been a man of words,
either in times past or now that You have spoken to Your servant;
I am slow of speech and slow of tongue." (Exodus 4:10)

"They won't believe me; they won't listen to my voice. They will say,
'God didn't appear to you.'" (Exodus 4:1)
Of course the Children of Israel wouldn't believe Moses. The people
would wonder why anyone with a stutter, slur or mumbling pattern of speech
— or whose words come so slowly it is agony to listen — would be chosen as
Leader and Teacher (רבינו). What kind of diplomat could possibly succeed if
he or she can't put a sentence together without visible strain?
The people will whisper in their hovels — and justifiably so — "This
must be some kind of joke."

Some Answers Students Have Given Why Moses —
Of All People — Should Have a Speech Impediment:

1. It is a constant reminder to Moses and the people that no one is perfect, that there is no danger of mistaking Moses for some supernatural or divine
being. By the same Midrashic line, it teaches the lesson that humility is an absolutely essential quality for leaders, as the Torah states later on, "Moses was
very humble, more humble than any person on earth." (Numbers 12:30)
2. Listeners must listen that much more carefully to catch the meaning of
the words. (Someone once told me — though I can't say for sure it is true —
that Chaim Weizmann always spoke very softly, so people would have to pay
closer attention.)
3. So no one would accuse the Jews of accepting the Torah because
Moses was a dazzling speaker. To the contrary, Moses's inarticulate mum-
blings prove it was *the content* of the Torah, not the mode of delivery that
moved them to say, "We will do and we will listen." (Exodus 24:7) (The late
Professor Saul Lieberman, ז״ל)

4. So Moses and his brother, Aaron, would become particularly close, since Aaron would actually speak Moses's words to Pharaoh. (Reply: Not always true. Imagine Moses, alone, coming down the mountain, proclaiming just one phrase of the Ten Commandments. Reply #2: Danger of pathologic dependency. As students of Torah, we must review all cases where Moses did it himself, spoke God's words and his own himself, did what he had to do without using Aaron. That is one reason why blind people should own their own automobiles.)

5. It is living proof of the ability of disabled individuals to succeed. (Reply: This can sound patronizing. Reply #2: True, but only sometimes. Not *everyone* has a success story. We never read about the others in the newspapers. Still, there is much to learn from the Winners.)

Our Job in Life:

1. To question diagnoses.

2. To try *all* methods, *absolutely all* methods to differentiate between genetically-caused or trauma-induced limitations and false or temporary disabilities that can be eliminated through (a) the Mitzvah of Tzedakah, i.e., what is just and right, (b) love and care, (c) creative therapeutic techniques, and (d) a constant reminder to ourselves that a certain percentage of the irreversible (17%?, 29%?, 68%?) is not irreversible.

I owe this insight to a very sensitive and bright 13-year-old young man, president of his day school student body who described visits to the local residence for elders. They visit, they talk, they listen, they sing and entertain, but underlying it all, as he described it, is that most of them are "gone," irrevocably condemned to a Zombie-like state.

He is wrong. Until everyone involved in the lives of those Elders re-assesses which ones are absolutely irreparably *biologically* damaged, the 13-year-old's job is to discover and develop any and all methods to bring out the best, most glorious, and noble aspects of their beings back into the light of day.

We need to find out what is caused by weak or damaged genes, cellular degeneration, poor nutrition, and depression, loneliness or uselessness so we can proceed accordingly with the appropriate acts of Tikkun Olam — fixing things.

That's our job, no less than the physician or psychologist.

Three Common Examples:

1. Helen Keller and Annie Sullivan.
2. The Special Olympics.
3. Wilma Rudolph, world record holder in the 1960's of the 100 and 200 meter dash ...despite having a damaged leg in childhood, a leg supported by orthopedic braces. Her childhood reality included polio, scarlet fever, and double pneumonia.

We, The Teachers:

1. We would do well to apply the First Rule of Special Education to all education and human interrelationships, namely: Look at the other person fairly and lovingly, discover by any and all methods what the person's abilities and talents are, and use any and all methods to actualize those abilities and talents, i.e., to always seek out the glorious soul within, the נשמה גוטע, the good, sweet divinely-given soul from which all human grace and poetry spring.

2. We should buck the trend of complicating terminology. On résumés, on tax forms, on applications, and when referring to ourselves, we should write and say, "Teacher." There is really no need for the word "Educator" or "Pedagogic Specialist". Making it longer doesn't help. Think of the medical term P.I.E. — pyrexia of indeterminate etiology, compared to F.U.O. — fever of unknown origin. If it was good enough for Moses to be called רבינו- Our Teacher, it should be good enough for us. Indeed, we would do well to consider that, of all the descriptives the Talmud and Midrash could give Moses — Our Leader, Our Prophet, Our Liberator — they chose, רבינו- Our Teacher.

And so, it would seem that what we might want to be when we grow up is a Teacher, the one who reveals all that is hidden in the human soul, reveals the grandeur and the glory to the person himself or herself and to all others who would meet that human being in the course of a natural lifetime.

Why Young Chileans Are 6 Inches Taller
Than Their Parents and Grandparents Were
in the 1950's:

Suppose you and a friend are traveling through Scandinavia. At some point, perhaps while savoring the herring in Reykjavik or Oslo, you might remark on the striking height and build of the Icelanders or Norwegians. Finishing the meal with some unusually tasty flatbread, you might add, "What marvelous genes these folks have!"

Suppose you and a friend are on vacation, strolling around Santiago or Valparaiso or Antofagasta. You might never remark, "How short the children are compared to ours in America!"

...because Dr. Fernando Monckeberg set up infant nutrition centers throughout Chile.

...because Dr. Fernando Monckeberg established a system of intensive treatment centers for infants throughout the country.

And another statistic: Whereas in the 1950's more than two-thirds of Chile's children age 6 and younger were undernourished and mentally damaged, today, about 8% are undernourished, most of them to a mild degree.

And another statistic: In the 1950's, the infant mortality rate in Chile was more than 130 deaths/1,000 live births. Today it is less than 16/1,000.

Let us, then, consider, all those Chileans in their early and mid-child-hood, their teens, 20's, 30's and 40's who are bright, active, animated citizens, because of The Good Dr. Monckeberg.

Let us, then, consider all those Chileans in their early- and mid-child-hood, teens, 20's, 30's, and 40's who might not be alive today were it not for The Wise Dr. Monckeberg who suspected all along it wasn't in the genes at all.

And so, what we might want to be when we grow up is a Fernando Monckeberg.

Rachel:

According to those who knew her, Rachel died at age 100. Born in Kurdistan, she came to Jerusalem many years before, perhaps in the late 1940's or early 1950's.

In her old age, for reasons unknown to me, she became one of Jerusalem's street beggars. Into her 80's she sat there, hand extended, rattling her coins to get the attention of passers-by. And sometime in Rachel's 80's, Myriam Mendilow, God rest her awesome soul, came along and put her to work at Life Line for the Old. She made ceramic beads that became beautiful jewelry. Hundreds, perhaps thousands, of Jerusalemites and tourists from around the world wear jewelry fashioned by her ancient hands.

This is what Mrs. Mendilow wrote me a number of years ago, "I regret to inform you that we lost Rachel, from Ceramics. She was 100 years old when she died — she just lay down and fell asleep forever. For me, she represented the story of Life Line. I shall always remember her. From a beggar in the streets, we made of her an honourable and beautiful citizen."

She might have lived her last years and died a nobody, just another beggar whose body was found one day in her room by some neighbor. No one would have noticed. No one would have missed her.

That is why, when we grow up, we might want to become a Myriam Mendilow.

The Economics of Mitzvahs

I. Numbers

1. The lower school of Ramaz Yeshiva in New York has been donating leftover food from the lunch program to soup kitchens.
    A. First-year donations: 3,000 pounds.
    B. Second-year donations: 7,000 pounds.
    C. Third-year donations: 15,000 pounds.
    D. Fourth-year donations: more than 20,000 pounds (as of mid-March, 1995, with three months still to go in the school year.)
2. David Levitt of Seminole, FL, convinced Pinellas County's superintendent of schools to institute a program of donating leftover food from all the schools. Total donations: I don't have the figures, but I am sure they are staggering. (David was in the 6th grade when he made his suggestion.)
3. The Baltimore Orioles gave Steve Chaikin and his friends permission to pick up leftover food at the end of the games. In one season (81 home games) Steve gathered the equivalent of 81,000 meals for local food programs.

Imagine if every Jewish day school, every public, parochial, and private school, and every major and minor league team, and every college and high school team donated the leftovers.

4. Ranya Kelly redistributed food and goods stores used to throw out — perfectly good items — to the extent of $1,500,000 worth of items in one year.
    A. Her operating budget for that year was approximately $15,000.
    B. The $1,500,000 is a low figure, some sort of tax reckoning for the stores. True market value is much higher.
    C. About 10 years ago, she started with new shoes that were being dumped. By February, 1995, she had gathered and distributed over 160,000 pairs of shoes.

Imagine if there were 20 or 50 or 150 Redistribution Centers around the country.

5. At one of Dr. William Thomas' Eden Alternative nursing homes — the cost of medications was cut in half in 2 1/2 years. In the first year of his program, the dollar amount dropped dramatically: from $220,006 to $135,901 for 80 residents.

Imagine if every old age residence in the country could do the same...how much that would save America and Americans in health care costs.

6. Janet Marchese has facilitated the adoption of more than 3,400 infants with Down Syndrome in adoptive homes in the last 10 years.
    A. She takes no salary, though she is entitled to it.
    B. In any given year, she personally is involved in placing more infants with Down Syndrome *than any agency* in the country.

Imagine...if adoption agency employees came to her to find out how she does it. Imagine, purely from the hard cash standpoint, how much money would be saved.

7. One study[1] showed that using service dogs for individuals with spinal-cord injuries, muscular dystrophy, multiple sclerosis, and traumatic brain injuries, the average annual savings per person was $13,000.

Imagine if, in all applicable situations, service dogs could be provided — imagine, in pure dollars and cents, how much would be saved.

8. Professor Jack Daly founded the Case Engineering Support Group (CESG) at Case Western Reserve University in Cleveland to encourage his students to play a part in what we would call Tikkun Olam-Fixing the World. He had them use their training and talents to design devices (including toys) that would benefit people with disabilities. The particular story that caught my eye was an article about an elbow sleeve for a child with cerebral palsy. For purposes of this article, the details are not that important. What is significant is that the students made what was needed for $16. A commercial firm, presented with the same problem to solve, bid $8,000 for the same job.

Imagine what a world we would have with all that extra Mitzvah money lying around waiting to be used for Good Things. In this one case alone, it would equal $7,984. Multiply that by thousands of similar cases Out There, and we are on to many millions of Tzedakah dollars.

In another example of CESG's efficiency-through-creative-Mitzvahs, the Clevelanders set up a workstation at a medical center that would simulate a working environment so that patients who had been injured could prepare to return to their jobs without fear of re-injury. The workstation is a room with electrical, plumbing, and construction job layouts, cars, stairs, a platform — all kinds of configurations similar to employment situations the workers would return to. On this project, CESG spent $3,000. The commercial estimate was $120,000. That equals another $117,000 in Mitzvah savings.

Between these two projects alone: $117,000 + $7,984 = $124,984 saved.

When more complete statistics are in, i.e., all the comparative savings from the group at Case plus all other groups established around the country on the Cleveland model, I am certain the sum will be in the millions of dollars.

II. The Two-Sentence Overview

Wherever we stand on the argument of government involvement in the cure of society's ills and injustices (and I stand with those who say it is impossible to do, absolutely impossible without government financial support) — we must take into account that the Mitzvah heroes provide many vital insights. Why, in 1995, experts and consultants and leaders and legislators and other powerful people are not coming to learn from them and to put their Mitzvah work into action is beyond me.

III. The Jewish Text

When I teach, I often use the text:

אַל־תִּגְזָל־דָּל כִּי דַל־הוּא

Don't rob poor people because they are poor.
(Proverbs 22:22)

I ask, "What could you possibly steal from poor people?" The usual first answer is, "Their dignity." It is a very good answer. But, as we have seen by the few statistics I have gathered, *not* being more efficient in our Tzedakah work is also a form of denying them what they could easily — and rightfully (which is the meaning of the word "Tzedakah") — receive.[2]

6 Ways to Sharpen Your Tzedakah Skills
Brief and To the Point

In no particular order of importance. Start with whichever ones you as a person are most comfortable with:

1. Gather newspaper and magazine articles and books and videos and materials from electronic bulletin boards about Mitzvah projects and Mitzvah heroes.

2. Meet the Mitzvah heroes and join them in their work.

3. Study Jewish texts on Mitzvahs and Tzedakah.

4. Learn the distinctive Jewish vocabulary and integrate it into your thinking and speech.

5. Do Mitzvah projects: one-time projects, short-term projects, long-term projects, once-in-a-lifetime projects, small-size, medium-size, or large-size projects...whatever fits your nature as a human being.

6. Keep giving your money away.

All six will interplay more and more as you go along.
Trust me.

Sunset Sam, the Mighty Mitzvah Dolphin, enjoying a moment of relaxation.

Final Exam

I remember having to remember names like "Chickamauga" and "Chancellorsville" and dates like 1787 for an American history course in high school. I remember memorizing the names of the 13 children of Jacob (in order of birth) for Hebrew school, and, later on in college, the Kings of Israel and the Kings of Judah (in order). Learning 40 new words a night for Spanish was not unusual, "sueño," "encontrar," and "lentamente" among the early ones. I remember the satisfaction of mastering the lists, and, at the same time, I remember rebelling against having to memorize. My mood varied day by day. It was partially a mental thing, and partially, no doubt, teen-age hormones.

Late on, I became an educator. Then I remembered the many discussions about the importance of knowing a mass of factual material, and the secondary importance of factual material and the primacy of learning to think, and the shortcomings of knowing how to think but having no facts at the ready to help make sense of all the thinking. Most, I remember feeling like a tennis ball being whacked back and forth across the court: facts, thinking, thinking, facts.

Without taking sides on the age-old debate, here is my list of Names to Know (which I update regularly). If I were teaching a semester's course, I would want my students to be able to identify all these people, programs, and animals...and the simple math equation at the end. (Naturally, there are a few trick names. "Tzedakah" and "Ziv," for example, do not refer to Mitzvah work, but rather to Black Labradors being trained by Canine Companions for Independence for a productive life working with individuals who use wheelchairs.)

Not everything on this list has been covered in the book. If you score a 50%, you have probably read the material very thoroughly. For the rest, you have to read my other essays, come to a seminar I am doing, or take a long, long Shabbat walk with me.

Enjoy! לחיים!

ALYN
Caridad Asensio
Ashley, Ashlie, Tova, and Maia
Misha Avramoff

Dr. Bonnie Bergin
Trudi Birger
Charna Blumberg
Sheda Braunhut
Erin Broadbent
Dr. Anne Brooks
Ray Buchanan
Buttercup

Steve Chaikin
Chase and Sanborn
Susanna Cheung
Tova Cohen
Comet
Kimberly Cook
David Copperfield

Daddy Bruce Randolph
John Francis Xavier Daly
Dave
Joël Dorkam

Eden

Elana Erdstein

Bruce Feldman
Trevor Ferrell
John Fling
Reb Osher Freund
Shaul F'taya, ל״ז

Victoria Ginsberg
Barbara Ribacove Gordon
John Graham
Teddy Gross
Rabbi Danny Grossman

William Halamandaris
Clara Hammer
Yehudit Harris
Lis Hartel
Linda Hines
Brenda Hirsch
John Holt
Ken Horne
Carol Hutton

Dr. Eliezer Jaffe
Jeannie Jaybush
Jubilee

The Rabbanit Bracha Kapach
Katie
Dr. Martin Kieselstein
Marianne Klingel
Kosmic

Justin Lebo
Lois Lee
Hadassah Levi
David Levitt
Grandma Lewis
Dr. Jesse Lipnick
Little John
Joseph Lordi
Uri Lupoliansky

Yaakov Maimon, ל״ז
Janet Marchese

Ann Medlock
Myriam Mendilow, ל״ז
Fernando Monckeberg
Dr. Ronald Myers

Ari Newman

Chana Ovadia
Simcha Ovadia
Yehuda Ovadia

Paul Margolis
Pearl

Reverend John Steinbruck
Mark Ross
Joy Rothenberg

Yossi Samuels
Kalman and Malky Samuels
Serra
Anita and Giora Shkedi
Ethel Shull
Sister Anne Brooks
Sister Margaret McCaffrey
Travis Stout
Stumpy
Sunset Sam
Sweet Pea

Target
Dr. William Thomas
Warren Toltz
Tzedakah

Sigrid Ueblacker

Shoshana Weinstock
Windsong
Windwalker
Stuart and Ellen Witkin
Wolfman

Ziv

$220,006-$135,901= $84,105

Biblical Verses[1]

The following selections from Biblical texts are printed to offer the reader the opportunity to study them for a variety of purposes:

1. Personal Torah study and enrichment. I have selected these in particular because they are open to many possible interpretations.

2. A Dvar Torah, i.e., a word of Torah presented at the beginning of a meeting, to set the tone for the deliberations at hand.

3. Study with a friend. I recently took a walk with my teacher, Dr. Abraham Gittelson, selecting Psalm 119:2 as the text. We spent nearly an hour developing the ideas the verse suggested to us, and had barely begun to penetrate the depth of meanings this one verse offered.

The texts are in no particular order. They should be used freely, and, I believe, frequently. Each will produce additional insights into Mitzvahs and Tzedakah, and their relationship to Life.

From Psalm 119[2]

1 אַשְׁרֵי תְמִימֵי־דָרֶךְ הַהֹלְכִים בְּתוֹרַת יְהוָה:

Happy are those whose way is innocent,
following God's teaching.

2 אַשְׁרֵי נֹצְרֵי עֵדֹתָיו בְּכָל־לֵב יִדְרְשׁוּהוּ:

Happy are those who observe God's Mitzvahs,
searching for God with a whole heart.
[The more heart the Seeker puts into the search, the greater the rewards of the Search.]

7 אוֹדְךָ בְּיֹשֶׁר לֵבָב בְּלָמְדִי מִשְׁפְּטֵי צִדְקֶךָ:

I will praise You with a sincere heart
as I learn Your just rules.

10 בְּכָל־לִבִּי דְרַשְׁתִּיךָ אַל־תַּשְׁגֵּנִי מִמִּצְוֹתֶיךָ:

I have sought you out with all my heart;
Do not let me stray from your Mitzvahs.

13 בִּשְׂפָתַי סִפַּרְתִּי כֹּל מִשְׁפְּטֵי־פִיךָ:

I speak about
all the rules You proclaimed.
[It is not enough to merely __think__ *about Torah. We should verbalize our thoughts, review the words, listen to what we are saying.]*

14 בְּדֶרֶךְ עֵדְוֹתֶיךָ שַׂשְׂתִּי כְּעַל כָּל־הוֹן:

I rejoice over the ways of Your decrees
as over great wealth.

15 בְּפִקֻּדֶיךָ אָשִׂיחָה וְאַבִּיטָה אֹרְחֹתֶיךָ:

By talking about your Mitzvahs,
I see more clearly the way You would like things to be.
*[Torah was originally Spoken Torah. Passionate discussion, lively give-and-
take, and enthusiastic Torah-talk produce greater and greater insight.]*

17 גְּמֹל עַל־עַבְדְּךָ אֶחְיֶה וְאֶשְׁמְרָה דְבָרֶךָ:

Treat Your servant kindly,
so I may live to keep Your word.

19 גֵּר אָנֹכִי בָאָרֶץ אַל־תַּסְתֵּר מִמֶּנִּי מִצְוֹתֶיךָ:

I am in this land [of Life] only for a little while;
do not hide Your Mitzvahs from me.

24 גַּם־עֵדֹתֶיךָ שַׁעֲשֻׁעָי אַנְשֵׁי עֲצָתִי:

Your Mitzvahs are my delight,
my intimate companions.
*[Mitzvahs are so intimate a presence in the Psalmist's Life, they are personified
as people.]*

28 דָּלְפָה נַפְשִׁי מִתּוּגָה קַיְּמֵנִי כִּדְבָרֶךָ:

Though I have times of enormous grief,
give Me Life through Your words.
[Torah and Mitzvahs give us the strength to survive the most trying times.]

32 דֶּרֶךְ־מִצְוֹתֶיךָ אָרוּץ כִּי תַרְחִיב לִבִּי:

I run on the way of Your Mitzvahs;
You give me greater and greater understanding.
*[The Talmud takes this idea even further, teaching that, as long as there is en-
thusiasm for doing Tzedakah, God will provide the means to what is needed.]*

ואמר רבי יצחק....
כל הרודף אחר צדקה
הקדוש ברוך הוא ממציא לו מעות ועושה בהן צדקה
רב נחמן בר יצחק אמר
הקדוש ברוך הוא ממציא לו בני אדם המהוגנים
לעשות להן צדקה

Rabbi Yitzchak said...:
The Holy One will provide sufficient Mitzvah money
for any who runs to do Tzedakah.
Rabbi Nachman bar Yitzchak said:
The Holy One will provide appropriate recipients
through whom to perform the Mitzvah of Tzedakah. (Bava Batra 9b)]

37 הַעֲבֵר עֵינַי מֵרְאוֹת שָׁוְא בִּדְרָכֶךָ חַיֵּנִי:

Keep my eyes from seeing worthless things;
Give me Life by means of Your ways.
[Tzedakah gives the human being a perspective about what is precious in life,
what is somewhat or slightly less-than-precious, what is of little value, and
what is of no value whatsoever.]

45 וְאֶתְהַלְּכָה בָרְחָבָה כִּי פִקֻּדֶיךָ דָרָשְׁתִּי:

I will walk about at ease,
for I have carefully examined your Mitzvahs.
[The Psalmist is not naïve. Life has many painful moments. Life has
heartache, the ache of the body diseased, the agony of separation from loved
ones, catastrophe beyond human control. Yet the poet makes the bold state-
ment: ultimately one may be at ease, because Life is meaningful through
Mitzvahs, through Tzedakah, doing for others. See the following verse.]

50 זֹאת נֶחָמָתִי בְעָנְיִי כִּי אִמְרָתְךָ חִיָּתְנִי:

When I am suffering, this is my comfort:
Your word gives me Life.

52 זָכַרְתִּי מִשְׁפָּטֶיךָ מֵעוֹלָם | יְהֹוָה וָאֶתְנֶחָם:

I remember Your ancient Mitzvahs, O God,
and find comfort in them.
[The continuity of thousands of years of Jewish tradition gives the Jew a sense
of being connected to Life as something far greater than any single lifetime. We
are a part of a very long and great history.]

54 זְמִרוֹת הָיוּ־לִי חֻקֶּיךָ בְּבֵית מְגוּרָי:

Your Mitzvahs are a source of strength to me
wherever I may live.
["זמירות,"translated here as "source of strength" ³ also means, "song".]

64 חַסְדְּךָ יְהֹוָה מָלְאָה הָאָרֶץ חֻקֶּיךָ לַמְּדֵנִי:

Your steadfast and profound caring, O God, fills the earth;
teach me the [Mitzvah-] laws.
[Chessed-חסד is reliable love. Acts of Chessed can be relied upon. The
Mitzvah Person trusts that God fills Life with Chessed-חסד, and that God's
Presence manifested as Chessed-חסד can be discovered — even in the most
unlikely places — if we but look for it.]

66 טוּב טַעַם וָדַעַת לַמְּדֵנִי כִּי בְמִצְוֹתֶיךָ הֶאֱמָנְתִּי:

Teach me the insight and knowledge needed to do Mitzvahs,
because I trust in them.
[Though human beings are naturally endowed with the talent to do Mitzvahs,
God teaches us how to refine our talents to do them more skillfully and effi-

ciently, achieving greater measures of Tikkun Olam-Fixing the World, with each act. By analogy: even a great musician, one endowed with perfect pitch and an astonishing feel for the keys say, of a piano, needs teachers...and needs to practice constantly to take his or her music to greater heights.]

105 נֵר־לְרַגְלִי דְבָרֶךָ וְאוֹר לִנְתִיבָתִי:

Your word is a lamp to my feet,
a light for my path.

123 עֵינַי כָּלוּ לִישׁוּעָתֶךָ וּלְאִמְרַת צִדְקֶךָ:

I pine away for Your deliverance,
for Your promise of victory.
[This is one of many verses in the Torah where the root "Tz-D-K=צדק" means "victory". The victory is, of course, a just, peaceful, and Menschlich world.]

From the Book of Proverbs

וְצַדִּיק יְסוֹד עוֹלָם:

The very foundation of the world is Good People. (10:25)

יֵשׁ מְפַזֵּר וְנוֹסָף עוֹד וְחוֹשֵׂךְ מִיּשֶׁר אַךְ־לְמַחְסוֹר:

People who give generously end up with more;
Those who restrain themselves from doing the right thing, lose. (11:24)
[People who do Mitzvahs claim they get more out their work than what they put into it. In their eyes, it is not sacrifice. Tzedakah is pure enrichment, its own reward, each Mitzvah bringing others in its wake. My teacher, Rabbi Jack Riemer, taught me a humorous, yet true, analogy: Mitzvahs are like potato chips. Just as you can't eat just one chip, so, too, you can't just do one Mitzvah.
My translation of the second half of the verse hints at a fact of human nature: people are by nature inclined to Mitzvahs, and not doing them takes an active effort of restraint. The losses are many: human energy is used inefficiently and for the wrong purpose, less Mitzvahs produce a less decent, livable society, people suffer.]

רָשָׁע עֹשֶׂה פְעֻלַּת־שָׁקֶר וְזֹרֵעַ צְדָקָה שֶׂכֶר אֱמֶת:

The wicked person earns illusory wages,
but those who sow Tzedakah have a true reward. (11:18)
[As the Yiddish phrase goes, תכריכים האבן נישט קיין קעשענעס, *"Shrouds have no pockets."]*

יֵשׁ מִתְעַשֵּׁר וְאֵין כֹּל מִתְרוֹשֵׁשׁ וְהוֹן רָב:

One person pretends to be rich and has nothing;
Another professes to be poor and has much wealth. (13:7)[3a]
[The first half of the verse is very troubling. People need to be educated to be the recipient of Tzedakah when it is truly needed. There is no loss of dignity and no need for embarrassment. Receiving Tzedakah is not the same as "taking

charity" which implies weakness. The recipient receives only what is rightfully his or hers. Two examples: (1) Some Jews who have to use food stamps travel far from their neighborhoods to shop for groceries. They don't want to be seen by people who know them. (2) Synagogues that have sound systems for hearing impaired people often find that people who need them won't use them. In general, many synagogue Mitzvah committees find that, though they have announced they wish to serve the needs of members as well as serve the general community — they find that few members who are in need are willing to come to them. People need to be educated to receive as well as to give.]

Some people are rich and have nothing;
Others are poor but have great riches. (13:7)[3b]
[Daddy Bruce Randolph died at the age of 94 in March, 1994. For many years he fed thousands of people on Thanksgiving and other holidays from his Denver restaurant, Daddy Bruce's Barbecue. I met him when he was 90 years old, and — to use a Biblical tone — God's radiance was upon his face. Fifteen hundred people — the famous and the homeless among them — came to his funeral. The Denver Broncos paid for the funeral, and Daddy Bruce was driven to his final rest in a Cadillac, and though he died poor, until his dying day he considered himself the richest person in the world. One of the ministers who eulogized him, the Reverend James Peters of New Hope Baptist Church said, "No one can deny that we lost a friend....Wouldn't you like to have been in Glory when he came walking in?" The crowd responded with a unanimous "Amen!"]

עֹשֵׁק דָּל לְהַרְבּוֹת לוֹ נֹתֵן לְעָשִׁיר אַךְ־לְמַחְסוֹר:

To profit by withholding what is due to the poor
Is like making gifts to the rich — pure loss. (22:16)

וְאֹרַח צַדִּיקִים כְּאוֹר נֹגַהּ הוֹלֵךְ וָאוֹר עַד־נְכוֹן הַיּוֹם:

The path of Good People is like radiant sunlight,
ever brightening until noon. (4:18)

וְצָפַן [יִצְפֹּן] לַיְשָׁרִים תּוּשִׁיָּה מָגֵן לְהֹלְכֵי תֹם:

God reserves ability for Upright People
and is a shield for those who live blamelessly. (2:7)
[Creativity in Mitzvah work has no limit. God shows new ways to do Tzedakah with every Mitzvah act a person performs. The mind is stimulated, the hands — indeed, the entire body — are enlivened. New talents are discovered at every turn. An example: though a computer hacker may use creativity to break into other computers and security systems, it is still a very one-sided affair — breaking the law. Were that person to use the computer for Mitzvahs, at the keyboard and on the screen are infinite possibilities to rebuild the lives of hungry people, shattered people, people who need an education but cannot afford it, lonely people, people who arrive on safe shores with only the clothes on their bodies, addicted people screaming for a way out of their slavery to sub-

stances, people plagued by stalkers, people haunted by hateful people who scrawl graffiti on their houses of worship and wear metaphorical white sheets to terrorize the innocent...the list is endless.]

From Other Biblical Books:

וְאֵרַשְׂתִּיךְ לִי לְעוֹלָם
וְאֵרַשְׂתִּיךְ לִי בְּצֶדֶק וּבְמִשְׁפָּט וּבְחֶסֶד וּבְרַחֲמִים:
וְאֵרַשְׂתִּיךְ לִי בֶּאֱמוּנָה וְיָדַעַתְּ אֶת־יְהוָה:

I will betrothe you to me for all eternity,
I will betrothe you to me
by means of true justice, infinite love and care, and ultimate trust.
In that way you shall know God intimately. (Hosea 3:21-22)

כִּי־לְעוֹלָם לֹא־יִמּוֹט לְזֵכֶר עוֹלָם יִהְיֶה צַדִּיק:

That person shall never be shaken;
the Good Person will be remembered forever. (Psalm 112:6)

קוּמִי אוֹרִי כִּי בָא אוֹרֵךְ וּכְבוֹד יְהוָה עָלַיִךְ זָרָח:

Arise, shine, for your light has dawned;
The Presence of God has shone upon you. (Isaiah 60:1)

פִּזַּר ׀ נָתַן לָאֶבְיוֹנִים צִדְקָתוֹ עֹמֶדֶת לָעַד קַרְנוֹ תָּרוּם בְּכָבוֹד:

One who gives freely to poor people —
his or her beneficence lasts forever;
he or she shall be treated with dignity. (Psalm 112:9)

לֹא־תַעֲשׂוּ עָוֶל בַּמִּשְׁפָּט בַּמִּדָּה בַּמִּשְׁקָל וּבַמְּשׂוּרָה
מֹאזְנֵי צֶדֶק אַבְנֵי־צֶדֶק אֵיפַת צֶדֶק וְהִין צֶדֶק יִהְיֶה לָכֶם
אֲנִי יְהוָה אֱלֹהֵיכֶם אֲשֶׁר־הוֹצֵאתִי אֶתְכֶם מֵאֶרֶץ מִצְרָיִם:

You shall not falsify measures of length, weight, or capacity.
You shall have an honest balance, honest weights,
an honest ephah, and an honest hin.[4]
I , God, am your God who freed you from the land of Egypt.
(Leviticus 19:35-36)
*[*צדק*, used four times in these verses means "justice," the same as the word* צדקה*. In the world of Jewish values, they are the same issue: conducting business honestly is the same as providing Passover food for poor people, insuring access for people with disabilities, or finding homes for abandoned children. In every case, something is wrong and needs to be set right.]*

אִישׁ כְּמַתְּנַת יָדוֹ כְּבִרְכַּת יְהוָה אֱלֹהֶיךָ אֲשֶׁר נָתַן־לָךְ:

...each with his [or her] own gift,
according to the blessing
that God has bestowed upon you. (Deuteronomy 16:17)

[Everyone has to give Tzedakah, however great or small quantitatively God's blessings may be. As the Talmud states it:

אמר מר זוטרא
אפילו עני המתפרנס מן הצדקה יעשה צדקה

Mar Zutra said:
Even a poor person who is sustained by Tzedakah
must give Tzedakah. (Gittin 7b)]

טוֹב־אִישׁ חוֹנֵן וּמַלְוֶה יְכַלְכֵּל דְּבָרָיו בְּמִשְׁפָּט:

All goes well with the person who lends generously,
who conducts his or her affairs with equity. (Psalm 112:5)

וְכִי־יָמוּךְ אָחִיךָ וּמָטָה יָדוֹ עִמָּךְ וְהֶחֱזַקְתָּ בּוֹ גֵּר וְתוֹשָׁב וָחַי עִמָּךְ:
אַל־תִּקַּח מֵאִתּוֹ נֶשֶׁךְ וְתַרְבִּית וְיָרֵאתָ מֵאֱלֹהֶיךָ וְחֵי אָחִיךָ עִמָּךְ:
אֶת־כַּסְפְּךָ לֹא־תִתֵּן לוֹ בְּנֶשֶׁךְ וּבְמַרְבִּית לֹא־תִתֵּן אָכְלֶךָ:
אֲנִי יְהוָה אֱלֹהֵיכֶם אֲשֶׁר־הוֹצֵאתִי אֶתְכֶם מֵאֶרֶץ מִצְרָיִם
לָתֵת לָכֶם אֶת־אֶרֶץ כְּנַעַן לִהְיוֹת לָכֶם לֵאלֹהִים:

If your kinsperson, being in straits, comes under your authority,
and you hold that person as though a resident alien,
let that person live by your side:
do not exact advance or accrued interest,
but fear your God.
Let that person live by your side as your kinsperson.
Do not lend that person money at advance interest,
or give your food at accrued interest.
I, Adonai, am your God,
who brought you out of the land of Egypt,
to give you the land of Canaan, to be your God. (Leviticus 25:35-38)
[This is one of the verses upon which the ancient — and modern — Jewish practice of interest-free loans is based.]

5 וְאִישׁ כִּי־יִהְיֶה צַדִּיק וְעָשָׂה מִשְׁפָּט וּצְדָקָה:...

...If a person is good and does what is just and right:... (Ezekiel 18)
[The opening statement is in generalized terms. Ezekiel then gives more concrete examples, finally concluding the passage with a general summary. Ezekiel is teaching that generalities without specifics won't work when it comes to trying to make a just and decent world.]

7 וְאִישׁ לֹא יוֹנֶה
חֲבֹלָתוֹ חוֹב יָשִׁיב
גְּזֵלָה לֹא יִגְזֹל
לַחְמוֹ לְרָעֵב יִתֵּן
וְעֵירֹם יְכַסֶּה־בָּגֶד:

not having wronged anyone;
returning the debtor's pledge,
taking nothing by robbery;
giving bread to hungry people
and clothing to those who are naked,

8 בַּנֶּשֶׁךְ לֹא־יִתֵּן וְתַרְבִּית לֹא יִקָּח
מֵעָוֶל יָשִׁיב יָדוֹ
מִשְׁפַּט אֱמֶת יַעֲשֶׂה בֵּין אִישׁ לְאִישׁ:

not having lent on advance interest or exacted accrued interest,
having abstained from wrongdoing
and executed true justice between one person and another....

9 בְּחֻקּוֹתַי יְהַלֵּךְ
וּמִשְׁפָּטַי שָׁמַר לַעֲשׂוֹת אֱמֶת
צַדִּיק הוּא
חָיֹה יִחְיֶה
נְאֻם אֲדֹנָי יְהוִה:

if having done this,
he or she has followed My laws
and kept My rules and acted honestly —
that person is righteous.
Such a person shall live — declares God.
(Ezekiel 18: 7-9)

A Selection from the Prophetic Reading for Yom Kippur Morning, Isaiah 58:5-12

5 הֲכָזֶה יִהְיֶה צוֹם אֶבְחָרֵהוּ יוֹם עַנּוֹת אָדָם נַפְשׁוֹ
הֲלָכֹף כְּאַגְמֹן רֹאשׁוֹ וְשַׂק וָאֵפֶר יַצִּיעַ
הֲלָזֶה תִּקְרָא־צוֹם וְיוֹם רָצוֹן לַיהוָה:

Is such the fast I desire,
a day for people to starve their bodies?
Is it bowing the head like a bulrush
and lying in sackcloth and ashes?
Do you call that a fast,
a day when God is favorable?

6 הֲלוֹא זֶה צוֹם אֶבְחָרֵהוּ
פַּתֵּחַ חַרְצֻבּוֹת רֶשַׁע הַתֵּר אֲגֻדּוֹת מוֹטָה
וְשַׁלַּח רְצוּצִים חָפְשִׁים וְכָל־מוֹטָה תְּנַתֵּקוּ:

No, this is the fast I desire:
to unlock fetters of wickedness,
and untie the cords of the yoke

to let the oppressed go free;
to break off every yoke.

7 הֲלוֹא פָרֹס לָרָעֵב לַחְמֶךָ וַעֲנִיִּים מְרוּדִים תָּבִיא בָיִת
כִּי־תִרְאֶה עָרֹם וְכִסִּיתוֹ וּמִבְּשָׂרְךָ לֹא תִתְעַלָּם:

It is to share your bread with the hungry,
and to take the wretched poor into your home;
when you see the naked, to give them clothes,
and not to ignore your own kin.

8 אָז יִבָּקַע כַּשַּׁחַר אוֹרֶךָ וַאֲרֻכָתְךָ מְהֵרָה תִצְמָח
וְהָלַךְ לְפָנֶיךָ צִדְקֶךָ כְּבוֹד יְהוָה יַאַסְפֶךָ:

Then shall your light burst through like the dawn,
and your healing spring up quickly;
Your Vindicator shall march before you,
the Presence of God shall be your rear guard.

9 אָז תִּקְרָא וַיהוָה יַעֲנֶה תְּשַׁוַּע וְיֹאמַר הִנֵּנִי
אִם־תָּסִיר מִתּוֹכְךָ מוֹטָה שְׁלַח אֶצְבַּע וְדַבֶּר־אָוֶן:

Then, when you call, God will answer;
When you cry, God will say: Here I am.
If you banish the yoke from your midst,
the menacing hand and evil speech,

10 וְתָפֵק לָרָעֵב נַפְשֶׁךָ וְנֶפֶשׁ נַעֲנָה תַּשְׂבִּיעַ
וְזָרַח בַּחֹשֶׁךְ אוֹרֶךָ וַאֲפֵלָתְךָ כַּצָּהֳרָיִם:

and you offer your compassion to the hungry
and satisfy the famished creature —
then shall your light shine in darkness,
and your gloom shall be like the noonday.

11 וְנָחֲךָ יְהוָה תָּמִיד וְהִשְׂבִּיעַ בְּצַחְצָחוֹת נַפְשֶׁךָ
וְעַצְמֹתֶיךָ יַחֲלִיץ וְהָיִיתָ כְּגַן רָוֶה
וּכְמוֹצָא מַיִם אֲשֶׁר לֹא־יְכַזְּבוּ מֵימָיו:

God will guide you always;
God will slake your thirst in parched places
and give strength to your bones.
You shall be like a watered garden,
like a spring whose waters do not fail.

12 וּבָנוּ מִמְּךָ חָרְבוֹת עוֹלָם מוֹסְדֵי דוֹר־וָדוֹר תְּקוֹמֵם
וְקֹרָא לְךָ גֹּדֵר פֶּרֶץ מְשֹׁבֵב נְתִיבוֹת לָשָׁבֶת:

People from your midst shall rebuild ancient ruins,
You shall restore foundations laid long ago.
You shall be called "Repairer of fallen walls,
Restorer of lanes for habitation."

Rabbinic, Legal, and Kabbalistic Texts

1. Mitzvah Messengers

איתמר אמר רבי אלעזר
שלוחי מצוה אינן ניזוקין
לא בהליכתן ולא בחזירתן

It was stated that Rabbi Elazar said,
"No harm happens to people on Mitzvah missions,
neither on the way,
nor on the way back." (Pesachim 8b)[1]

2. Shedding Those Extra Few Pounds

דרש רב עוירא
זימנין אמר ליה משמיה דרבי אמי
וזימנין אמר לה משמיה דרבי אסי....
אם רואה אדם שמזונותיו מצומצמין
יעשה מהן צדקה
וכל שכן כשהן מרובין....

Rabbi Avira explained,
(sometimes in the name of Rabbi Ammi,
and sometimes in the name of Rabbi Assi):
....[1a]
If a person sees that his or her financial resources are limited,
that's the time when he or she should be doing Tzedakah,
and, so much the more so,
when he or she has abundant financial resources....

תנא דבי רבי ישמעאל
כל הגוזז מנכסיו ועושה מהן צדקה
ניצל מדינה של גיהנם
משל לשתי רחילות שהיו עוברות במים
אחת גזוזה ואחת אינה גזוזה
גזוזה עברה
ושאינה גזוזה לא עברה

It was taught
in Rabbi Yishma'el's school of Torah study:
Whoever shears[2] away some of his or her money
and uses it for Tzedakah
will be saved from the Judgment of Gehinnom.
A parable will explain this —
It is like two ewes that need to cross a river,
one that has been shorn
and one that has not.
The one that has been shorn makes it across,
while the other does not. (Gittin 7a)

3. On the Road and Temporarily Out of Money

בעל הבית שהיה מהלך לעיר

ותמו לו המעות בדרך

ואין לו עתה מה יאכל

הרי זה מותר ליקח לקט שכחה ופאה ומעשר עני

וליהנות מן הצדקה

ולכשיגיע לביתו אינו חייב לשלם

שהרי עני היה באותה שעה

הא למה זה דומה

לעני שהעשיר שאינו חייב לשלם

If a person was traveling from one place to another and ran out of money and has nothing to eat at the moment, he or she is permitted to take from the Gleanings, Forgotten Sheaves, and Corners of the field, from The Poor Person's Tithe, and to benefit from other Tzedakah. When the person returns home, he or she is not required to repay, since he or she was poor at the time [he or she benefited from the various Tzedakah portions.] What other legal situation does this resemble? That of a poor person who later became rich and who also is not required to repay what he or she had received at an earlier time when he or she was poor.
(Maimonides, Mishnah Torah, Hilchot Matnot Ani'im 9:15)[3]

4. Preparing to Face God

רבי אלעזר יהיב פרוטה לעני והדר מצלי

אמר דכתיב

אֲנִי בְּצֶדֶק אֶחֱזֶה פָנֶיךָ

Rabbi Elazar would give a coin to a poor person.
Only then would he pray.
He explained,
The Biblical verse says,
"I, by means of Tzedakah, am entitled to see Your Face."[4]
(Bava Batra 10a, Psalm 17:15)

5. A Different View of Old Age

איתיביה אביי המביא גט והניחו זקן

אפילו בן מאה שנה נותן לה בחזקת שהוא קיים

Abayye objected
[to the flow of the discussion], saying:
If a person is delivering a divorce document
on behalf of an old man,
even if he is a hundred years old,
it is delivered with the assumption that he is still alive
[when it reaches the wife.] *(Gittin 28a)[5]*

6. The Power of Life and Death

עובדא הוה בחד גבר דהוה סלק מן בבל
יתיב למקרטא באורחא
וחמא תרתין ציפריא מתכתשין באורחא חדא עם חדא
וקטלת חדא מנהון חברתא
אזלת ההיא אחריתי ואיתיית עשב ויהבית עלה
ואחיית יתה
אמ' טב לי נסב מן הדין עישבא
מסיק מחיי מיתיא דארע דישראל
מיפרי וסליק חמה תעל מית מקלק באורחא
אמ' טב לי מנסייא בהדין תעלה ויהב עילוי וייחי
והלך וסליק עד שהגיע לסולמי דצור
כיון שהגיע לסולמי צור
חמא חד ארי קטיל מקליק באורחא
אמ' טב לי מנסייא בהדין אריא
יהב עילוי מן ההוא עישבא וחיה
קם ואכלתיה

Once upon a time, a man was coming to Israel from Babylonia. When he sat down to rest, he saw two birds fighting with each other in the road. One of the birds killed the other, then flew away. It brought back a certain herb, which it placed on the dead bird, and revived it.

The man said, "It would be wonderful if I could get some of that herb. I could take it with me and bring the dead of the Land of Israel back to life!"

[Having found some of the herb], he continued on his way. He saw a dead fox lying by the roadside. The man said, "It would be good to test this on the dead fox," and touching the fox with the herb, he revived it.

Continuing still further on his way, the man reached the Ladders of Tyre, [near the border of Israel]. At that place he saw on the road a lion that had been killed. The man said, "It would be good to try this on the lion."

He touched the lion with the herb, and it was brought back to Life.

The lion then got up and ate the man.[6]

(Leviticus Rabbah 22:4, Margoliot 3:510)

7. Wise Investments

זכות יש לה קרן ויש לה פירות

Tzedakah has both principal and interest. *(Tosefta Pe'ah 1:3)*[7]

8. Good Deeds

דעובדין טבין דבר נש דעביד בהאי עלמא.
אינון עובדין משכי מנהורא דזיווא עלאה.
לבושא לאתתקנא ביה לההוא עלמא
לאתחזאה קמי קב"ה. ובההוא לבושא דלביש.

The good deeds a person does in This World become threads of light from the Sublime Radiance of God. Those threads are woven into the garments which The Good Person will wear in the Next World when it is time to appear before The Holy One. *(Zohar, Pekuday, II, 229b)*

In Case of Emergency:
Discretionary Tzedakah Money
For Youth Group Presidents

By Ari Newman
GARIN MITZVAH NETWORK, Inc.
14 Upton Rd.
Providence, RI 02906
401-861-3474

FOR IMMEDIATE RELEASE...
August 5, 1994, Jerusalem

All the hands went up.

The sixty teenagers raised their hands when answering the question: "Who has ever talked a friend out of suicide?" This was the norm this past Summer.

THIS IS AN APPEAL AND WILL BE DIRECT AND TO THE POINT.

While working with Danny Siegel this past Summer, I met, and launched Tzedakah projects with over 600 teenagers from North America. One out of two will raise their hands to tell me that they have talked a friend out of suicide. Perhaps the Talmud is right when it says, "If the eye only had the power to see, no human being could handle all the harmful things in the world." (Berachot 6a) And perhaps this is why we don't think to ask our children such questions.

The second part of the problem is that when Danny and I ask the question, "Whose parent is in a lifesaving profession?" ONLY THE DOCTORS' KIDS WILL RAISE THEIR HANDS — not the teachers' kids nor the social workers' kids. If this continues to be the case for our nice Jewish boys and girls with strong Jewish educations, then I'll be the first to say that we have failed as Jewish educators.

So, let's start with one lifesaving act — talking friends out of suicide — and help them, the talkers, on their way. Let's assume that the non-social workers (the students) can prevent only 10% of the suicides in our high schools. (I believe the percentage is much higher, but I'll play the cynic. Then let's connect with the people who have the power — the teens.

Listening to the kids, it is quite clear that students often will go to a peer for the "big problems" before going to a Rabbi, Youth Director, etc. In addition, although many schools have peer support/peer mediator groups, the teens are telling us that such programs simply aren't enough. While the ear is very much needed, sometimes critical cash can make the miracles happen.

I know from my United Synagogue Youth experience that when the regional presidents gather annually to allocate hundreds of thousands of dollars to Tzedakah, for some, this moment is a life changing experience. Well, let's give the same opportunity to all teen leaders, locally as well as nationally. Let's start discretionary funds for our youth group and student council Presidents. The students tell us that the money is needed, and kids are falling through cracks because the money isn't there. (All this ignores the incredible educational experience it is for a teen to be trusted with funds and the challenge of making every penny count!) The suicide example is perhaps the most shocking; however, there are others such as poverty, pregnancies, drugs, loss of dignity, etc. Sit with the teens and ask them how much money could be used; you'll be somewhat shocked by their replies.

Therefore, my fund is making an appeal (from now, August 5, 1994, 4:45 p.m. Jerusalem time) for contributions that will be forwarded for teen discretionary funds. Every time $100 comes in specifically for this project, a teen leader will be selected and a check written. A supplemental guide is currently being developed for the teens who will administer these funds. However, there are no restrictions as to how the funds may be used — except "every penny must make a difference." (Don't be led astray by all the stupid people who say that teens can't be trusted with money.) An accounting will be asked of the leaders at the end of the year to determine where money is most needed and for what types of problem — no names, for reasons of confidentiality.

To contribute, make checks payable to GARIN MITZVAH NETWORK and make sure they state "Discretionary Fund". All checks should be mailed to the above address and are tax deductible. HINT: I'd like to give out $1,000 before Yom Kippur.

TO CONCLUDE with another passage from the Talmud (Shabbat 11a): "Any pain rather than pain in the heart." With these new funds, when a kid knocks on the door black and blue and beaten and crying, ready to end it all, the other person can say, "sleep over and we'll rent movies and hang out all night". (Every night doors are knocked on throughout North America. Call the experts and they'll tell you what the teen suicide rate is.) Of course, fifteen dollars for movies will not solve any of this kid's problems, but it will heal the pain in the heart. All too often the wrists are cut and the pills are downed because of the pain in the heart. In the morning, when the movies are over and the tears are dried, (using the supplemental manual) the Lifesaver will be able to contact the much needed "expert".

We've taught our kids that they have power with their hearts, minds, and hands; now let's complete the process and give them the cash. Wouldn't it be a real shame for a kid to die simply because another kid couldn't say, "Come, we'll watch movies instead"?

Setting Our House in Order

I. The Lyrical Introduction

It would be good to begin this piece by remembering that the word "ecology" comes from the Greek word "oikos," meaning "house". As we read the words, it will remind all of us that we are living together in one big house, and that, Jewishly speaking, Shalom Bayit-Peace in the Home, depends on whether or not we create mansions and estates out of hovels and scroungy-looking and litter-strewn vacant lots, and whether or not, ultimately, the world will be a clean, well-lighted, and Menschlich place in which we can do our Mitzvah work. In that environment, we will be refreshed each day and have the vigor needed to perform the Jewish and human tasks at hand.

II. The 1990's — Ecology and the Jews

The decade of the Nineties goes beyond having just a fashionably passing interest in ecology. More and more people are becoming aware of the growing desperation of the problem. Every day our consciousness is being raised as to how much we are all in this together, and that the damage done somewhere ostensibly far away from home is really something quite proximate and immediate, something that will hurt us and the generations that will inhabit this universe after we are gone.

An oil spill over there, somehow will play into our own lives over here. They are usually a little far from us geographically, but we *know* it is hurting us wherever we are.

The litterers down the road bother us more than oil spills. They are closer. We understand that — somehow — *their* junk by *our* roadside is going to hurt us up the road where we live, which turns out to be only a couple of hundred yards or a few miles away.

The tree-cutters in the distant jungles, we learn, not only effect the exotic, wild, and gorgeous creatures in Brazil, but somehow, we, too, will pay a much higher price than we had thought if the tree cutting is done poorly or wastefully. But, Rainforest Crunch and all, that, too, is far away.

Second-hand smoke hurts the non-smoker in the room....Now *that's* when we really get particularly touchy about ecology.

We become more sensitive, it seems, when whatever happens is going to harm us *personally*. And that's all right. So the woeful world won't be set aright for the highest-of-the-high reasons. It'll happen more selfishly.

If that's what it takes to get more Mitzvahs rolling, that's fine, too, as long as things get fixed.

There are cynics who say people only do Mitzvahs for selfish reasons anyway. We'll even grant them some small nod of assent.

III. *Tzedek*/צדק-*Justice*, *Tzedakah*/צדקה-*Doing The Right Thing*

We should be thankful for these trends, or rather, these ecological concerns that are much more pressing than mere trends. If they were only trends, then when they would fall out of fashion, we would be, (as they say in Yiddish) *off tzalochus*, out of luck. We should hope that ecology will remain in fashion and beyond trendiness for many years into the human future, until there will be no more fears of disappearing ozone layers, plutonium hazards, and landfills bursting with industrial wastes that poison for nearly-forever.

What we have here, I believe, is a good old-fashioned case of Tzedek and Tzedakah. Something is wrong on this planet, and Tzedek/צדק-Justice can help set it right, and Tzedakah/צדקה-Doing the Right Thing can make it even "righter". It happens every time we pitch in with our clean-ups and lawsuits against the polluters and our pressure-politicking and boycotting, and because we do these things, we can literally hope to breathe more easily.

But, as is often true in the earlier stages of enthusiastic revolutions, some aspects of the ecological movement seem off the mark. For example, it feels uncomfortable listening to some Jews still ranting and raving about the few homeless and hungry people who might be phonies, who play the system for a sucker, the handful who might intimidate us on the street, and then somehow let slide with a sigh of "Oh, well!" the scandals of the Savings and Loans. They are both issues of Tzedek, and our *Jewish* reactions should be fine-tuned differently: (1) For poor and hungry and homeless people, Jews are supposed to refrain from berating the hungry people, the homeless people (even if there are some who deceive). Maimonides explicitly warns against that kind of arrogance. (2) With the lending institutions, all we need to do is pause for a moment and figure (a) how long we and our descendants will be paying for that one, and (b) how many times over the money lost in those crimes could have paid for the recovery of all hungry and homeless people (*and* for the re-settlement of refugees, *and* for the clean-up of toxic wastes, *and* for literacy campaigns, *and* for AIDS research, *and* for....)

But we are slower on the S&L's. It bothers us, and we might make a breakfast-table comment or do some low-key railing about the enormity of it all at some party, but we just don't seem to get our blood boiling as much as we do about endangered birds or seal pups (which *are* in danger and need to be cared for) or millions of styrofoam cups at Dunkin' Donuts (which *are* an issue).

What we have here is a problem of logic, and Talmudic logic at that.

IV. *Kal V'Chomer*-קל וחומר

Kal V'Chomer is a form of Talmudic reasoning.

It goes something like this: if something should not be done on Shabbat, then, *Kal V'Chomer*, it should not be done on Yom Kippur, since Yom Kippur is a much more important and weighty day in the Jewish calendar. Or, if we should respond to the need for clothes for a poor person, then, *Kal V'Chomer*, we should hurry to provide for food, since food is a much more pressing issue. Or, to give a third example, if Mrs. Fields can donate her leftover cookies and brownies to hungry people, your local bakery can certainly do it.

At this point, I would offer two examples of *Kal V'Chomer* in relation to the issues of the ecology movement:

(1) If we are so concerned for endangered species, we should always remember that — when it comes to fixing up this world — destroyers of animals are secondary to destroyers of people. Poachers who wipe out elephant herds for the tusk money need to be dealt with as severely as necessary to stop the outrageous slaughter. But savings and loan institutions that wipe people out, and HUD corruption machines that eat up the Life's savings of human beings need to be dealt with more severely and more immediately. No hungry hawk's, mustang's, or chimpanzee's pain will ever equal that of a human infant without milk. That is a *Kal V'Chomer*...because, it would appear to me, people are more weighty creatures in this world than animals are.

(2) When we read about companies that declare their product biodegradable, but the courts rule that their advertising text constitutes deceptive and false advertising, we should take that fact, and our anger over that deception, and shove the problem much higher up on our priority list of concerns. More of that happens every day than tree-cutters destroy rain forests. The more we accept the fact that people are excused for white-collar crimes (mis-labeled in conversation as "shenanigans" or "playing the game, all they did wrong was get caught" or sometimes "misdemeanors"), the more our house, our *oikos*, goes to ruin. And the less we will have true Shalom Bayit, peace in our home. That is a *Kal V'Chomer*.

V. The Siddur, Our Prayerbook

From our earliest childhood, many of us were taught that, if we drop a Siddur, a prayerbook, or Chumash, a volume of readings from the Torah, or any other holy book, when we pick it up, we kiss it. It is a delicate and lovely gesture and a very lovely symbol of our true affection and reverence for the sacred words contained in the books.

Recently, though, I have found this custom very unsettling, to the point where I am almost ready to stop doing it. *That* thought is even more unsettling, but I am so troubled by the fact that I lift the Siddur and Chumash with great love, respect, and care — to the point of kissing it before setting it gently down on the desk or table or back on the shelf — and that I *don't* do the same for *people* who have fallen down to the ground, I feel the act and the symbol have lost much of their meaning. That's a *Kal V'Chomer*. No Siddur feels the pain of the battered spouse with no safe place to flee, no Chumash knows the loneliness of the abandoned Elder with no one to talk to, or the person with AIDS starving to death because no one will come in and cook for them at home.

It seems that, at least in this case, we Jews lost the skill of our Talmudic logic.

Now, it is true that curricula are being written to teach ecology, and I very much encourage educators to continue to do that. They'll teach the best of texts, including the one (Ecclesiastes Rabba 7:28) where God takes Adam around the Garden of Eden and says, "This is all yours. Take care of it. If you dirty it, you will have to clean it up. *I'm* not going to do it for you." And that's just one of the many powerful Jewish sources waiting to be gathered, anthologized, taught, learned and acted on.

The teachers will give Jewish insight on pollution and smog, on infection and contagion, on earth and sky and air and water, but without this most basic human *Kal V'Chomer*, it simply won't be enough.

VI. *The Address and Phone Number.*

I usually give an address or phone number of some Mitzvah hero or some awesome project already solving a particular Tzedakah problem. This issue is too new, too much on the rise. I have no addresses or phone numbers.

If someone will establish the Jewish Commission on Tzedek/Tzedakah Kal V'Chomers, we will all welcome the address and phone number, which will be published in some future article or book.

It's time, high time.

Why Congregation B'nai Israel of Millburn, NJ, Sold a Sefer Torah
(And a Second One)

I. Why, After More Than Thirty Years on the Road,
I Still Travel and Lecture

People ask me — after thirty years of traveling and lecturing in just about every Jewish community in North America except Little Rock, Boise, and a few others — they ask (and kindly), "Doesn't it get boring after so long?"

The answer is a definite and emphatic, "No!" On one level, there are always interesting things to see in every city and town. In New Orleans, I always enjoy a walk in the French Quarter. In Denver, the mountains never fail to dazzle me with their beauty. In Miami and Boca Raton and Ft. Lauderdale in the Winter — well, who would turn down two or three or four days in the sunshine while everyone in Detroit and Chicago and particularly Minneapolis is freezing?

And, of course, there is that lovely perk: the frequent flyer programs. I have all those glorious air miles adding up in my accounts waiting for me to cash in and take a week away in Hawaii where I can study Torah more intensively and with a clearer mind, of course. It should be obvious to all how much more insight one gets into some difficult Talmudic passages while sitting in a beach chair on the sands of Maui or admiring God's wonders with a snorkeling mask and fins.

On a more serious level, there are two essential reasons why the travel never bores me: (1) I meet great Jews wherever I go — quiet Jews doing their Mitzvah work without anyone knowing, Jews with incredibly sensitive hearts, young Jews and very young Jews, old Jews and middle-aged Jews that perform acts of Tzedakah and caring lovingkindness so delicate and gentle, it moves me to a sense of great joy to hear of them and their work or to see them in action or to hear them tell their stories, their faces radiant, and (2) there is always something new and exciting in the Torah study and/or world of Mitzvah work that comes out of the week-end or the seminar or evening lecture. I can recall many times when, after working with a Talmudic text for five or ten years and reaching a dead end, someone in the audience or class comes up with a fine piece of breakthrough wisdom that releases my creative energies. Or, after a talk, someone comes up to me and tells me of a particular Mitzvah project he or she is involved in that fires my imagination. All this happens, always, besides the hundreds of people who have been my hosts and hostesses, who have opened their homes to me, taken me in, and shown me many kindnesses. I have become an expert in the Mitzvah of Hachnassat Orchim-Hospitality because of the many, many people who have been very good to me.

After all these years on the road, I have discovered that my post-roadtrip exhaustion is as much emotional as physical. We — my students and myself — have been through intense and profound times together, and the rewards are *very* great. Not infrequently I will remember a specific audience or incident years later: the room, the nosherei (of course), the give-and-take, the moment of revelation, and the person who opened my eyes and mind to some vastly warm and wonderful aspect of Torah and Mitzvot.

II. *One Particular Week-end in the Fall of 1991*

If someone were to open my Macintosh and go to the file, "Calendar," he or she would scan a long list of dates and places I have to be during High Season, September to June. To the casual observer (and to myself before I do the programs), all of the places may seem the same: somewhere to be at a specific time to do such-and-such a talk on Mitzvah heroes or 116 Practical Mitzvah Suggestions or Bar and Bat Mitzvah Kinderlach and What They Can Do to Make This World a Nicer, More Menschlich Place to Live. But by late Spring, as I begin to review the season's travels, each visit stands out with a distinctive texture and tone. This is the story of one of those trips a few months ago, and a relatively simple story it is — once you think about it:

Steven Bayar is the Rabbi of Congregation B'nai Israel in Millburn, New Jersey. I have known him for a number of years, and, indeed, he used to live right next door to my publisher and was kind enough to let us use some shed space to store cartons of my books. His wife, Ilene, is another one of my friends, a fine educator, and someone who had had me do some talks for her students at different times and in different places where she was the principal. So when I got a call from the Bayars to come up to Millburn for a week-end, I was delighted.

As we developed the week-end plans, it sounded to me fairly standard: this talk and that, and ideas for short-term and long-term follow-up once I had gone home on Sunday, and, naturally, the anticipation of meeting a few of the fine Jews I described above. In brief, the usual staggering stuff.

As the week-end actually developed, though, it became clear that this particular congregation was ready for some more extraordinary possibilities. The President, Naomi Eisenberger, left no doubt that whatever Mitzvah projects I might suggest, they were ready to do it. This was confirmed on Saturday night when we established a synagogue Mitzvah Committee, complete with a preliminary list of initial programs to begin *now* rather than *later*, that all-encompassing and oft-disappointing cover-up term.

With such a positive atmosphere, at one point in the week-end I made a suggestion I had made a few times before, reminding the congregants that the project must be done with the utmost sense of respect: Sell one of the Torahs and use the money for Tzedakah.

It wasn't my idea. It came from the Talmud (Megillah 27a) and was later codified in the Shulchan Aruch:

מוכרים בהכ"נ וכן שאר דברים שבקדושה
ואפי' ס"ת
להספקת תלמידים או להשיא יתומים בדמיו

"We may sell a synagogue, and, similarly, all holy objects — even a Sefer Torah — in order to provide for students of Torah or to marry off orphans with the proceeds of the sale. (Orach Chaim 153:6)

The Tosafot — medieval Talmudic commentators — add that the money may also most certainly be used for redeeming captives. (Bava Batra 8b) How striking a passage in our tradition! As holy as a Sefer Torah may be, if the human needs are so great out there in the Big World, we are permitted to sell a scroll to raise money to meet those needs.

Some synagogues found the idea appealing.

No group has disagreed: there is never enough Tzedakah money to provide food, clothing, shelter, and jobs for all poor people, for all people who need scholarships, for access for all people with disabilities (large print Siddurim cost money, special sound systems cost money, interpreters for the deaf cost money, making bathrooms accessible is *very* expensive), for resettlement of Jews from the former Soviet Union, Ethiopians Jews, Syrian Jews...

A few synagogues — after their initial astonishment — liked the idea very much.

But only B'nai Israel of Millburn *did something about it..*   And this is what they did:

1. Within a week, the Board had given its preliminary approval to sell a Torah and set up an endowment fund and use the proceeds of the sale for Tzedakah projects to be supervised by the Mitzvah Committee.

2. Shortly thereafter, final approval was given.

3. Shortly thereafter, a specific Torah was selected.

4. A while later, a Sofer (Scribe) was hired to examine the Torah to insure its Kosher status.

5. Shortly thereafter, B'nai Israel began to pass the word around that a Sefer Torah was now available for some congregation to purchase, perhaps a synagogue just getting started that would need one for Shabbat, holidays, and Monday and Thursday morning Minyan.

6. A while later, another congregation inquired, discussions began, and the sale was completed.

7. The congregation that purchased the Torah did what many congregations do: they sold letters, words, and sections of the Torah, and the proceeds of their efforts went into a Tzedakah endowment, too.

8. Another congregation purchased a second Torah from B'nai Israel.

III. Symbol and Need

The commentators — and common sense — tell us that all other efforts should be made to raise the necessary Tzedakah money before considering taking such drastic action as selling a Torah. Yet one more Tzedakah campaign is a prerequisite.

The next step might be selling the silver from the Torahs. This would have to be done, of course, with the consent of the original donors if there were individuals or families who gave the breastplate or crown or pointers. Sale of these items must also be done with utmost respect and care.

Ultimately, the selling of a Torah, or the silver, or other precious synagogue objects, should be explained and conducted *not* as a symbolic act. Rather, it is as real as can be, the result being that many in need will benefit.

For one set of beneficiaries — those who need scholarships for Torah study — there is a particularly important quote, "Since we may sell a synagogue to purchase a Torah and other texts, we may certainly sell it (a Torah) for the purpose of Torah study, since what good is it buying texts and a Torah if we are not able to study from them? [In this case, by comparison,] the student is more important than the Torah, as is stated in the last chapter of Tractate Makkot." (Rabbi Yosef Karo [1488-1575, in Bet Yosef to Tur 153] quoting Rabbeynu Asher [1250-1357, Teshuvah Clal 13, Section 14]

And what applies to Torah study certainly would apply to redeeming captives, i.e., securing the release and resettlement of Jews from the former Soviet Union and the freeing of other Jews in danger.

And, as for providing for the needs of orphans: there are so many Jews today that might be considered orphans: Jewish elders on fixed incomes and living alone, Jews in need of hospice, and Jewish battered spouses seeking refuge, just to mention a few — Tzedakah money could be put to immediate use.

Many of our people who are otherwise beyond our reach could benefit.

IV. *"Call me sometime."*

Actually, the Rabbi and members of the synagogue, and Naomi in particular, call me frequently. They want me to know about their latest projects and the progress being made on the programs we launched that Saturday night in the Fall.

And I call them frequently, the Rabbi or a congregant or Naomi. Whenever some difficult or unusual or a just-run-of-the-mill Tzedakah project comes my way, they are among the first I call, because I know it will be taken care of in the all-important framework of *now*. *Later* doesn't seem to be part of their thinking.

And if you would like to look into doing the same — selling one of your Sifray Torah for the sake of Tzedakah work — call Rabbi Bayar at 201-379-3811 or Naomi Eisenberger at 201-763-9396. They will review the entire process with you, from Alef to Tav, and with the great Simcha appropriate to such a Mitzvah.

Appendix I
Mitzvah Videos

The following is a small sampling of particularly moving and insightful videos that I have discovered over the past few years. Most are brief and can be used as trigger films for discussion or as a final note to a talk on Tzedakah, to summarize exactly what is meant by a particular Tzedakah project or what a person who lives the Life of Mitzvahs fully looks like, talks like, and acts like in his or her daily actions. As with my other resource materials, I recommend each person assemble his or her own list of audio-visual resources that will bring home the message of Tzedakah.

The rating system is simple:

No asterisk means "Highly recommended".

* means "Stunning, moving, and essential,"

** means, "Astonishing, revolutionary, a *must* resource to do major World Repair."

1. **Animals in Hospitals: Fabulous, incredible! Beautiful to behold! Dogs, cats, turtles, birds, chinchillas — some resident pets, some visitors *in hospitals*. This goes beyond old age homes. *A must!* Call The Delta Society, 1-800-869-6898 (V/TTY), fax: 206-235-1076. $22 + shipping. (Send $30.)

*2. **Mitzvah Dogs** trained to work with individuals with disabilities. Ask for the tape about Travis Stout and his dog, Kosmic. My reaction on seeing the video for the 1st time and for the 100th time was, "Wow!" Canine Companions for Independence, 1215 Sebastopol Rd., Santa Rosa, CA 95407, 707-579-1985, fax: 528-0146. (Send a $25 contribution.) 6 minutes. They also have other wonderful, instructive tapes.

*3. **Mitzvah Horses:** Fabulous — hippotherapy (special physiotherapy on horseback) at the Therapeutic Riding Club of Israel, near Netanya. Shows individuals with a wide range of disabilities taking their riding lessons, and the personal reactions of the riders to the experience. Miraculous stuff. (About 15 minutes.) ($18 contribution to Ziv Tzedakah Fund.) Contact: Naomi Eisenberger, 384 Wyoming Ave., Millburn, NJ 07041, 201-763-9396.

*4. **Jewish Poverty in Montreal**: The story of the lives of a few of Montreal's 18,000 poor Jews. Very powerful! Free, but send $18 contribution. 13 minutes. Danyael Cantor, 514-345-2600, fax: 735-8972. (Federation CJA).

5. **Miracle Workers**: A "48 Hours" show, five or six segments on amazing people and Mitzvah projects; 2 or 3 superb, teachable pieces, including the Mitzvah Monkeys and incredible ophthalmologists who fly around the world to do their good work. 1-800-338-4847. $33+.

*6. **The Giraffe Project**: "It's Up To Us". Giraffes — people who stick their necks out to make good things happen in the world. 1-360-221-

7989, fax: 228-7817. $30.00; $24.00 if you are a member of the project. (Sign up. They also have fine curriculum materials.) 28 min.

*7. **Trevor Ferrell** (the boy who feeds homeless people in Philadelphia), 6 min., excellent, the best: $25 contribution to "Trevor's Endeavors," send to Frank Ferrell, Box 21, Gladwyne, PA 19035, 610-642-4633.

*8. **Shelter Boy**: *Very* powerful 12-15 minute TV segment on a 12-year-old boy who lives in a shelter with his family. Contact the Union of American Hebrew Congregations (UAHC) Religious Action Center 202-387-2800. Teaching materials about the film are also available.

9. **Bet Tzedek:** 6 segments about people who were saved from ruin by the *pro bono* lawyers of this marvelous project in LA. Narrated by the actress, Bea Arthur. $18.00 contribution to Bet Tzedek, c/o Ralph Gottlieb, 145 S. Fairfax Ave., LA, CA 90036, 213-939-0506, fax: 939-1040. 14 minutes. (Another video came out in 1994.)

10. **Shalva:** Marvelous project for children with disabilities in Jerusalem. 8 minutes, $18 contribution to Ziv. Contact Naomi Eisenberger for tapes (see #3 above.)

11. **Best Boy**: Oscar-award winner. Documentary story of an adult Jewish man's transition from living with his parents to a group home. Check film catalogues for availability

12. **Breaking Through Denial**: A workshop and documentary footage on Jews and alcoholism. About 30 minutes.

13. **A Test Of Love:** An incredible film based on the true story of a young woman erroneously placed in an institution as an infant — they diagnosed her as being a retarded child. Upon reaching majority, she sues the institution for the right to live on the outside...and wins! Beautifully done. The movie is sometimes listed as **Annie's Coming Out.** (There's a book by the same name.) Consult video stores and catalogues.

Appendix II
Synagogue Mitzvah Committees

For front-line Mitzvah work, there are many groups who devote themselves to reaching individuals and families. Sometimes Jewish Family Service is the best way to insure everyone will have enough Passover food to have a joyous holiday. Where there is a Jewish community chaplain, that person is often the one to serve as your critical link to working with Jewish prisoners or families with specific short-term or long-term needs. Jewish hospice groups exist in many places. Congregational sisterhoods or men's clubs cover many other areas, as do B'nai B'rith, National Council of Jewish Women, Hadassah, Jewish Federation Young Leadership or Women's Division or the Board. In many, many situations, a meeting with the congregation's rabbi produces the best possibility for an individual's involvement.

Every community is different. In some places, the "juiciest" Mitzvah work might be accomplished by the youth groups or by a spontaneously-formed informal gathering of friends within the context of the Jewish Community Center. So, too, with friends who simply get together, see a need, and set themselves the task of doing whatever is necessary to solve the problem.

In recent years, there has been a revival of what I call synagogue Mitzvah Committees. They go by different names: Social Action or Social Justice Committee, Chessed Committee, Tikkun Olam Committee. Whatever the name, they are a marvelous vehicle for individuals who want to make New Americans more comfortable in their new environment, who want to make certain people get rides to community events, who make sure the kids get to religious school if — God forbid — one of the parents is in the hospital for an unexpectedly long stretch.

Over the past number of years, I have met members of many of these Mitzvah committees. Their enthusiasm for their work, their efficiency in cutting through red tape to solve the problems, their human kindness has impressed me greatly. I offer my partial list as an example of what I have seen — keeping in mind that chairpersons leave and are replaced or that Mitzvah committees have more active and less active years. Call one or two of them to exchange ideas about what your respective committee are doing, or if you want to start a similar committee in your own congregation. Most of all, make a personal list appropriate to your own community and your own interests in direct Mitzvah work. (Since many of the committees have regular columns in the synagogue bulletin, ask to be put on the mailing list.)

It's good for everyone.

1. Congregation Har Shalom, Potomac, MD, Robert Sunshine, 301-340-2787.

2. Temple Shalom, Succasunna, NJ: Rabbi Joel Soffin, 201-584-5666 (o). *(He is also one of the experts on getting special sound systems for hearing impaired people into synagogues.)*

3. The Marlboro Jewish Center, Marlboro, NJ: Anita Bogus, 201-536-3358 (h), 201-431-1777 (o).

4. B'nai Israel, Millburn, NJ: Naomi Eisenberger (President), 201-763-9396 (h), 226-3351 (w).

5. Temple B'nai Israel, Boca Raton, FL, (CFJ-Committee for Justice): Rita Bogen, 407-369-3732. *(Ask about their Tzedakah Newsletter, "Tikkun Olam".)*

6. Kehilath Jeshurun (KJ) in Manhattan (Rabbi Haskel Lookstein): Robert Leifert, 212-427-1000 (o).

7. Temple Beth Am, Miami, FL: Sheila Stieglitz, 305-271-9000 (w), 305-667-5353 (h).

8. Beth El Tzedakah Collective, Sudbury, MA: Robert Lindenberg, 508-443-5483.

9. Ohr Kodesh, Chevy Chase, MD: Zelda Segal, 9412 Linden Ave., Bethesda, MD 20814, 301-530-9492.

10. Congregation Ohev Shalom, Orlando, FL: Saul and Lea Zatz, 407-629-4085.

11. Temple Israel, Omaha, NE: Judy and Barry Siff, 402-493-4112.

Glossary

(H=Hebrew; Y=Yiddish)

Bema/Bima (H): The synagogue platform where the rabbi and cantor stand to lead religious services.

Boker (H): Morning. "Boker Tov" - "Good Morning."

Challah (H, pl.: Challot): The twisted loaves of white bread traditionally eaten on the Sabbath and holidays.

Chassidic (H): referring to a Jewish religious movement founded in Eastern Europe in the 18th century by the Baal Shem Tov. Chassidism is known for its sense of joy and ecstasy, particularly manifested in prayer, song, and dance.

Chumashim (H, sing.-Chumash): printed copies of the Torah.

Gelt (Y): money.

Havdalah (H): the ceremony at the end of the Sabbath and holidays that makes a separation between the holy days and the secular days.

Hilchot (H): The Laws of...

Hamentaschen (Y): 3-cornered, hat-shaped, prune-or-poppyseed pastries baked for the holiday of Purim.

Kal V'Chomer (H): a form of Talmudic logical reasoning.

Kavod (H): dignity, respect.

Kiddush (H): the blessing over wine, also the food served in synagogue after Sabbath services.

Kippot (H-pl., s.: Kippah): small, round head coverings worn by religious Jews.

Kashrut (H): The Jewish dietary laws.

Kosher (H): literally "fit," "appropriate". Food that meets the requirements of the Jewish dietary laws.

Kup (Y): head. "Areingefallen in Kup," "Fell into someone's head, suddenly occurred to someone."

Machzor (h): High Holiday Prayerbook.

Matzah/Matza (H): unleavened bread eaten on Passover.

Megillat Esther (H): The Biblical Book of Esther, read in synagogue on the Purim holiday.

Mensch (Y; adj.-Menschlich; abs.-Menschlichkeit): an upright, responsible, decent, caring, compassionate person.

Midrash (H): Jewish literature from the first 7 or 8 centuries of the Common Era containing stories, aphorisms, and narratives. Also, any non-legal portion of the Talmud. Also used to refer to a specific story or tale.

Minyan (H): a quorum of 10 people, needed for the recitation of public prayers and certain other Jewish ceremonies.

Mishigossen (Y): idiosyncrasies.

Mishnah (H): the earlier portion of the Talmud, edited around the year 200 C.E.

Mishnah Torah (H): Maimonides' 12th Century Jewish Law Code.

Mishpat (H): Justice.

Mitzvah (H): literally "commandment" or "instruction" — good deeds done by people according to the prescriptions of traditional Jewish texts, such as visiting the sick, comforting mourners, and giving Tzedakah. In this book, Mitzvah is usually synonymous with Tzedakah.

Parve (Y): food that is neither milk nor meat.

Purim (H): Jewish holiday celebrating the victory of the Jews of Persia over the wicked Haman. The holiday is celebrated with great joy, dancing, parades, masks, and merrymaking.

Rabbanit (H): a Rabbi's wife.

Rebbi (H-Y): teacher *par excellence*, not necessarily a rabbi. Also, a leader of a Chassidic sect.

Rosh HaShana (h): the Jewish New Year holiday.

Shabbat (H, Y=Shabbas): the Sabbath. "Shabbat Shalom," a Shabbat greeting — "A peaceful Shabbat to you."

Shlep (Y): haul, drag.

Shoah (H): the Holocaust.

Shulchan Aruch (H): major code of Jewish Law.

Siddur (H, pl.: Siddurim): a prayerbook.

Simcha (H): joy, a joyous occasion.

Simcha Shel Mitzvah (H): the joy of doing Mitzvahs.

Sukkah (H): a flimsy boothlike structure where traditional Jews live during the days of the Sukkot Festival.

Sukkot/Succot (H): the Fall festival celebrating a good harvest and commemorating God's kindness to the Children of Israel during their wanderings in the wilderness.

Talmud (H): an immense compendium of discussions, tales, aphorisms, legal give-and-take, and insights about Judaism, developed in Jewish academies (Yeshivas) during the first five centuries of the Common Era.

Tchatchka (Y): a toy.

Tikkun/Tikun (H): fixing up, repairing. Tikkun Olam=repairing the world.

Torah (H): literally "teaching". Originally meaning the Five Books of Moses, expanded to include the entirety of Jewish study and learning. "To talk Torah" is to discuss these texts.

Tov (H): good.

Tzaddik (H): a Righteous Person.

Tzedakah (H): the distinctly Jewish method of performing charitable acts. From the word "Tzedek," Justice.

Tzedek (H): Justice.

Yid (Y, pl.-Yiddn): A Jew.

Yom Kippur (H): The Day of Atonement.

Ziess (Y): sweet.

Ziv (H): radiance.

Notes to the Chapters

The Helen Keller of Israel

[1]DPT stands for "diphtheria," "pertussis" [whooping cough], and "tetanus," a standard immunization for infants.

[2]Shoshana, the Samuels, and Israelis pronounce her name "Veinshtock".

[3]The Hebrew word for "table". My teacher, Dr. Abraham Gittelson, pointed out to me how astonishing Shoshana's and Yossi's achievement was. "Table" is a difficult concept to grasp: legs or some other support, a top, etc.

[4]Or it could have been on his shoulder or chest or arm or back of his head....He can read anywhere he can feel someone's fingers spelling out the words. I just don't recall from the way Kalman told me the story where this particular word was spelled on Yossi's body.

[5]Kalman and Malky have founded their own project for exceptional children in Jerusalem, שלוה-Shalva. Among other things, children with all kinds of special needs come to their place in the Har Nof section of the city for a variety of activities. Some USY Israel Pilgrims have had a chance to visit during the Summer. You are welcome to call Kalman or Malky and arrange a visit of your own next time you are in Israel: 02-651-9505 or 651-8260.

[6]I met a young man — President of his Solomon Schechter Day School class, who described the good things the students would do when they would visit the local Jewish old age home. It was exhilarating to hear, but there was something disturbing about his summary of events. When I asked him to describe the residents they went to visit, he gave me the impression that the students thought that most of them were essentially zombies. I explained to him that he and the other students had to re-examine their observations. They had to learn to sort out which individuals might have irreparable *organic* problems, and which ones might seem listless or disoriented for other reason: loneliness, no will to live, lack of activity, etc. Once the students reviewed that aspect of their work, they could then expand their methods of enlivening them....by computers, by dressing up as clowns and putting on a show, by having permanent pets at the home, or by any other means at their disposal.

[7]The Talmud often refers to blind people as סגי נהור, i.e., "people who are full of light."

[8]Contact Marianne Klingel, 813-441-1790.

[9] I frequently use the archaic English term "Elders" for its connotative power to communicate a sense of respect and wisdom acquired through years of Life's experiences. A passage in the Talmud (Kiddushin 33a) expresses the idea quite clearly:

איסי בן יהודה אומר
מפני שיבה תקום
ואפילו כל שיבה במשמע

Issi ben Yehuda says,
The verse, "You shall rise before the Elders" (Leviticus 19:32)
applies to *all* old people."

    I was recently at The Temple, Congregation B'nai Jehudah, in Kansas City. During a break in the week-end's activities, I had the opportunity to admire the windows from the old synagogue building that have preserved in the more modern present structure. All of them, except one, had English and Hebrew terms that corresponded exactly to each other. "Shabbat" in English was the equivalent of "שבת" in the Hebrew. The one exception was for Old Age, the Hebrew was "סיני- Sinai," implying insight, inspiration, and teachers of the Torah of Life. In the same Talmudic passage quoted above, Rabbi Yochanan explains why he would rise before all Elders, "כמה הרפתקי עדו עלייהו-How many experiences these people have had in their lifetimes!"

    "Senior" and "senior citizen" never appealed to me.

The Poster

[1]1313 Fifth St., SE, Box 84, Minneapolis, MN 55414, 612-379-3858 (voice/TTY), 612-379-5972 (fax).

The Wilderness Inquiry people know the reality of people with disabilities very well. I got to know about Wilderness Inquiry because of an article someone sent me. Another recent piece I received is about the Worldwide Disability Solutions Group, Apple Computer, Inc. (1-800-776-2333.) This division of Apple will send a reprint of a special advertising section from *Business Week*, May 30, 1994, which is filled with insight about opportunities in the workplace for people with disabilities. One particular statistic brought home the message very powerfully: Robert J. Eaton, CEO of Chrysler Corporation states, "....it's estimated that more than 7 million mobility-impaired people with mobility impairments who *can't* use public transportation *could* drive a vehicle — if it were converted to meet their special needs." (They have a program called Physically Challenged Assistance Program (P-CAP) which covers this are of the automobile industry. 1-800-255-9877. General Motors has a Mobility Program, and the company will send a videotape called "On the Move Again". 1-800-323-9935, 1-800-TDD-9935 ([TDD=TTY].) Apple will also send a very useful diskette about adaptability of computer hardware and software programs for people with disabilities. Call The Apple Computer Disability Solutions Store, 1-800-600-7808, 1-800-755-0601 (TTY).

How to Solve All the World's Problems (Well Almost All of Them)
    By Making Just One Phone Call
[1]*Intermountain Jewish News*, February 28, 1992.
[2]The North American Riding for the Handicapped Association.

The Mighty Mitzvah Horses of Israel
[1] There is good news, though. Canine Companions also named one of their puppies "Tzedakah". Mr. Hudson writes in the same report, and I quote, "Tzedakah was scheduled for a July turn in. However, his puppy raiser chose to return him a little early. He has passed through all preliminary procedures and is beginning his training as I write this letter. It is too early in his training to report more at this time." Tzedakah's fans are rooting hard for him, and I hope Mr. Hudson's next letter will include a picture of him happily matched with a human partner, ready to embark on a life of opportunity and independence for his owner. For information, contact Canine Companions in Santa Rosa, CA, 707-528-0830 (V/TTY).
[2] The Full Circle Program, Clearwater Marine Science Center, 249 Windward Passage, Clearwater, FL 34630, Ms. Marianne Klingel, 813-441-1790 X 21, fax: 813-442-9466.
[3] This was also the first Olympic Games that allowed women to compete in this event.
[4] I saw some of these gorgeous horses once, one Summer on the way back from Israel. Icelandic Airlines was offering a special layover deal, so I stopped in Reykjavik for a couple of days. I ate the salmon and herring, took the tours, saw the steam from the natural hot springs, enjoyed the people, and at some point, got to see the horses through the bus window. I never knew that 15 years later I'd have a desire to buy one or two of them. We had a lead recently, but our connections for buying a few of them from someone in Norway fell through.
[5] POB 33150, Denver, CO 80233, 1-800-369-RIDE or 303-452-1212, fax: 303-252-4610.

From Newspapers, Magazines, Letters from Friends,
    Or Just Heard or Seen Around
[1] *The Denver Post*, January 25, 1994.
[2] *The Chicago Tribune*, June 5, 1994.
[3] *The Rocky Mountain News*, May 15, 1994.
[4] *USA Weekend*, January 13-15, 1995 and April 15-17, 1994.
[5] *The Rocky Mountain News*, June 28, 1994.
[6] *The Jerusalem Post*, July 20, 1994.
[7] *The Washington Post*, November 9, 1994. Lest some readers think Mr. Dornberger was not in command of his faculties and could not take care of Mizzen, the two of them were also on

the nightly news. Both looked and acted well enough to take care of each other. (Mr. Dornberger's daughter, Deedee, also lives with them, but works during the day. Ms. Dornberger is the one who administers Mizzen's two insulin shots a day to keep the diabetes under control.)

[8] Note sent to me by the veterinarian. I have preserved the original spelling of the letter.

[9] *The Miami Herald*, March 2, 1995.

[10] *The Miami Herald*, no date on article sent to me.

[11] *The Toronto Globe and Mail, August 26, 1994.*

[12] *The Denver Post*, August 10, 1994.

[13] *The Miami Herald*, February 22, 1995. Article by Ms. Joan Fleischman.

[14] To contact Sandy at school for details and additional Mitzvah suggestions for school age children, call 914-948-3111

[15] *The Wall Street Journal, November 1, 1993.*

[16] *Canine Companions for Independence, Northeast Companion*, Winter, 1995. For more on the versatility of the Canine Companions, see "Mitzvah Economics," Section 7.

[17] For obvious reasons of confidentiality, we cannot reveal more details about the source of this piece.

[18] *The New York Times*, November 27, 1994.

Life Is The Good People

[1] There is a certain mystery to the human phenomenon of action. What exactly is the relationship of thought to action? What makes someone *do* something, anything, good or bad, exquisite, exalted, or tragic or merely disappointing? The very nature of thinking is a subject that has held the attention of great minds for centuries: philosophers, inventors, artists, psychologists and psychiatrists. All of this is worthy of study, but I would work backwards: starting with action, amassing data and trends, discovering patterns, and examining what brings people to *think* the way they do, as a result of the kinds of things they *do*.

[2] *After the Rain*, Town House Press, 1993.

How to Make Your Old Age Home a More Menschlich Place

[1] Sotah 46b:

וילך האיש ארץ החתים

ויבן עיר ויקרא שמה לוז

היא שמה עד היום הזה

תניא היא לוז שצובעין בה תכלת

היא לוז שבא סנחריב

ולא בלבלה נבוכדנצר ולא החריבה

ואף מלאך המות אין לו רשות לעבור בה

אלא זקנים שבה

בזמן שדעתן קצה עליהן

יוצאין חוץ לחומה והן מתים

[2] Dr. Thomas is no longer associated with Chase Memorial. The phone number listed is an independent office of The Eden Alternative, the concept behind revolutionizing old age homes. He is presently consulting and speaking and working exhaustively at getting Edenized homes everywhere (among other projects), and is very much in demand on the speakers' circuit.

[3] On the issue of "Who will take care of the birds?" — I wanted to know how much care is needed for a pair of canaries, parakeets, finches, or love birds. I went into a nearby pet shop and asked. The Person Behind the Counter said, (I am paraphrasing), "Changing the water, putting seed in the cup, putting fresh newspapers on the bottom of the cage, and, once a week, cleaning the cage itself." I also asked how much canaries would cost. He quoted me the price and told me they stock canaries bred by someone whose birds are particularly noted for their beautiful singing voices. He mentioned some kind of rating system or competition and assured me that these birds were *very* high up on the scale. I didn't even know there were such Canary Music Awards ratings.

Kids, of course, know the answer to "Who will take care of the birds?" When I talk to groups of students — the younger ones in particular — inevitably one of them says, "The residents."

Selections from the Friends of the Eden Alternative Newsletter

[1] Dr. William Thomas' column, "Three Nursing Home Plagues," Fall, 1994, Newsletter.

[2] Wendy Lustbader, *Counting on Kindness: Dilemmas of Dependency*, quoted in Fall, 1994, Newsletter.

[3] Maria K. Landy, Nursing Home Administrator (NHA), Senior Care Coordinator, at Tioga Nursing Facility, Waverly, NY, from *Guthrie Newsletter,* Spring, 1994, quoted in the Friends of The Eden Alternative Newsletter, Fall, 1994.

[4] Since the article was written by Ms. Landy, things are in place. One may now happily read, "Tioga is now home to...."

[5] Ms. Tish Thomas, Project Life Coordinator, on a visit to Chase Memorial Nursing Home. From the Fall, 1994, Friends of The Eden Alternative Newsletter.

The Confusion of Care, Treatment and Kindness, or
The Story of Kahlid the Kind

[1] University of Missouri Press, 1994. Dr. Thomas is a very gentle man, and yet, this is an extremely brutal tale. I hesitated to use it in this book, but I knew of no better piece to describe the absolute necessity to consider the needs of the other person. Though Dr. Thomas tells the parable in the context of revolutionizing the nature of old age homes, the principle is applicable to many other human situations. The starting point of the concept and reality of Human Dignity-כבוד, is recognizing the needs of *the other person.*

The Gerbils and Bunnies of Kindergarten

[1] The Delta Society is the best resource for any and all relevant material on the issue of animals and their interactions with humans. They are in Renton, WA, near Seattle, and welcome calls and inquiries. Call 1-800-869-6898 (V/TTY), fax: 206-235-1076. They have articles, videos, scientific studies, newsletters, phone numbers and addresses — everything you need to launch a project such as resident pets in housing for Elders. There isn't even a need for you to read this article. Just call them, and they will tell you everything you need to know.

This article was prepared after discussions with many people. I thank the following people for sharing their experiences and ideas with me: Dr. Diane Jacobstein, Dani and Aaron Shneyer, Professor Ron Wolfson, Dr. Jay Masserman, David and Darryl Kuperstock, Stewart and Irene Bolton, Laura Rubin, Arnie Draiman, Janet Rickles, and Ms. Regina Carmel's Consolidated Hebrew School's Shabbat morning classes at Congregation B'nai Israel of Rockville, MD.

[2] I began to consider writing this article when I was scholar in residence at a synagogue one recent week-end in New Jersey. Wherever I go to lecture I carry hand-out materials and Show and Tell items. Since I need storage space, and since some of the items are one of a kind, I look for a room that can be locked. At this one particular synagogue, as I was unpacking my suitcase and the cartons of other items sent on ahead of my arrival, I heard sounds, something like scurrying. I turned around, and there was a gerbil or guinea pig in a cage. (After I heard it, then saw it, I could smell it.) During the week this room was used for pre-school classes. Throughout the week-end, as I was teaching about the need to re-think our position on the environment and program at old age homes and independent housing units, I kept thinking about this animal and why it was there.

[3] I once met a woman whose conversation I enjoyed very much. She seemed pleasant, decent, and devoted to the Good Causes. I even thought, "Were she not so young, I would consider asking her out on a date." That was until she mentioned her pets: rats. As soon as she mentioned the magic word, she went on and on about them, no less affectionately than others speak of their kitty or hound. That put a quick and total stop to my musings.

[4] I had a lovely tour of the Louisiana bayous. Our guide spotted many an alligator — far away — and I suffered no adverse reaction, reptiles though they be.

5 A classic example is a Jewish residence for Elders in Omaha. I was brought into a sitting room by a staff member to see their bird, an Australian dove. As I expected, it was sitting in its cage, thinking whatever thoughts these doves think when they are left alone for a while. What surprised me (and most pleasantly so) was that the staff member took the bird out of the cage, had it sit on her hand, and then let it fly freely around the room. It was very exciting.

6 See, for example, "Hospital Dogs Raise Spirits, Not Infection Rates," S.M. Lander and J. Reid, *Hospital Infection Control,* December 19 (12) (1992), pp. 162-164. Also, *The Medical Post,* January 5, 1993, p. 12, "Infectious Disease Control Going to the Dogs". The latter article reviews a session at the Interscience Conference on Antimicrobial Agents and Chemotherapy. Dr. Sandra Wallace, chairwoman of the infection control committee at Huntington Memorial Hospital in Pasadena, CA, responded to the serious and penetrating questions raised by the attendees about the spread of disease from the dogs at their hospital. The study's statistics are impressive: Over a five year period, using 34 dogs and their human volunteers, making visits to 1,690 patients and totaling 3,281 visits — to quote Terry Murray, the author of the article, "the hospital had *no* [Italics mine] instances of zoonotic spread of disease to patients, and the dogs don't seem to have carried any bugs from one patient to another." (Stedman's *Medical Dictionary* defines "zoonosis" as: an infection or infestation shared in nature by man and lower vertebrate animals. An excellent guide to preventing zoonotic disease transmission is *Good for Your Animals, Good for You: How to Live and Work with Animals in Therapy and Activity Programs and Stay Healthy,* Available from Delta Society, 1-800-869-6898 (V/TTY), Fax: 206-235-1076. ["Nosos" is Greek for "disease".] Phone number of Huntington Memorial Hospital: 818-397-5000.

Denver Children's Hospital has a visiting dog program. Contact Ms. Donna Miedema, 303-861-8062.

Walter Reed Army Medical Center in Washington, DC, has an animal assisted therapy program in its Department of Psychiatry. Contact Ms. Brenda Botts, Department of Psychiatry, Recreation Therapy, Walter Reed Army Medical Center, 6900 Georgia Ave., NW, Washington, DC 20307-5001.

7 It's the old joke we used to tell when we were in elementary school. "What does a 500 pound canary say?" "Chirp!" In most cases, choosing a standard canary, i.e., one that has not been genetically altered by toxic waste in the water system, would suffice.

7a In the middle of editing and revising this article, the latest issue of *InterActions* (Vol. 13, No. 1, 1995) arrived. *InterActions* is the magazine of the Delta Society, and this particular issue was devoted to the topic of loneliness. The cover is marvelous: a man petting two white cockatoos with their heads resting on his shoulder. There are too many topics to list, but, to mention a few (a) Dr. Juana P. Lyon's Guest Editorial, "An Antidote to Loneliness," mentions the phrase "emotional atrophy," a very eloquent term. She also quotes Charles Schultz's famous line, "Happiness is a warm puppy." (b) Susan L. Duncan, RN, in her article, "Loneliness: A Health Hazard of Modern Times," reviews a number of books and studies. Among the points she makes: (1) "Physiologically, loneliness can trigger the same stress response as a broken leg. This causes our bodies to alter the production of hormones which in turn alters the function of many other systems in the body. (2) Looking at an aquarium filled with fish lowers blood pressure more than staring at a blank wall. (From *Language of the Heart,* Dr. James Lynch, N.Y., Basic Books, Inc., 1985.) (3) Various scientific definitions of loneliness are given. (4) A notice that the Delta Society will provide sample leases and policies for property owners that would encourage them to allow pets. Ms. Duncan also provides abundant references to articles and studies. Titles include, "Hospital Dogs Raise Spirits, Not Infection Rates," "Benefits and Liabilities of Pets for the Homeless," and "Intimacy, Domesticity and Pet Therapy with the Elderly: Expectation and Experience Among Nursing Home Volunteers". This issue of *InterActions* is a good point of departure for anyone who wants to launch pet projects in residences for the Elders.

7b This is also one of the points to be made when introducing computers for Elders — in old age homes, in independent apartments, or living in their own homes. Any time day or night they can't sleep, they will just turn the machine on and play with the graphics, write a story or letter, set up their calendar, play solitaire or poker against the house at Caesar's Palace, or do anything else they want to with this 20th Century wonder of wonders and Mitzvah tool.

On the issue of aquariums:

I recently heard from my friend, Rabbi Gerry Walter, that dentists, particularly pediatric specialists, have aquariums in their waiting room. Apparently watching the fish calms the nervous patient, a real advantage particularly when little children are waiting to have a cavity filled.

Carol Hutton — the Bird Woman of Indianapolis — has expanded her activities to include aquariums. She believes that they work well particularly for children and adults who have experienced mental problems. The sense of calm would be very therapeutic.

In addition, in the last few months I heard a very strange story about The Fish Channel on cable TV. As best as I can recall, the story goes like this — One channel did not produce enough shows for 24 hours of programming. The producers would fill in the empty time slots with a camera trained on a big aquarium. Hours on end, viewers would see nothing but swimming fish. The station's fortunes continued to spiral downward. Fewer and fewer programs came on screen, and more and more hours of swimming fish replaced them. Eventually the channel ran out of money and was about to close, when a number of calls and letters came in urging them not to shut down operations. The viewers found that sitting in their easy chair and watching the fish was very enjoyable and was a very calming influence in their harried lives. Thus, the story of The Fish Channel. Anyone who can track down the facts should write to me so I can know the full story.

[7c] My most recent occasion for reciting the blessing was when I bought a new printer for my computer. While I was talking to the friend on the phone, I began printing a few pages of text. I recited the blessing, and she answered the appropriate "Amen".

[8] See the chapter "From Newspapers, Magazines, Letters from Friends, Or Just Heard or Seen Around" where the story is told in full.

[8a] One would suspect that an eight-year-old child in a coma or a teen-ager seriously injured in a diving accident would not be denied *all* options for recovery. The element of prejudice is cause for worry.

I recall visiting a synagogue in the Berkshires. Among the many people I met was the oldest member of the Jewish community, a woman who had recently celebrated her 90th birthday. She appeared to be very much an active, alive person, and I was stunned to hear that just a year before she had begun to decline. Her many friends were certain it was an irreversible turn for the worse. I would have never suspected it. Why she had declined and why she recovered — the details — are merely details.

For more Marvelous Bird Tales, call the Bird Woman of Indianapolis, Carol Hutton: 317-630-3063 (daytime), 845-8829 (evenings). She has been bringing birds to Elders for several years and has an abundance of fine stories.

[9] The real problem, then, is teaching the reality of death, but that is another subject for other teachers and experts to study and explain.

[10] Several years ago, I was involved in a program for teen-agers who would go visit children in an institution for people with mental disabilities. At one point, the staff at the institution suggested we stop the visits, the reason being that the kids enjoyed our visits so much, it took them a long time to calm down, and they were disappointed if such high moments didn't happen all the time. It was a surprising suggestion that shocked some of our own staff. Some of the responses would be: (1) A constant state of calm, lack of stimulation — in some case, a stupor — is most certainly not the preferred human condition. (2) What are they doing with the kids the rest of the time that this is one of the few Great Highs in their lives? This is also a parallel argument for having resident pets rather than visiting pets. They are *always* there. (3) This is the reason why some institutions accept only *regularly scheduled* visits from outsiders, so the once-a-day or once-a-week rhythm can be counted on by the residents. I invite others to review the literature and set the record straight once and for all, particularly on point #1.

[10a] *InterActions*, the magazine of the Delta Society, Vol. 13, No. 1, 1995. Dr. Lyon, now retired, served as Manager, Program Development Operations, Aging and Adult Administration, Arizona Department of Economic Security.

[11] The Massachusetts Society for the Prevention of Cruelty to Animals (MSPCA, phone: 617-522-7400) has a wonderful pamphlet called "Pets in People Places — Responsible Pet Ownership in Multi-Unit Housing." Chapter 2, "Pets in Housing and the Law," explains the

essential legal material. Further investigation of the applicability to a specific housing project requires (a) reading the law, and related laws such as the Department of Housing and Urban Development rules of 1986 in the Code of Federal Regulations, found at 24CFR, Part 243, in their entirety, and/or (2) consulting experts who have experience in the field: veterinarians, humane societies, the Delta Society, and others.

11a Quoted in the MSPCA pamphlet mentioned in the previous footnote.

12 And similar housing situations for people with disabilities. An interesting comparative study might be — how many places have denied tenancy to a blind person with a guide dog vs. how many denied tenancy to Elders for having a pet.

13 For a superb study of prejudicial thinking and action by children against the Elders, see Dr. Leora Weinstein Isaacs' doctoral dissertation "The Development of Children's Attitudes Towards the Aged," 1983, City University of New York Graduate Center.

14 This, in itself, is not the right way to do things. The blind individual prefers to take *your* arm.

15 And into a multitude of other government and public buildings, and on trains and other public forms of transportation. The right of access for other service animals — for people who use wheelchairs and for hearing impaired people, for example, is similarly protected by law. In restaurants and stores, the law is the same. How does the problem of people with allergies or people who are afraid of dogs or don't like dogs balance with the right of access for blind people with guide dogs? Why would the law favor them, and not the Elders?

16 I.e., both people with disabilities and people without disabilities.

17 The law is based on ancient Talmudic material. I am not certain if the original setting was eating at home with a family servant bringing the food, or at a private or public banquet, or in some public eating establishment. Whatever the situation, the principle is still valid.

17a To order copies, call the Eden Alternative office in Sherburne, NY, 607-674-5232, or fax: 674-6723.

18 And while they are discussing the topic of animals, let them suggest that an abundance of plants would also be most beneficial to the people who live in their buildings.

19 Huntington Memorial (Pasadena, CA): 818-397-3495; Denver Children's (303-381-8062); Albany Medical Center Hospital, St. Peter's Hospital (Albany) (call Linda Marowitz, 518-489-4706 [daytime, Congregation Ohav Sholom, where she works], 456-4781 (evenings) From the age of four months until her death at age 15, Linda's golden retriever, Buff, accompanied her to work and stayed by her side in the office.)

The Ziv Tzedakah Fund Annual Report

1 The Ziv Administrator (Volunteer) is Naomi Eisenberger, 384 Wyoming Ave., Millburn, NJ 07041, 201-763-9396. Board of Directors: Danny Siegel, Edythe Siegel, Dr. Gordon Gondos. Treasurer: Gerry Eisenberger. Educational Consultants: Rabbi Steven and Ilene Bayar. Israel Resource Person, David Morris. The separate fund in Canada is called Ziv Tzedakah Foundation. Board of Directors: Danny Siegel, Chairman; Merle Gould, Treasurer; Robert Silberstein, Board Member. Contact person: Merle Gould, 31 Glen Rush Blvd., Toronto, Ontario, Canada M5N 2T4, 416-486-7425.

2 Allocations include the Ziv Agent Educator and 1994 Summer intern program. Expenses include last year's April printing and mail costs, but not this year's. All costs for the Winter mailing were covered by a special grant from a Ziv contributor. In addition, some expenses technically belong under the entries for specific projects. We placed them under general expenses because it simplified the bookkeeping.

3 We repeat our note from previous years concerning terminology, namely that much of the terminology about individuals with disabilities remains in flux. While some people find certain words acceptable, others object to the same terms. Consider for example the use of the term "TDD," an abbreviation for Telecommunications Device for the Deaf. The more accepted term nowadays is "TTY," for the earliest models, known as the teletypewriter. The change is so recent, I recently reviewed an article from *Business Week*, May 30, 1994, which still refers to phone numbers for "TDD users". We will do the best we can.

4 The actual costs (purchase of the horses, veterinarian fees, shipping, and miscellaneous expenses) were about $19,000. $5,372.00 was transferred back to our account from the

Therapeutic Riding Club from money we had given them last year toward this project. Some of the miscellaneous expenses (phone calls, faxes, etc.) appear under our general expenses.

[5] For information on a cat sanctuary in Hawaii, contact Mary O'Loughlin, Noah's Ark, 6037 Olohena Rd., Kapaa, Kauai, HI 96746, phone/fax: 808-822-2067. Contributions are welcome.

[6] The Ferrells are no longer officially affiliated with Trevor's Campaign.

[7] This year, because of the Laws of שמיטה - Shmitta, we received our certificate, and the tree itself was planted after the New Year.

[8] Funding for this aspect of our program came from special contributions. No money was taken from our general allocations for the internship program.

Why People Who are Blind Should Own Their Own Cars

[1] Personal conversations, newspaper articles, television coverage. In February, 1994, I was with Mr. Fling once again, and he reminded me of a child, about 11 or 12, who was dying of a brain tumor and who had already become blind. She had said she really wanted a TV. When Mr. Sig Friedman, one of Mr. Fling's friends offered to donate one, it was a black and white set, but she said she would prefer a color TV. Her reason was that the sound was better on the color set, but Mr. Friedman and Mr. Fling both understood that it was really for her parents. It was both heartbreaking and eye-opening to hear the story told to me. Many similar tales come from the Make-a-Wish Foundation.

[2] Personal conversation on a Shabbat walk.

[3] Personal correspondence.

[4] Personal conversation, Shabbat (prime Mitzvah-thinking time), Dr. Schwartz's kitchen. David is a former International President of USY.

[5] Personal conversations. Ms. Hutton's evening phone number is: 317-845-8829.

[6] Personal conversations, personal contact with dog owners and their dogs.

[7] Meeting, personal conversations, demonstrations.

[8] Personal visits.

[9] The 800 number will provide you with the location of your nearest rehabilitative riding organization.

[10] The Full Circle Program, Marine Science Center Aquarium, Ms. Marianne Klingel, 813-441-1790.

[11] Personal contact, contact with many Giraffes.

[12] Personal contact, on-site visit.

[13] *The Baltimore Sun, Ocean City Supplement*, May 16, 1993.

[14] *The Baltimore Jewish Times*, January 29, 1993. On May 18, 1993, one of the administrators at Ramaz Yeshiva in New York reported that the students there are saving 60 pounds of food a day.

[15] *The St. Petersburg Times*, November 9, 1993 and November 11, 1993.

[16] Ari Newman called the White House kitchen to ask what they do with their leftovers. Contact him at 401-861-3474 to try similar governmental projects.

[17] Steve Chaikin did it for Orioles Park. 410-528-1637.

[18] Ari Newman has the leftovers taken directly to hungry Jews in the Boston area. (To contact him, see footnote 16.)

[19] For a fictionalized biography, read *The Cry and the Covenant* by Morton Thompson.

[20] *Reform Judaism* Magazine, Winter, 1992, and personal conversations.

[21] *The Toronto Star*, March 21, 1992.

[22] Personal conversations.

[23] *First* Magazine, April 27, 1992, personal conversations.

[24] *The New York Times*, February 24, 1993.

[25] *The Boston Globe*, January 30, 1993. On the subject of using one's talents for Mitzvahs, compare the story of the young man who is working on translating the Bible into Klingon, alien tongue of *Star Trek* fame. He has finished the *Book of Jonah* and was about to start on *Esther* and *Ruth*, but he got sidetracked tackling *Hamlet*. (By the way, according to the article, Klingon does not have a verb "to be," making the task extremely difficult.) On would

hope that his Biblical endeavor, once completed, will bring the Klingons to a gentler, kinder pattern of behavior. (*The Southern Shofar*, March, 1995, reprint of an article by Donna Ezor, *MetroWest Jewish News.*)

[26]*The Denver Post, March 31, 1993.*

[27]Flyer, personal conversations.

[28]*In Jerusalem*, October 1, 1993; *The Canadian Jewish News*, March 15, 1993.

[29]*The New York Times*, November 7, 1993.

[30]*The Washington Post*, March 21, 1993

[31]Flyer, personal conversations, personal participation in the first Faire

[32]Flyer, personal conversations.

[33]Flyer, personal conversations.

Feeding Hungry Jews

[1] This article was edited by Louise Cohen, and slightly modified and re-formatted by myself for the purposes of this book. Ari's personal style has been preserved according to the pamphlet he gave me, with only slight adjustments.

We consider this article to be something like "Just About Everything You Need to Know About Donating Leftovers," and since Ari and I would hope it will lead to great changes in the wasteful habits of many food establishments, we hereby give permission to anyone who would wish to use it, to reproduce it and circulate it as you see they see fit for the sake of Tikkun Olam-Fixing the World.

[2] [n.b. from D.S.: Ari has told me of a conversation with Alan Hassenfeld, CEO of Hasbro Toys. They were talking about the big play room called the "fun lab" where kids, little kids come in to play with the toys, to see which ones they really like. Ari asked Mr. Hassenfeld what percentage of the toys they market results from the kids' opinions. Mr. Hassenfeld said, "50%". Ari has used this on many occasions to reinforce the sense of the power kids have.]

[3] [n.b. from D.S.: Each community food bank decides eligibility requirements that best suit the local needs. As important is an understanding, an unspoken policy, a "feel" for how many exceptions are to be made and for what reasons. For many food banks, the human factor — specific individual need — more frequently than not overrides rules and requirements.]

[4] Who heard it on different occasions from Beth Huppin and Malka Edelman (who had heard it, no doubt, from some motivational speaker).

[5] The Massachusetts Good Samaritan Law concerning donations of food to non-profit organizations is reproduced later in this article.

[6] [n.b. from D.S.: By all means discuss the Law with an attorney and with soup kitchens or shelters or food pantries that are already in operation. But do as Ari did — balance their experience with the sense of urgency that something needs to be done sooner rather than later.]

[7] Ari Newman, c/o Garin, 14 Upton Rd., Providence, RI 02906, 401-492-6500.

[8] Ari suggests you try the Governor's Mansion, State Supreme Court, and state Legislature (if you live in the capital), and, certainly, your municipal and other local government agencies: Office of the Mayor, City Council, etc.

[9] [n.b. from D.S.: Michael J. Bohnen of Nutter, McClennen & Fish, Boston, kindly supplied Ari with a copy of this law. Several years ago he provided a copy of the laws for every state and the District of Columbia to me, and I make it a practice to carry the specific law for the state where I am speaking, offering copies to people who want to begin work on getting leftovers donated. At a program in New Jersey in March, 1995, 75 people (out of about 125) asked for copies.]

[10] 1983, 99, § 2, approved May 17, 1983, (effective by act of Governor, May 17, 1983).

[11] This section was added by D.S., with Ari's approval, after conversation with Jonathan T. Howe, author of the agreement. If you would like to discuss the matter further, Mr. Howe welcomes calls and may be reached at Howe & Hutton, Ltd., in Chicago at 312-263-3002, Fax: 312-372-6685.

[12] Reed Publishing, Secaucus, NJ. Mr. Howe does not recall in which issue this article appeared. When I spoke to him, "A couple of years ago," is the best he could do without access to his reference library.

13 A flyer Ari circulated in the Boston Jewish community, included in the pamphlet.

Revelations

1 *The Newark Star Ledger,* June 1, 1994

2 320 A St., NE, Washington, DC 20002, William Halamandaris, Director, 202-547-4273, fax: 546-8968.

3 Vision and insight do not depend on intellectual powers. My own mild learning disability sometimes manifests itself in the following way: I will be reading some written text and I feel like a steel plate has been placed behind my eyes, blocking the information from going to my brain. It is a bothersome feeling. I am curious about it, but not frightened. It happens; that's just the genetic way some of my cerebral circuits are connected.

4 My teacher, Rabbi Joseph Braver, pointed out to me a well-known interpretation made by several Biblical commentators: the Hebrew word for "ladder" [spelled in its "full form"] is סולם. Its numerical value is 136, the same as the Talmudic word for money — ממון. Tzedakah money brings Heaven and earth together.

5 The verse uses the word והנה twice. The word usually means additional emphasis is to be given to the statement. In older translations of the Bible, it was often translated "Behold!" I have employed an exclamation mark, though the Torah does not have any punctuation marks. The text is not merely describing that there was a ladder and angels were going up and down. The verse means to convey that this was a most astonishing vision. הנה in its various forms appears more than 225 times in the Five Books of the Torah, more than 120 times in the Book of Genesis alone. Many of those occurrences mean the student of Torah should understand how emphatic the meaning is, i.e., ! The most famous example is, of course, in Genesis 22:1 when God calls out to Abraham and he replies, "הנני," meaning, "I am most certainly here, ready to do whatever it is You require of me!"

5a Two other (of the many) examples of not seeing what was always there: God opens Hagar's eyes, and she sees the well. (Genesis 21:19). Her feeling of desperation at watching her son, Yishmael, dying, prevented her from noticing that there was water right there for her to give to him. [Taught to me by my teacher, Rabbi Marc Wilson.] The other example is more striking for its irony: Balaam, a Seer, fails to see the angel standing right in front of him. (Numbers 22:31). God limited Balaam's vision because he had set out to use his talent for the wrong purposes, to curse the children of Israel.

6 I.e., a hint, a taste of prophecy. In the same Talmudic passage is a more disturbing statement: שינה אחד מששים למיתה- Sleep is 1/60 of death. The connection between sleep and death is a common human fear. And yet, even in the midst of that dread of never waking up, even in the deep darkness and helplessness of sleep, we are capable of receiving messages from God about Life. It is an interesting contrast to Freudian dream analysis.

Tzedakah — Tree of Life

1 When it all began, some people thought that Habitat for Humanity was a nice symbolic gesture attempting to overcome the problem of low-income housing for poor Americans and for others around the world lacking a decent home. World wide, Habitat for Humanity has built 35,000 houses. Habitat has not solved the problem, but it long ago ceased being a symbol.

2 On my last trip to Hawaii, I saw a video of Hurricane Iniki at its most destructive moments. The bartender at the Hyatt on Kauai took quite a bit of footage, including at the height of the storm when 140 mile-an-hour winds were tearing away at the property and the vegetation. Of course many of the trees were torn away. But the wondrous thing is how many "stood their ground."

3 Rashi, the Medieval Biblical and Talmudic interpreter makes a very interesting comment on the verse in Numbers 13:20. Moses instructs the scouts who are about to enter the Promised Land. He wants them to make sure to see (among other things) if the soil is rich or poor and היש בה עץ אם אין — are there any trees there at all? Rashi's comment on "trees" is: are there any Good people by whose merit, by whose Menschlich life, the Children of Israel can expect to be protected by God (אם יש בהם אדם כשר שיגין עליהם בזכותו)? The

Good Person's deeds and way of Life are a shield against the ravages of a decayed or decaying society.

Tzedakah: Beyond the Merely Human

[1] Rabbi Gordon Tucker has pointed out to me that the Chassidic Master, Dov Ber, The Maggid of Mezerich made an interesting comment on the syntax of the verse in Psalm 118:17 — לֹא אָמוּת כִּי אֶחְיֶה, reading, "I will not die *while* I am yet alive," meaning I would not waste this glorious gift of Life, merely breathing and existing. Rabbi Tucker fills in the end of the verse, וַאֲסַפֵּר מַעֲשֵׂי יָהּ, "I will speak of God's great deeds," interpreting that, following God's ways is the best method for living the most fulfilling, meaningful life.

Jewish *Jewish Leadership: The Element of Mitzvah Work and Tzedakah*

[1] I am grateful to Richard H. Meyer, Executive Vice President of the Milwaukee Jewish Federation and members of his staff, and to Dr. Judith Fine Dach of Ft. Lauderdale, FL, who offered useful comments on the initial draft of this article. I have tried to incorporate some of their suggestions into my revisions.

[2] For the past several years, CLAL, The National Jewish Center for Learning and Leadership has taught extensive Torah to the leadership of the North American Jewish community. Their efforts have had significant impact on the community in general, and on the lives of those individuals whose leaders respond to the sounds, images, and meanings of the texts.

[3] A word on my methodology.

As a student of Torah, I needed to move into the '90's with all due speed.

While still a student at the Jewish Theological Seminary, I had built a rather fine library of traditional Jewish literature. For more than 20 years, I have had in my possession numerous Biblical works and their ancient, Medieval and modern interpretations, Talmuds (Babylonian and Jerusalem, varied texts of the Mishna and their commentaries), Law codes (Maimonides, Tur, Shulchan Aruch, later codes), and the classic texts of the Midrash (many).

Add to that dictionaries, thesauruses, concordances, monographs, and studies *about* Jewish tradition, and one may readily understand my reluctance to pack up and relocate from time to time. There were just too many cartons of books to face.

Imagine my astonishment when about a hundred of these volumes were magically transformed on to a CD-ROM.

Imagine my greater astonishment when I placed one of these CD's on my postal scale and discovered that, if I put it in an envelope to mail to a friend, it would still come in under one ounce, a mere 32¢ to put in the mail!

Not that the one precludes use of the other. The computer tool by no means eliminates the need to study from the books. The interplay of words on the huge page of Maimonides' *Mishna Torah*, reveals to the eager student insights no touch of the keys on a Mac keyboard could ever produce.

Still, on a topic as important as "What is so Jewish about Jewish leadership" I needed to start somewhere. As our tradition states it:

Rabbi Chanan of Tziporin [said....]:
What does the unwise person say?
"Who could possibly study all of Torah?
The section Nezikim alone is 30 chapters!
The section Kilim alone is 30 chapters!"
What does the person-of-insight say?
"I will study two laws today, and another two tomorrow...
until I have recited the entire Torah." (Leviticus Rabba 19:2, Margoliot 2:417)

ר' חנן דציפורין.....
מי שטיפש מהו אומר מי יכול ללמוד את התורה
נזיקים ל' פרקים כילים ל' פרקים
מי שפיקח מהו אומר
הריני למד שתי הלכות היום ושתי הלכות למחר
עד שאני קורא את כל התורה כולה

This article is a result of the books and the marvels of the computer's vast scanning powers. On the latter, note one typical example: scanning the two Talmuds and about 20 classic Midrashic texts, and scanning only for one of the words for "leader" (פרנס-Parnass) 63 texts flashed on the screen in about the time it would have taken for me to press the stopwatch button on my wristwatch.

[4] The Hebrew text is from Prof. Burton I. Visotzky's edition of *Midrash Mishle, A Critical Edition based on Vatican MS. Ebr. 44,*...Jewish Theological Seminary, New York, 1990.

[5] The printed text reads: רחמנא, but the late Professor Saul Lieberman understood this as a scribal error, the original text being: רחמא.

[6] References in brackets are to the selections in my book *Where Heaven and Earth Touch (The Combined Anthology of Midrash and Halachah)*, Town House Press, 1988.

[7] For details on how the community dealt with this tremendous problem, contact Federation CJA, 514-345-2600. Their insights may well be useful in working with Jewish poor people in other communities.

[8] On the emotionally charged problem of being inundated with solicitations for so many Tzedakah projects, how to overcome the feeling of "I can't do everything," how to decide how much to give and to whom, how to manage the feelings of being intruded upon, and similar questions, see Arthur's Kurzweil's excellent piece, *Brother Can You Spare a Dime, The Treatment of Beggars according to Jewish Tradition*, Tikun Olam pamphlet of United Synagogue Youth (212-533-7800), reprinted from *Moment Magazine*, Volume 56, #10, November 1981, and *Gym Shoes and Irises*, Danny Siegel, Town House Press, Pittsboro, NC, 1982. His article records a bare hint of quantity and quality of fine Torah insights he has taught me. My Teacher.

[9] Two of the texts were discovered while I was scanning on the CD. I had originally known only one of them, but the computer picked up the two others, each with an all-important variation in Rabbi Yona's words.

Tzedakah as Radiance

[1] The Talmud records the following statement:

דרש רבי דוסתאי ברבי ינאי....
אדם נותן פרוטה לעני זוכה ומקבל פני שכינה

*Rabbi Dostai expressed the following insight
in the name of Rabbi Yannai:*

....

*If a person gives even the smallest coin to Tzedakah,
he or she senses God's Intimate Presence. (Bava Batra 10a)*
It doesn't take sweeping or earthshaking acts of Tzedakah to be moved into the sublime realms of Life. The most ostensibly insignificant acts are blessed with God's Intimate Presence.

[2] Buber Edition, with a note, "an additional text on the section Chukkat, Chapter 1, according to a second Oxford manuscript".

The Economics of Mitzvahs

[1] Study reported in The Delta Society's *Alert, Service Dog Center Newsletter*, Vol. 5, #4, 1994. Reported by Dr. Karen Allen, University of Buffalo's Center for the Behavioral and Social Aspects of Health at the Delta Society's 1994 Annual Conference. The two-year study involved 48 people. For details, contact the Delta Society, 1-800-869-6898 (V/TTY), fax: 206-235-1076.

[2] For further insight into the meaning of this verse — how not giving the prescribed Tzedakah is seen as robbing poor people of what is *rightfully* theirs — see the Midrash Numbers Rabbah 5:2.

Biblical Verses

[1] Many of the Biblical translations in this section (as in other parts of the book) are taken from the Jewish Publication Society's (JPS) version, © 1962, 1985, 1989. A number of the

translations are mine, building on those of the JPS. For my own, I usually choose free, poetic translations, most notably for reasons of syntax and when translating Hebrew words such as עדות, משפטים, פיקודים and similar terms as "Mitzvahs". My additions to the translations, and my comments are enclosed in brackets.

2 This is the longest of the 150 Psalms, containing 8 verses for each letter of the Hebrew alphabet. The style of most of the verses is brief, two halves, usually both halves parallel in meaning. With free-style translation this offers many rich opportunities for variations. The original intended meaning (the פשט-Pshat), though, would be closer to Part A = Part B than my translations show.

3 See, for example, Exodus 15:2.

3a Jewish Publication Society Translation.

3b My translation.

4 The ephah and hin are Biblical measures.

Rabbinic, Legal, and Kabbalistic Texts

1 Many explanations are given for the protection the Mitzvah-messenger receives on the way back, even though he or she has completed the mission. One is that it is the messenger's reward for having completed the Mitzvah mission. Another is that God's Intimate Presence is with the person, and continues to be present, so that the messenger does not *feel* any harm, even if something bad happens on the way home. There are probably a dozen wonderful explanations for Rabbi Elazar's words, and this is one of those texts that people should live with and review every so often to see what new insights they yield as Life changes and as we change in relation to the text.

1a The explanations in this text are based on a very complicated verse in Nachum 1:12. I have omitted the Biblical interpretations because communicating them in English would have been very complex. Some of the richest interpretations in Rabbinic literature originate in difficult, sometimes obscure verses in the Bible.

2 There is a play on the Hebrew root גז, meaning "to shear sheep," based on one of the words in the verse in Nachum.

3 One would expect, of course, that once the traveler returns home, he or she would feel moved to contribute to Tzedakah. Having been a recipient, the person would be particularly sensitive to what it feels like to be in need. I am grateful to Rabbi Gordon Tucker, who pointed this text out to me, as well as the Talmudic argument upon which it is based (Mishna Peah 5:4). Rabbi Tucker related Maimonides' statement to forgetting your credit cards at home and running out of cash while out on the road. Shades of the advertisements by American Express about their credit cards, "Don't leave home without it."

4 Even the simplest Mitzvah act is part of Life's greater context: the human being is setting things right, is feeding people, is saving lives, is Fixing the World. The sense of power that comes from Tzedakah allows the person doing the Mitzvah to have a fix on Life and a sense of self dignity. By doing Mitzvahs, a person becomes a person of great worth, precious in God's sight, as described by the metaphorical language "to see Your Face". The Biblical term "כבוד" means not only "person, self," but also "dignity." When used in relation to God, it means God's Presence, equal to the Talmud's term "שכינה".

5 Some Talmudic texts explain that, in the case of the 100-year-old man, since he has reached such an extraordinary age, the odds are he will continue to live on.

6 The story is open to many interpretations. I have been working with it for years, with a number of students, classes, and audiences. One meaning is simply that the power of Life and death that humans have extends only up until the time of death. I can't quite figure out what the man did wrong: how did he abuse this incredible plant? Another 10 years and 50 discussions will hopefully yield a better understanding of the text. Still, it is a marvelous story.

7 According to the commentary of the late Professor Saul Lieberman, זכות=צדקה, see text and comments in תוספתא כפשוטה, זרעים, חלק א, pp. 126-127.

DANNY SIEGEL, a 1993 recipient of the prestigious Covenant Award for Exceptional Jewish Educators, has been described by writer Leonard Fein as "American Jewry's leading expert in micro-philanthropy." As chairman of the Ziv Tzedakah Fund, which he founded 14 years ago, he has collected nearly $2 million for grass-roots community projects worldwide. He lectures to synagogues, Jewish Federations, religious schools, and university student groups about the dozens of mitzvah people he has met, and encourages his audiences to get involved, to fix the world, to make a difference.

Professor Gerald Bubis once referred to Danny Siegel as the "feeling person's thinker."

When not on the road, Danny lives, works, and writes in Rockville, Maryland. He is the author of 20 books of prose and poetry, and has also written three books for children.